TO HELL

TO HELL AND BACK

Race and Betrayal in the Southern Novel

Jeff Abernathy

The University of Georgia Press
Athens and London

© 2003 by the University of Georgia Press

Athens, Georgia 30602

All rights reserved

Designed by Mindy Basinger Hill

Set in Walbaum by Bookcomp, Inc.

Printed and bound by Maple-Vail

The paper in this book meets the guidelines for
permanence and durability of the Committee on
Production Guidelines for Book Longevity of the
Council on Library Resources.

Printed in the United States of America

07 06 05 04 03 C 5 4 3 2 1

07 06 05 04 03 P 5 4 3 2 1

Library of Congress Cataloging-in-Publication Data

Abernathy, Jeff, 1964–

    To hell and back : race and betrayal in the southern novel / Jeff Abernathy.

    p. cm.

    Includes bibliographical references (p.   ) and index.

    ISBN 0-8203-2486-8 (hardcover : alk. paper) — ISBN 0-8203-2578-3 (pbk. :
alk. paper)

    1. American fiction—Southern States—History and criticism   2. American
fiction—20th century—History and criticism.   3. Twain, Mark, 1835–1910—
Influence.   4. Southern States—In literature.   5. African Americans in
literature.   6. Race relations in literature.   7. Social ethics in literature.
8. Betrayal in literature.   9. Race in literature.   I. Title.

    PS261.A38 2003

    813'.509355—dc21

2003007992

British Library Cataloging-in-Publication Data available

FOR A BROTHER—
James Goss Ferneyhough III
1962–2001

CONTENTS

ACKNOWLEDGMENTS

At the end of his story, Huck Finn writes, "If I'd a knowed what a trouble it was to make a book I wouldn't a tackled it." While I have at moments felt deep sympathy for his position, I have managed to avoid sharing his sentiment because I have not had to bear his substantial burden of writing from the isolated Territory. I am grateful to have worked in the company of others.

John Seelye directed me in the early development of this book when I was a graduate student at the University of Florida; I am deeply grateful for his sustained direction and support. John and Alice Seelye continue to be good friends and good company. Anne Goodwyn Jones guided me from my first days in Gainesville and this book from its beginning. Her scholarship and her pedagogy have taught me much, and her thorough, nuanced reading of a recent draft of the book has made it by far the richer. David Leverenz read an early draft with such care that, years later, his thoughts guide me still. Bertram Wyatt-Brown and Andrew Gordon each contributed in many ways to the development of my argument. The idea for this book developed out of my conversations with Harry Crews on the southern novel. I am obliged to Padgett Powell for the use of an early draft of *Edisto* and for instruction in the art of writing that extended from theory to praxis.

David Roediger's work in whiteness studies and his thoughtful analysis of this manuscript have shaped my thinking through my last revisions.

I am grateful to the University of Georgia Press for sending the manuscript to two anonymous readers, whose incisive critiques helped me write a better book. The staff at Georgia has been a pleasure to work with, and I am especially grateful to Nancy Grayson, Jennifer Reichlin, Erin McElroy, Mary Koon, and Malcolm Call. Copyeditor Mary M. Hill has improved the final draft immensely through her careful reading. Peter Ripley directed me to Georgia some years ago.

A National Endowment for the Humanities Summer Institute led by Cecelia Tichi at Vanderbilt University helped to broaden the focus of this work.

Colleagues in the Society for the Study of Southern Literature have been especially helpful with their comments at our meetings in recent years. Margaret Bauer has long been a friend and confidante. Dorothy Scura read the manuscript and helped me bring the argument to final form.

Illinois College is a rich academic community in which to teach and write, and my years there were rewarding. I am grateful for the opportunity to take a year's sabbatical and a year's leave while I was writing. I am indebted to all my faculty and administrative colleagues and in particular to Jim Davis, Kelly Dagan, Bernd Estabrook, Bob Koepp, Bob Kunath, Jim and May Marshall, Paul Spalding, Winston Wells, and Lisa and Larry Zettler, each of whom offered insightful critiques of my argument. Dean Richard Fry read the manuscript in its entirety and helped to bring the book to its final form. Scott Belobrajdic, Malinda Carlson, Martha Church, John Gibbons, and Bob Lane have likewise offered support. At Schewe Library I found unflagging support from Pat Bone, Stuart Gaetjens, Martin Gallas, Laura Sweatman, and Mike Westbrook. President Richard A. Pfau supported my work on this book throughout his years at Illinois College; Dean Frederik Ohles read the manuscript and gave me invaluable direction and encouragement. I am grateful as well to Kathy Bandy and Jill Shoemaker for their assistance. I learned much from my students at IC, and Josh Bluhm, Julie Bodam, Jill Friday, Peri Gonulsen, Jamie LaMarche, and Rick Willbanks commented on portions of this work. Kelly Payne and Tammy Hamilton served ably as research assistants. Tammy's remarkable insight and her gifts as a researcher made it possible for me to complete the project; her substantial contributions include primary preparation and the index.

I completed this work soon after arriving at West Virginia Wesleyan College. I am grateful to the many colleagues here who have given me encouragement. The staff at Annie Merner Pfeiffer Library has been very helpful; library director Kathy Parker critiqued the index and helped me to complete that final portion of my work.

At Longwood College Martha Cook first showed me the fascinations of southern literature, and I hope this work will serve to show that I was listening. In more recent years, Martha has been my professional guide and mentor, and I owe her much. I am grateful for her painstaking readings of the manuscript. Michael Lund has offered advice and guidance since my days in Farmville.

During two recent years in Virginia, the staff of the library at Mary Washington College was generous beyond measure. Carla Bailey, Jack Bales, Tim Newman, and Elizabeth Perkins were also excellent company through many an afternoon of conversation overlooking the Rappahannock River in Fredericksburg. Jack Bales read a portion of this manuscript and gave insightful comments.

I am indebted to library staffs at Augustana College, Florida State University, Monmouth College, Randolph-Macon College, the University of Florida, the University of Illinois, the University of Richmond, and the University of Virginia.

My family—Richard Abernathy, Lois Abernathy, Robert Marshall, Stephanie and John Allison, Laura Wade Abernathy, Doug Abernathy, Don Laugherty, Ron Abernathy, Cheryl Abernathy, Alice and Bill Talbot, and Richard and Neta Abernathy—have given me their love and support throughout the writing of this book.

Without the friendship of a group known to its members as the Fifth Column of the University of Florida English Department (namely, Mike Crocker, Joan Pinkham, Mike Disch, Jim Papian, Andrea Tyler, Jim and Chris Iddings, and Dawn Corrigan), I would hardly have begun this work, never mind brought it to a close. Bill Beverly has helped to shape this book through his careful analysis. I owe much as well to my friends Clay and Kathy Mullican and their three boys—Sean, Jake, and Dylan—as well as to Brad and Deborah Krueger. Joe Johnson has read the manuscript twice and offered sage advice. Linda Ferneyhough has given me much encouragement.

I am grateful to Rebecca Wee for her love and for her patience with me in the final year of this project. She read the entire manuscript and brought a poet's reflection to the process of editing.

This book is dedicated to Jim Ferneyhough, who in twenty years of friendship won most of the arguments we had on the vexing issue of race in America and whose principles on race as on so many more subjects helped to shape my own. His wife, Janice Ferneyhough, and their son, Goss, will be dear to my heart always.

TO HELL AND BACK

INTRODUCTION

Crossroad Blues

The real American melting pot was the formation of
African American culture out of diverse African and American
materials in slavery, a culture so fundamental to American
development that it became the port of entry for various ethnic
cultures wanting in on America.

ERIC LOTT

Every human identity is constructed, historical; every one has
its share of false presuppositions, of the errors and inaccuracies
that courtesy calls "myth," religion "heresy," and science
"magic." Invented histories, invented biologies, invented
cultural affinities come with every identity; each is a kind of
role that has to be scripted, structured by conventions of
narrative to which the world never quite manages to conform.

K. ANTHONY APPIAH

Americans speak of race as static and knowable, but we experience it as dynamic and inscrutable, ever shifting and ever elusive.
In seeking to reconcile this dissonance between representation
and reality, we turn to cultural productions that attempt to define
racial identity as a mythic movement from white to black, as a
journey toward transcendence. American culture tirelessly gives
forth images of these racial crossings, from our earliest written
narratives, in which the settlers at Jamestown—not Americans,
surely, but no longer entirely English either—saw themselves as
a race apart, to the minstrel performers who founded their art
on journeys across the color line, to the new millennium rock and

hip-hop performers who market a bricolage of racial identities. In myriad texts, as in our history, we predicate stories of the American self on journeys through the crossroads where races meet, a markedly unstable milieu where, no longer fixed, race becomes an amorphous catalyst for transcendence from the certainty of old biases to the possibility of new hope.[1] Our repeated meetings at the crossroads of race engage us in a conversation about our highest ideals even as they compel us to confront the underlying tensions of Americanness itself.

This work addresses the representation of these racial crossings in the southern novel from Mark Twain's *Adventures of Huckleberry Finn* to the present and in the broader American culture that has time and again defined race in distinctly southern terms. I assess a broad range of southern fiction in my discussion.[2] In early chapters, I look to William Faulkner's *Go Down, Moses* and *Intruder in the Dust*, Elizabeth Spencer's *A Voice at the Back Door*, Carson McCullers's *Member of the Wedding*, and Harper Lee's *To Kill a Mockingbird*. Each of these major works of American literature repeats the racial drama at the center of *Huckleberry Finn* while responding to the particular cultural context in which it was written. In a later chapter, I consider more recent works of southern fiction like Kaye Gibbon's *Ellen Foster* and Sara Flanigan's *Sudie*, works in which the pattern I identify emerges as a popular standard. Next, I address novels by African American writers—*Native Son, Invisible Man, Meridian*—that contest the account of race to be found in the southern novel. In my last chapter, I consider works by white writers—Padgett Powell's *Edisto*, Ellen Douglas's *Can't Quit You, Baby*, and W. Glasgow Phillips's *Tuscaloosa*—that begin to undermine the racial assumptions of this central drama of American culture in intriguing ways. Throughout I place these southern novels in cultural context by means of references to texts from popular culture: a Lou Reed song, a Spike Lee film. In my coda, I assess the significance of the pattern within the larger context of American history.

I argue that southern novels—many of them among the most prominent works of American literature—frequently express directly the national ambivalence over race: the journeys across the color line I identify are founded in American culture writ large, so that the South has become the locus of a national engagement with race, the main stage upon which race is performed in America. These stories seek to render race certain and fixed, yet we find that instead race becomes ever more uncertain and ductile.

These southern stories find their basis in the broader culture, and in reading the best-known works of American literature we find countless images of companionship across the color line; taken together with myriad parallels in American culture, these cross-racial literary relationships constitute a distinctly American response to a set of social and historical conditions unique to the United States. As Winthrop Jordan has observed, the existence of slavery in America made white Americans more conscious of their freedom; if one result is the leitmotif of freedom in American literature, another is a mythic, metaphoric journey away from whiteness. From the narratives of John Smith through the fictions of James Fenimore Cooper, Herman Melville, Harriet Beecher Stowe, Mark Twain, and William Faulkner and into the contemporary period in the work of Cormac McCarthy and Toni Morrison, mainstream American writers have time and again portrayed an American cultural frontier at which races join. Thus our writers have reflected upon the central question that has haunted American history: how do we reconcile our higher ideals with our baser reality?

In these pages, I examine in particular the place of these cross-racial companionships—along with the betrayals that almost inevitably accompany them—in the southern novel. In doing so, I look to *Adventures of Huckleberry Finn* as a tutor text, for, of all our novels, it remains at the nexus of the American obsession with race. The innocence readers have so often assigned to Twain's Huck reflects an American dilemma: utterly complicit in the failings of American race relations, we nevertheless aspire to shed that complicity for a carefree raft ride down the Mississippi, shut off from the burden of our troubled history. That Huck himself can never escape his own past doesn't affect our nostalgia for the book one whit.

Mark Twain's America

A persistent theme of American literature traces a white character's development through his or her relationship with a man or woman of color. Among nineteenth-century works, one thinks of Cooper's *Leatherstocking Tales,* Melville's *Moby Dick,* and Joel Chandler Harris's *Uncle Remus, His Songs and His Sayings,* to name only the most prominent. In each of these works, a man of color attends the physical or intellectual development of a white protagonist, whether through the wild wisdom of a Chingachgook or a Queequeg or through the folktales of an Uncle Remus.

In *Adventures of Huckleberry Finn,* the novel most frequently associated with America itself, Mark Twain alters the pattern of his literary forebears—and so the course of American literature— in portraying a white character who experiences moral growth through his relationship with a black man. Where Leatherstocking and Ishmael come naturally to sympathy for their companions, Huck Finn must be converted. Huck's river companion, Jim, who initially resembles the minstrel and mammy figures of earlier American novels, grows more complicated in Twain's portrait of his emotional and physical longings. Huck's moral identity ultimately depends upon his ability to remove Jim from the essentialist stereotypes posited by his southern society. When Huck apologizes to Jim following their separation in a fog, he has begun to acknowledge Jim's basic humanity, and when he decides at the climax of the novel to "go to hell" and steal Jim out of slavery, he ostensibly escapes the hypocritical and corrupt southern society that formed him (271). In such scenes, Huck conceives of

Jim as an individual cut apart from the narrow and essentialist terms with which all other white characters in the novel define him. More significantly for Huck, he begins to share in Jim's black identity, sensing the degree to which a mysterious black culture contributes to his nascent understanding of self.

A return to stereotype accompanies Huck's return to white society, however, and this betrayal exposes the superficial nature of his moral development. On the Phelps farm, Huck, with the assistance of his deceptive friend Tom Sawyer, returns Jim to type. The moral growth that Huck experienced on the river never does affect his behavior on the river's banks, and his later efforts to free Jim consequently lack their earlier moral resolve. And though Mark Twain attempts, in the final third of his novel, to undermine Huck's reversals with irony, ultimately, he emulates his protagonist in returning Jim to the literary minstrelsy from which he had earlier rescued him.[3]

Having re-created himself by sharing Jim's alienated identity, Huck ultimately denies the significance of his journey. He thus refuses to admit otherness and, specifically, blackness into his sense of identity beyond the narrow locus of "the raft," enacting a classically American denial of the place of black identity in the formation of the American self. From the earliest moments in the story, Huck moves toward recognition of a shared identity with Jim, toward an understanding of the part played by otherness in the development of his own identity. Yet just when he is closest to this recognition, he recoils violently from it, unable to bear its implications.

With its roots in the print and performance cultures that emerged in the United States in the early nineteenth century, this pattern of engagement and betrayal—Huck's journey to hell and back—appears repeatedly in American and, specifically, southern novels following *Huckleberry Finn*. White liberal novelists in the South following Twain have frequently recast Huck Finn and Jim, ostensibly intending to portray African American characters transcending stereotype in the eyes of white, often adolescent, protagonists.[4] Thus these works specifically challenge the legacy of the blackface minstrel show, yet, like Twain, these writers nevertheless frequently portray their protagonists returning black mentors to type. By contrast, African American writers pointedly contest the pattern, portraying autonomous black and white characters who must earn their own salvation or fail to gain it at all.

Following Twain in their portrayal of a mixed white and black cultural identity in their protagonists, the novelists I consider reflect upon a central dilemma of the southern culture from which they write even as they help to define the racial ambivalence of the nation. As Grace Elizabeth Hale writes, "To be American is to be both black and white. Yet to be a modern American has also meant to deny this mixing, our deep biracial genesis" (3). In denying the participation of blackness in the development of their own identities, these characters thus proclaim at once their whiteness and their Americanness, qualities their narratives will often suggest are one.

In my consideration of *Huckleberry Finn*, I focus on the effect of the ending, the center of scholarly debate surrounding the novel throughout the twentieth century. A study focusing solely upon the critical treatment of Twain's conclusion is surely overdue; I am concerned primarily with those critics who most closely address the issue of Twain's representations of racial betrayal in the novel.[5] Though critics have long recognized Faulkner's debt to Twain, few have addressed Twain's influence on the southern novel more generally, in particular in the portrayal of race at the center of so much of southern fiction. In this shared theme, these works come to express the essential concerns of the nation, and this central paradox in Twain's work—as in the nation—emerges as a defining element of the southern novel following Twain. Further, I argue that Twain's novel expresses at once the persistent democratic vision at the heart of American culture as well as the racial hierarchy that has ever undermined that vision. The South, as Howard Zinn describes it, "far from being utterly different, is really the essence of the nation. It is not a mutation born by some accident into the normal, lovely American family; it has simply taken the national genes and done the most with them" (219).

Southern Stories

Many of the novels I consider are indeed "southern" in that they take place in the South (the exceptions are, by no coincidence whatever, two novels by African American writers, Wright's *Native Son* and Ellison's *Invisible Man*), but, more significantly, they are southern in their often strained efforts to address racial issues and racial interaction, usually through one of the extremes of absolution or denunciation of southern whites. Even as the influence of African American culture has provided the South with its distinctive regional identity, an engagement with African American culture defines southern letters as a field of study. Louis D. Rubin Jr. notes that no sense of southern identity existed until those living in the South were faced with the possibility of abolition and that "the very idea of a 'southern' literature, as distinct from an American literature, had its origins in the slavery controversy" (12).

A reversal of moral stance in regard to African Americans emerged as a critical factor in southern history, as C. Vann Woodward writes: in the 1830s, popular aversion to slavery, which had increasingly been tied to the region's ills, died away to be replaced by a celebration of slavery as the regional cause par excellence.[6] Southern racial mythmaking thus begins in earnest, and the plantation mythos, in which the history of the plantation comes to stand for the history of the South, suppresses any emergent egalitarian themes.

Southern writers following Twain are likewise bound up in a southern dialectic of race even as they try to critique it; they hold a critical mirror to southern culture while reproducing some of its more blatant offenses. But that should bring little surprise, for such duplicity has been the South's, and the nation's, central moral paradox ever since a southern slave owner wrote the defining words of his American society: "All men are created equal."

That the paradox has taken a central place in the nation's development suggests the importance of the region to the nation's identity. If the texts I examine are largely southern, the problem I reflect upon is distinctly not: the South remains an identifiable place in both southern and northern reckoning largely because white American anxiety over race is ever linked to the South.[7] As the nation found in the twentieth century in its battle against segregation, problems initially thought to be "southern" turned out to be anything but exclusive to the South. The pattern of southern protest that James Cobb describes in *The Most Southern Place on Earth*—"exotic and immutable beliefs, rituals, and relationships mysteriously persisting in outright defiance of the powerful innovative influences of American mass society" (x)—does not obtain here: American popular culture persistently patterns itself in parallel to the popular and literary culture of the South.

The specific pattern of denial in Twain's novel arises out of similar denials in the larger culture. As several critics have noted, Huck's betrayal of Jim—whatever layers of irony readers might attribute to it—at the end of the novel resembles a reenactment of the sad end of Radical Reconstruction that occurred as Twain was writing the novel. One finds similar treacheries in American letters before and after *Huck Finn*, acts that parallel the long history of broken promises to minorities in the United States.[8] These acts of betrayal emerge as the mudsill of the nation, upon which our very identity is founded. While I primarily intend to demonstrate the ways in which such betrayals develop as the central motif of the southern novel, I shall read the region in the context of the nation, considering the ways in which patterns within the form emerge out of historical conditions specific to the United

States. In making reference to a broader set of texts from popular culture, I show that the pattern of racial engagement—and disengagement—that I will trace in the southern novel is a reflection of a far broader pattern present throughout American culture, that, as I have noted, the South is but the stage upon which the drama of race in America is performed.

Jonathan Arac argues that the canonization of *Huckleberry Finn*—together with the vitriolic defense of the novel against those who would question its place as the book Americans love best—ultimately bolsters those structures within American society that continue to restrain minority culture. We might then question the politics of canonization that have exalted the southern fiction of race while consigning, for a time, other works (the slave narrative, sentimental fiction) to the dustbin of history. The pattern of reversal that Twain established emerges as a kind of American mythos and a central narrative pattern of American literature: in retelling the tale, our writers have often reaffirmed the very prejudices they intend to interrogate.

Blacking Up: Performances of Blackness

Though racial crossing has been a theme for "American" writers since the colonial period, from the middle of the nineteenth century these blendings in both popular and literary cultures emerged from the tradition of blackface minstrelsy. In the white gaze, as Eric Lott argues in his work on the minstrel show, the black world has ever held a lurid appeal. White artists adapt black identities in order to transform themselves from a whiteness they find alternately constrictive and loathsome: "Have you seen us, Uncle Remus?" Frank Zappa asks in mock blackface performance, turning—as will generations of southern writers—to the black figure as authority for white selfhood.

The opportunity to "black up" affords the white performer—as it will afford many a white protagonist following Huck Finn—a release from whiteness. David Roediger argues that, prior to the Civil War, "to black up was an act of wildness," and both popular and literary culture have reflected this same pattern long after the close of the war (*Wages* 118). Blackface enables performers to claim kinship with the other while also asserting *through the performance* their own whiteness.[9]

A shifting racial identity, for example, constitutes a central theme of American popular music from the middle of the twentieth century in work from artists as disparate as the King of Rock— a white man who sang and moved black—to the King of Pop—a black man who became white before our eyes—and in the work of myriad musicians since the emergence of jazz and the birth of rock. Lou Reed, whose "Walk on the Wild Side" ironically invokes the essentialist ideology with which white Americans approach black America, again parodies this movement to blackness in his song "I Wanna Be Black." Repeating the title line over and over, Reed laughs at the self-imposed limits of any movement toward supposed blackness: "I wanna be black, have natural rhythm . . . I wanna be black, I wanna be a Panther, have a girlfriend named Samantha and have a stable of foxy whores," he sings.[10] But the urge to engage with blackness is in part the product of a desire to escape a narrow and constricting whiteness: Reed continues, "I don't want to be a fucked-up middle-class college student anymore." In aspiring to shed whiteness itself, white Americans have frequently gravitated to identities on which they have projected an endless series of essentialist ideologies.

Popular music since the emergence of hip hop in the 1980s has reflected this pattern as well, if not always with the rich sense of irony that we find in the work of Zappa and Reed. White rappers like MC Serch and Eminem, for example, in drawing on black musical forms, often acknowledge a split existence. In a bragging black dialect, Eminem raps, "I'm not the first king of controversy / I am the worst thing since Elvis Presley, to do Black Music so selfishly" ("Without Me").

The pattern is even more apparent in American film, in which both the blending of race and the setting of the American South have been essential and inescapable: a narrow, vindictive view of race in the South was envisioned at its inception in *Birth of a Nation*, for example, and then again in the much-celebrated *Gone with the Wind*. More recently, the particular theme of racial crossing has emerged from the genre of buddy films as a distinct genre unto itself: *Guess Who's Coming to Dinner, 48 Hours* (the original and the sequel), the *Lethal Weapon* series (in which the comic weapon is race), *Clara's Heart, Driving Miss Daisy, Jungle Fever, Bulworth, The Legend of Bagger Vance, The Family Man, Happy Gilmore, Training Day, Monster's Ball, Changing Lanes*.[11] The list goes on. These films—some set in the South, others not—inevitably operate on the narrative terms of Twain's novel, portraying the moral development of white characters through their ability to shed the essentialist thinking with which they enter a relationship with persons of color. As on the big screen, so too on the small; on television, the pattern has become a staple.[12]

The essentialism in the texts I consider derives in part from the presentation of black identity—an abstracted blackness—in popular culture that white audiences often take for a genuine representation of African Americans. In his study of the minstrel show, Eric Lott argues that whites invested in the notions of blackness presented to them by white performers in blackface and so in "the idea of blackface as a people's culture" (34). This investment by white audiences in performances of blackness informs both the novels I discuss and the readers who read them. The southern novel has returned time and again to the images of both blackness and whiteness that Twain established in *Huckleberry Finn* largely because the concept of southernness itself is premised upon these narrow definitions of race. Indeed, race as a culturally held set of assumptions is partly formed in the southern novel.

This book addresses the ways in which our writers have repeated this pattern of racial crossing, but I am equally concerned with the implications for the American audiences that have invested in this movement to blackness over and over, celebrating it in every medium yet celebrating, too, the return to white culture that is its concomitant part. The journey into blackness comes ironically to define the pilgrim: "I wanna be black," Lou Reed sings. In America, who doesn't? Who isn't?

What does it mean that white Americans return to this story time and again and that a failure of moral resolve is almost invariably repeated in these works as in the larger culture? Wishing to redress cultural wrongs, wishing to overcome an abiding guilt over the treatment of minorities in American culture, white Americans find these cultural crossroads irresistible. American literature reflects these broad cultural choices, and the southern novel distills these choices precisely.

White on Black

In this study, I employ the terms *blackness* and *whiteness* to indicate cultural understandings of racial identity and racial characteristics rather than entities unto themselves.[13] Since the settlers arrived at Jamestown, Americans have spoken of race in essentialist terms, reducing racial identity to a perceived essence, an assumed set of behaviors. Indeed, as much recent scholarship has shown, whiteness itself has been founded upon these very assumptions.[14] This work responds to this body of criticism by examining the ways in which our writers play to and against these essentialist ideologies. Though I will not again use intrusive annotation such as quotation marks or italics in employing the terms *white* and *black* or *whiteness* and *blackness*, I believe that the assumptions associated with any such language are specious at best. Ultimately, such terms are essentially mythic in quality: they tell us more of our charged assumptions as a society than they do of the likely behavior of any individual. When the white characters in the novels I examine engage in blackness, they enter a fabled realm created in the national culture. Their movement toward blackness is thus metaphoric, archetypal, and literary, telling us much of our national obsession with race and racial boundaries, and their new understanding of themselves has as much to do with their ability to view American culture from the position of a marginalized other as with the blackness they think they know. But of course I must acknowledge as well that simply because race is a social construction does not mean individuals do not act on it as if it were a biological absolute: "Race—racism—is a device. No more. No less. It explains nothing at all," says a character in Lorraine Hansberry's play *Les Blancs,* "but the fact remains that a man who has a sword run through him because he refused to become a Moslem or a Christian—or who is shot in Zatembe or Mississippi because he is black—is suffering the utter *reality* of the device. And it is pointless to pretend that it doesn't *exist*—merely because it is a *lie!*" (qtd. in Kenan 6). Thus I use these terms advisedly.

Just as African American culture has attracted white audiences through mass culture productions ever since blackface minstrelsy, it enthralls and engages the white protagonists of these southern novels. The particular attractions are many. For some of these protagonists blackness is an exoticized other, a human region defined primarily by its opposition to themselves; they journey toward an imagined blackness because of a powerful desire to escape a white self. Other protagonists come to blackness through maronage: cast out from white society, they discover their common humanity with other outcasts. Still others are attracted out of a liberal paternalism that guides them to those less fortunate than themselves or a nostalgic longing for the maternal figure of a comforting black mammy. Most employ some combination of these variations.

Ultimately, otherness attracts these white protagonists precisely because their journey there is not permanent. They define themselves as white through a journey into blackness, as has ever been the case in American culture. Italians, Greeks, Jews, the Irish, all became white precisely by defining themselves in opposition to

American blacks. As David Roediger writes, "[T]he process of in-
clusion into whiteness has always been predicated on accepting
the exclusion of others" (*Colored White* 240). These white characters define themselves as black briefly in order to affirm their
whiteness the more profoundly after their return to white culture.
And of course the black characters who alternately accompany,
lead, or heal these white protagonists are most often cut off from
any sustained connection to black culture or black community:
the blackness they represent for their white companions has no
depth.

The boundaries of southern white identity, and especially
southern white male identity, are marked by the opposition of
white and black in the novels I consider. The southern protagonists do go to the forbidden place that is the black world. They
discover on the journey that the boundaries between the races
shift and overlap constantly; as a result, they begin to sense that
race itself is, at best, a fragile cultural construction. But such
a discovery—made in the absence of the social authority that
enforced their original notions of identity—untethers these protagonists from all they have known. Their growth is ultimately
determined by their ability to see that blackness is not the opposi-
tional force their southern culture had always defined it to be but
is instead an expression of themselves and of their culture long
denied. This makes their own ultimate denials of a moral kinship
with African Americans all the more troubling, especially since
the pattern reflects similar denials in American culture.

According to Carole Shammas, American history turns constantly upon the pattern of reversed identification of white-as-
victim that is at the heart of *Huckleberry Finn*. The thinking
of revolutionary leaders centered upon just such a role reversal:
"Having practically destroyed the aboriginal population and enslaved the Africans, the white inhabitants of English America
began to conceive of themselves as the victims, not the agents,
of Old World colonialism" (Shammas qtd. in Limerick 111). And

this is just what the protagonists of the novels I examine are up to. Persistently, they attempt to share with their marginalized companions a sense of victimization and hence to shed the role of the colonizer. Southern writers and their protagonists repeatedly lay claim to a racial innocence which they do not possess, denying their own participation in the oppression of minority communities in America. It is a claim that white America has made often enough, and so the southern novels here express the racial ambiguities of a nation. Thus it is that Americans continue to express a desire for a multicultural national identity even as we continue to segregate ourselves by racial categories that have less meaning every day.

The white protagonists in these novels come to know of a marginal identity within themselves that both comforts and terrifies. In one sense they thus recognize themselves as Americans for the first time, for where but in the United States is identity formed from so many cultural possibilities? But having begun to acknowledge a multicultural American self, they retreat swiftly from the implications such recognition might hold. This betrayal—and ultimately the betrayals I examine are as much of self as of another—of a vision of multicultural selfhood reflects the contradictory urges of white Americans identified by Winthrop D. Jordan: white Americans desire at once to liberate and to restrain African Americans, in whom they come to see a shared humanity. Jordan argues that white Americans felt a natural desire to liberate African Americans, and that desire emerged decades before the American Revolution, in the American Enlightenment, when whites recognized that the story of the New World would inevitably be multiracial in origin. Yet the desire to restrain African Americans—born of a refusal among whites to recognize the violence and degradation within themselves— was stronger still. The pattern in the southern novel reflects directly these sharply opposed desires. These novels represent in miniature the broad pattern of denial of an African presence in

American literature following from that conflict. As Toni Morrison suggests, "Africanism is the vehicle by which the American
self knows itself as not enslaved, but free; not repulsive, but desir-
able; not licensed, but powerful; not history-less, but historical"
(52). Many of the protagonists I consider return from a recognition of their own marginal identity in order to stake their claim
in history.

❋ 1 ❋
A RAFT OF HOPE
Mark Twain's Southern Strategy

> A moral drama that inflicts pain on black (and white) readers
> and raises acutely discomfiting questions about the color line,
> *Huckleberry Finn* has become the book we love to hate and
> wish had never happened. But it is impossible to imagine an
> American literature, and its obligation to engage with the
> historical facts of slavery and racism, without *Huckleberry
> Finn*. We are as bonded to this nettlesome book as
> Brer Rabbit was to Tar Baby.
>
> JUSTIN KAPLAN

Adventures of Huckleberry Finn is an American touchstone, a book that those who seek to define American culture ignore at their peril.[1] The fact that 120 years after its publication we still publicly and vociferously debate its merits suggests its importance to us. When was the last time Stowe, Melville, Poe, Hawthorne, or Faulkner made front-page headlines across the country, as Twain's novel does for one reason or another every few years, or generated passions so deep and so broad across the continent? Twain riles up new audiences with such regularity that one observer noted, "[N]othing has become as much an American classic as the continuing controversy itself" (*Adventures of Huckleberry Finn* 329). Like the Tar Baby, Huck Finn will not let us be.[2]

In *Adventures of Huckleberry Finn*, Mark Twain draws from both the minstrel show and the slave narrative to form his central dialectic of slavery and freedom. While his portrayal of Jim owes much to the minstrel show's constrained images of African Americans, his focus on freedom emerges from the liberating impulse of the slave narrative. These contesting sources and impulses leave Twain's novel forever moving back and forth between restraint and liberation, a vacillation that also comes to characterize his hero.

As Mark Twain sat down to write *Adventures of Huckleberry Finn* in the summer of 1876, he had just published *The Adventures of Tom Sawyer*, a book he would later call "simply a hymn" to boyhood (Kaplan, *Mr. Clemens and Mark Twain* 197). Unlike *Tom Sawyer*, the new book, he had claimed a year earlier in a famous letter to his friend W. D. Howells, "is *not* a boy's book, at all. It will only be read by adults" (Smith and Gibson 91). That summer, as the presidential campaign that was to figure so prominently in the formal ending of Reconstruction was heating up, Twain was "tearing along" (Kaplan, *Mr. Clemens and Mark Twain* 197) on the novel that would come to focus on just what the Radical Reconstruction had set out to do, namely, "setting a free slave free" (James Cox 175).

Twain did not immediately have in mind a narrative focused on race. Indeed, the opening pages establish a setting not unlike the one we encountered in the earlier work, with Huck and Tom once again involved in adventures that ostensibly set them against Hannibal society. Twain's choice with *Huck* was whether or not to repeat the earlier narrative (he planned, for example, to include a trial ending in the sequel), but he swiftly envisioned a much more complex narrative when he hit upon the racially charged relationship of Huck and Jim.

It was a topic that suited Twain, for few of his contemporary white writers held views on the question of race as liberal as those of this "desouthernized Southerner" (Howells 30).[3] Twain's "Twins of Genius" tour with George Washington Cable, like his quiet patronage of a young African American bound for college, demonstrates the depth of his racial liberalism.[4] For Shelley Fisher Fishkin, with *Huckleberry Finn* Twain became the first white writer to demonstrate the "emotional terrain" of slavery (100). In the present chapter, I address the nature of the racial dialectic in *Huckleberry Finn*, at the center of which we find our most celebrated literary companions.

We know something about Huck Finn's preoccupation with race and racial identity from our encounters with him in *The Adventures of Tom Sawyer*, in which we find a foreshadowing of the pattern of attraction and betrayal in *Huck*. Indeed, Huck provides a model for what Forrest G. Robinson calls the "bad faith" that typifies his relationship with Jim in the sequel.[5] When, one evening, Tom asks Huck where he will sleep, Huck's reply anticipates the relationship we find between white and black in the later novel:

> "In Ben Rodgers hay-loft. He lets me, and so does his pap's nigger man, Uncle Jake. I tote water for Uncle Jake whenever he wants me to, and any time I ask him he gives me a little something to eat if he can spare it. That's a mighty good nigger, Tom. He likes me, becuz I don't ever act as if I was above him. Sometimes I've set right down and eat with him. But you needn't tell that. A body's got to do things when he's awful hungry he wouldn't want to do as a steady thing." (Twain, *The Adventures of Tom Sawyer* 174)

Huck's relationship with Uncle Jake—and, specifically, his interpretation of that relationship—anticipates the central pattern of moral development and ultimate betrayal that we find in the later novel. As Robinson notes, while the two show compassion in their exchanges, for Huck's part, "[t]here may be hunger here, but there is much greater respect" (*In Bad Faith* 116). The relationship between Huck and Uncle Jake thus anticipates Huck's days spent with Jim on the Mississippi, when we find him initially bringing Jim food and, later, Jim generously sitting watch for Huck. Huck equates food—and maternity, for both Jake and Jim relate to him as mothers—with a kind of love, albeit a love checked by a deep ambivalence over race.

But if there is an ideal of racial parity in Huck's description here, there is also the affirmation of his society's ideology respecting African American culture, and we find the latter periodically throughout the novel and especially in its later chapters. " 'That's a mighty good nigger, Tom,' " Huck says, as if recognizing his friend's incredulousness, and then Huck offers a more overt analysis of the relationship between black and white than we will ever see in *Huckleberry Finn:* " 'He likes me, becuz I don't ever act as if I was above him.' " Twain here anticipates the compassionate relationship that he will later develop at length between Huck and Jim on the river, revealing that long before he had Huck apologize to Jim following the fog sequence and his mean-spirited deception, Twain knew that social and racial hierarchies undermine social relationships. The racially charged dogma at the conclusion of the passage foreshadows the failures of moral will that Huck experiences in the later work as well as his specific inability to maintain the courage of his intuitions in the presence of Tom Sawyer.

Like the protagonists we encounter later, Huck moves toward an awareness of the place of otherness within his identity that he ultimately comes to reject. At the center of the novel's dialectic, we find a movement toward a mutable racial identity: initially it comes in Huck's rejection of life at the Widow Douglas's home and later in his parallel rejection of life with Pap. Escaping these bewildering experiences, Huck discovers Jim on Jackson's Island, a fortunate meeting that leads to the novel's first gratifying domestic scene. Throughout much of the novel, Jim continues to serve as a silent mediator of the deep conflicts Huck feels in the presence of white society; Huck's union with Jim represents a merging with, and an emergence into, a black culture he intermittently rejects and finally cannot bear.

Huck and Jim

In his most-loved and most-loathed novel, Mark Twain demonstrates Huck's moral growth through his relationship with a marginalized mentor in Jim, who becomes a conduit for Huck's own growth. In the course of their experiences together, Huck casts off his essentialized view of his companion and, despite the imperatives of American and specifically southern culture, comes to see Jim's emotional capacity. He finds in his relationship with Jim more solace and relief than he has found elsewhere in the world.

We see that Twain valued the book's focus on racial enlightenment in his much-celebrated remembrance of *Huckleberry Finn* as "a book of mine where a sound heart and a deformed conscience come into collision and conscience suffers defeat" (qtd. in Lauber 109). By the end of the novel, however, Huck once again views Jim through the essentializing racial stereotypes of the southern society that neither of them can finally escape. By the end, that is, Huck has returned Jim to the stereotyped position from which he so lately rescued him, and Twain, for his part, has returned his narrative and his narrator to the boyhood world of *Tom Sawyer*. As Robinson has noted, if Huck cannot bear society, neither can he bear Jim, and he abandons both in leaving for the Territory (*In Bad Faith* 210).

Leslie Fiedler notes such a pattern in his still-luminous study, *Love and Death in the American Novel*, in which he argues that the relationship between Huck and Jim—like that between Ishmael and Queequeg—reflects the white American writer's unconscious longing for a prepubescent, homoerotic relationship with an older individual who represents a culture that white Americans have persistently oppressed. At the heart of the white character's embrace of the man or woman of color is, for Fiedler, a fear of repudiation: "Behind the white American's nightmare that someday, no longer tourist, inheritor, or liberator, he will be rejected, refused, he dreams of his acceptance at the breast he has most utterly offended" (*Love and Death* 670–71). Huck Finn is the first of many such characters who look to a black character for moral growth when forced to do so but ultimately turn from that character—and from recognition of the place of otherness

in the creation of their own identities—once they have achieved
the growth necessary to their development. Huck thus uses Jim
as a springboard for his own escape from a society that he finds
constricting.

For many contemporary critics, this betrayal points to the central failings of American culture. Rhett S. Jones argues that *Huckleberry Finn* "reflects and embodies white double-consciousness
as Mark Twain shifts back and forth in his perspective on Jim and
other blacks, now viewing them as full-fledged human beings,
now regarding them as inferior folk" (28). Arnold Rampersad
sees the return to stereotype in Twain's novel as the result of inherent bias within a "typically American 'twinning' of white and
dark-skinned characters." The motivation for employing such
characters, Rampersad argues, "is based on a sense of a black or
native American familiarity with Nature, noble in essence and
finally inaccessible to the white man" (50). Though such characteristics might suggest that the dark-skinned character plays
the more significant role in the relationship, Rampersad argues
that he remains "almost inevitably second in importance to the
white hero. He is only an acolyte in the ritual of American absolution from sin—when he isn't the sacrificial victim itself. In *Huck
Finn*, Mark Twain exalts Jim—just beyond the level of a white
boy—but finally cannot allow him to remain exalted. Jim then
becomes little more than a plaything, like a great stuffed bear,
for the white boys over whom he once stood morally" (51). For
these critics, the difficulty with Twain's ending is not a matter of
aesthetics or unity, the main reasons for which the book was at-
tacked before Fiedler published his fabulously controversial essay,
"Come Back to the Raft Ag'in, Huck Honey!" in 1948. For them,
Twain's ending reflects the central ideological contradictions of
American culture.

Other critics, however, have found that Twain's struggle with
his portrayal of Jim—his movement in and out of stereotype—
led to a portrayal of black characters significantly developed from

earlier types. Ralph Ellison argues that Twain, writing as he did in the midst of the popularity of the minstrel show and shortly after a war that had left white Americans weary of addressing the problems of blacks, "fitted Jim into the outlines of the minstrel tradition, and it is from behind this stereotype mask that we see Jim's dignity and human capacity—and Twain's complexity— emerge" (*Shadow and Act* 50). As I demonstrate in a later chapter, in *Invisible Man* Ellison in turn renders a black character who in some ways resembles Jim in full humanity even as he dismisses the role of the well-meaning whites in the development of African Americans.

But whatever the "human capacity" present in Jim, he is surely not a fully realized human character at the end of Twain's novel. James Cox persuasively argues in his seminal study *Mark Twain: The Fate of Humour* that Jim's position at the end of the novel reflects the position of African Americans in American society as Twain wrote the novel. In the end, I agree with Wayne Booth that such an elevated reading is remote from the experience of the vast majority of readers. And Twain himself, in his stage performances of scenes from the novel, encouraged an interpretation of the conclusion that heightened the comic effect of Jim's position, reducing what satiric emphasis might be found in the published novel.

Mississippi Crossings

Throughout the novel, Huck's emergent sense of Jim's humanity is linked to his determined struggle with his own identity. Huck adopts a lengthy series of memorable aliases: he is variously Sarah Williams, Sarah Mary Williams, Charles William Albright, and George Jaxon, among others; ultimately, of course, he becomes Tom Sawyer. Twain contrasts this series of guises with Huck's transcendent identity, an identity that is most clear in the river passages in which Huck is cut off from society and linked closely to Jim. Here, as Rampersad suggests, Huck is at one with nature, and here, as he recurrently reminds us, things are most "easy and comfortable" (155). Huck accepts a marginalized identity on the river, for there as nowhere else it will remain unchallenged. Away from Jim, however, Huck's identity—like that of the typical picaresque hero—always changes, suggesting that he will ultimately cast off whatever development he experiences through his relationship with Jim once they have returned to society, as of course they must. Thus Twain early on prepares us for Huck's ultimate betrayal of Jim, even if we have often hoped things will turn out differently.

For all his protean shifts in identity, the one identity Huck cannot accept, despite his glory in the fugitive's life, is that of a slave narrator. Already a marginalized figure in southern society, Huck adopts the tropes of the first southern genre of marginalization, the slave narrative, as trickster figure, autobiographer, escapee from a harsh southern environment. Through Jim, he confronts the very cruelties of slavery that the slave narratives specifically addressed: alienation within an absurd and chaotic environment, division of family, and movement toward autonomous selfhood. But while he shares in all these experiences with Jim, Huck finally cannot accept the idea of kinship between himself and Jim, and he betrays their relationship when he returns to a white southern community. It is a classic American story that no one before Twain had told and one he didn't quite know he was telling.

Huck in Limbo

We associate Huck with the African American community from our first encounter with him in *The Adventures of Tom Sawyer*, where he emerges swinging a dead cat that he invests with magical powers. Huck's superstition—like so many others he possesses—links him unwittingly to Jim and suggests that Twain always conceived of Huck as a character tied to the black community. In the first chapter of the sequel, Huck's anguish at having burned a spider in a candle ("I didn't need anybody to tell me that was an awful bad sign and would fetch me some bad luck" [4]) contrasts strongly with his indifference to Miss Watson's tale of Moses and the "bullrushers" ("I don't take no stock in dead people" [2]), and the opposition of the two demonstrates his predisposition toward engagement with black culture. Later, Huck gives up superstition for Tom's romantic claptrap, and this rejection amounts to his denial of his own engagement with a black world. But at the beginning, Huck's superstitions prepare us for his movement toward otherness and toward the novel's central relationship.

From the beginning, Jim is the primary agent of identity for Huck. As the second chapter opens, for example, Huck and Tom are escaping from the Widow Douglas's yard, and Huck's initial portrayal of Jim imparts the significance the relationship will come to have for both: "We scrouched down and laid still. Miss Watson's big nigger, named Jim, was setting in the kitchen door; we could see him pretty clear, because there was a light behind him. He got up and stretched his neck out about a minute, listening. Then he says, 'Who dah?' " (6). Twain depicts Tom and Huck "tip-toeing along a path" as they attempt to escape the house and bowing down in hiding from Jim. At this early moment, Jim ironically implements the moral codes of those who enslave him: as moral agent, Jim reminds the boys of the Widow's restrictive values, values that won't permit midnight flights from the house. While Jim later acts as catalyst for Huck's moral development and so inspires Huck's ostensible rejection of the "conscience" he equates with St. Petersburg's moral ideology, here he reminds Huck of his obligations to the Widow and Miss Watson.

Huck and Tom can see Jim "pretty clear" (though, with only a light behind him, they can see only his silhouette) as he searches the darkness for them, but Jim cannot determine the source of the noise that he has heard. " 'Who dah?' " he calls out, and Huck remains a vague moral figure for him at least until they join their two causes on Jackson's Island. Indeed, Jim questions Huck throughout, metaphorically demanding that Huck define himself, declare his identity, by aligning himself with or against Jim's flight. His initial question is one for all white Americans, asked in countless ways by America's minorities from the earliest days of the colonial presence. It is a question we'll encounter again in the southern novels that follow *Huck Finn*.

Hearing no response to his question, Jim continues to seek out the source of the noise he has heard:

> He listened some more; then he come tip-toeing down and stood right between us; we could a touched him, nearly. Well, likely it was minutes and minutes that there warn't a sound, and we all there so close together. There was a place on my ankle that got to itching; but I dasn't scratch it; and then my ear begun to itch; and next my back, right between my shoulders. Seemed like I'd die if I couldn't scratch. . . . Pretty soon Jim says:
>
> "Say—who is you? Whar is you? Dog my cats ef I didn' hear sumf'n. Well, I knows what I's gwyne to do. I's gwyne to set down here and listen tell I hears it agin." (6)

Twain's portrayal emphasizes the role Jim plays in relation to Huck throughout much of the novel. Jim literally and figuratively separates Huck from his companion Tom, whom Twain painstakingly portrays as a force aligned with this southern society.[6] If Huck feels physically uncomfortable here ("Seemed like I'd die if I couldn't scratch"), it is because Jim forces him outside that society in separating him from Tom Sawyer. Huck will ever be moving between a white world best represented by the duplicitous Tom and a black one represented by Jim, and, in this moment, we begin to see an inkling of the alienation that becomes central to Huck's character as, later on, he confronts the reality of slavery in America as well as the ideal of freedom in American culture. Huck's misery here anticipates the struggle of conscience he will face on the river, where his proximity to Jim compels him to confront the moral conflicts of a white identity.

The first of the many tricks Tom plays on Jim establishes both Huck's passive acceptance of Tom's machinations and Jim's vulnerability to both boys. When Jim falls asleep after lying down to wait out the source of the noise, Huck and Tom successfully escape. To Huck's consternation, however, Tom insists on returning to fool Jim:

> When we was ten foot off, Tom whispered to me and wanted to tie Jim to the tree for fun; but I said no; he might wake and make a disturbance, and then they'd find out I warn't in. Then Tom said he hadn't got candles enough, and he would slip in the kitchen and get some more. I didn't want him to try. I said Jim might wake up and come. But Tom wanted to resk it; so we slid in there and got three candles, and Tom laid five cents on the table for pay. Then we got out, and I was in a sweat to get away; but nothing would do Tom but he must crawl to where Jim was, on his hands and knees, and play something on him. I waited, and it seemed a good while, everything was so still and lonesome. (7)

Tom assumes a position of control by virtue of his ability to pay for his moral transgressions, something we see him do at the end of the novel, when he pays Jim forty dollars "for being prisoner for us so patient" (360). He thus provides stark contrast to Huck Finn, who, cut off from both Tom and Jim, experiences his first moment of reflection upon the racial themes of the novel as he feels "all still and lonesome," waiting for Tom to return from playing his trick upon Jim. When Huck cannot move between white and black worlds but is instead left to contemplate that movement, his thoughts invariably turn to a quietude that approaches death.

Tom's manipulations of Jim result in Jim's first subordination to minstrelsy, and it is a role he plays frequently. Yet Jim turns the minstrel's role to his advantage: in exaggerating upon his story of having been "rode by witches," Jim wins the respect of other slaves in the area: "Strange niggers would stand with their mouths open and look him all over, same as if he was a wonder" (8). David L. Smith argues that Twain portrays Jim's strategic efforts alongside racial stereotypes, thus "elaborat[ing] them in order to undermine them" (6).

Both author and character move into a black world with this first of Jim's tales—Fishkin demonstrates that Jim's story parallels the stories of slaves throughout the South who were warned by masters of ghosts and the like that wandered the countryside at night (81–86). Huck's ironic dismissal of Jim's story—"Jim was most ruined, for a servant" (8)—reveals his first moment of admiration for African American culture and specifically for the trickster figure that Huck himself comes to resemble. Conceding that Jim has turned things to his advantage, Huck admires him for the fabrication.[7] Jim is thus himself performing blackness—which is to say, the expectation his audience has of blackness—to his own advantage, and the performance carries a different meaning for each audience: for Tom, it affirms Jim's lowly status, since Tom himself instigated the trick; for the slaves who hear him, Jim is himself empowered. Between these two extremes we find Huck Finn struggling to comprehend the nature of Jim's performance and, ultimately, of race itself. In such moments, race is cut loose from all certainty for Huck.

The scene likewise further develops the dialectical opposition of Tom and Jim, of a white world and a black one, that serves to underscore Huck's central dilemma throughout. While Jim claims that he has been conjured by witches, Twain's reader might well have imagined a different fate entirely. Here is the first indication of the indictment of slavery to come: as John Seelye writes, "If slavery was a dead issue in the centennial year 1876 [when Mark Twain began writing *Huckleberry Finn*], intolerance was not, and in the hands of lynch mobs often became a burning issue" (Introduction xxv). Tom's "trick" turns upon the reader and evokes the larger themes that Twain addresses as his novel develops. In the midst of it all is Huck Finn, bewildered and torn between a white world that alternately constrains and abuses him and a black one he has been taught to resist.[8]

Jim will, from these early moments in the text, increasingly become the agent of moral growth for Huck as well as the conduit for Huck's passage toward a new understanding of himself that will be accompanied by his movement toward the margins of his American culture. Huck has a distant recognition that he must turn to black culture in order to fully understand his own place within southern and, ultimately, American society. In Huck's next encounter with Jim, he asks Jim to "do magic" and reveal the reason that Pap has returned to St. Petersburg. Huck asks Jim to consult a hairball: "What I wanted to know, was, what [Pap] was going to do, and was he going to stay?" (20). Huck seeks black magic, black knowledge, blackness itself in order to learn more of himself. In coming to blackness, Huck expects it to be certain and fixed: he is confounded when he discovers it is instead a performance, subjective and infinitely adaptable.

We see in this scene the extent to which the union of black and white that centers the novel is fraught with deceit and manipulation: Jim tells the gullible Huck that the hairball sometimes "wouldn't talk without money." In response, Huck gives Jim "an old slick, counterfeit quarter," but he fails to mention "the dollar I got from the judge" (21). Each keeps a close watch on the other, but if their relationship is thus characterized by deception, each nevertheless comes away satisfied: Jim is, after all, able to make use of that counterfeit quarter, and Huck gets the advice he seeks. Huck's movement toward a black world is checked not only by his own resistance but also by Jim's. Jim, perhaps suspecting Huck's role in Tom Sawyer's mock lynching, now warns Huck with a mocked-up lynching of his own: " 'You wants to keep 'way fum de water as much as you kin, en don't run no resk, 'kase it's down in de bills dat you's gwyne to git hung' " (22).

When Jim prophesies that Pap is wrestling with two angels, he seems to allude to the very moral dilemma in which Huck soon finds himself: " 'One uv 'em is white en shiny en t'other one is black. De white one gits him to go right, a little while, den de black one sail in en bust it all up' " (22). Jim's language ironically alludes to the essentialized assumptions of race against which Huck struggles as he later helps Jim to escape. Further, Jim's explanation alludes to Huck's own predicament, caught as he is between black and white identities. Indeed, Jim says that Huck too is caught between a dark presence and a light one: " 'Dey's two gals flyin' 'bout you in yo' life. One uv 'em's light en t'other one is dark. One is rich en t'other is po'. You's gwyne to marry de po' one fust en de rich one by en by' " (22). The dark and poor one we know already, of course, following Fiedler's thesis, but Huck remains a reluctant suitor. If Jim has earlier been asking Huck's identity (" 'Who dah?' "), Huck has now come to ask his own identity of Jim, probing cautiously into a black world to which he senses he must go in order to discover himself.[9]

On Jackson's Island, a Crusoe-like Huck initially celebrates his own cultural autonomy: "I was the boss of it; it all belonged to me," Huck declares as he explores the island (48). But his discovery of Jim's campfire challenges his fantasized independence, and as in their initial encounter, Huck attempts to conceal his identity as long as possible. Returning to the camp the next morning, Huck approaches cautiously: "By and by I was close enough to have a look, and there laid a man on the ground. It most give me the fan-tods" (50). Huck's discomfort in Jim's presence—like his short-lived failure to recognize Jim—anticipates the abstract distance he will feel from his companion throughout the novel.

Huck's initial supposition that a white man is on the island threatens his autonomy as well as the fictional death he created in his escape from Pap's cabin. With the "gray daylight" dawning upon them, however, Huck soon recognizes Jim and immediately loses all trepidation, as he is able to rely on the tropes of race that he knows so well—and that he will persistently employ in his dealings off the river—in interacting with Jim (50). He knows now that it is not a "man" but a slave he has happened upon:

"[I]t was Miss Watson's Jim!" In Jim's reaction, Twain reasserts his character's superstitious nature, which invokes a characteristic white fantasy of black behavior:

> He bounced and stared at me wild. Then he drops down on his knees, and puts his hands together and says:
>
>   "Doan hurt me—don't! I hain't ever done no harm to a ghos'. I awluz liked dead people, en done all I could for 'em. You go en git in de river agin, whah you b'longs, en doan' do nuffn to ole Jim, 'at 'uz awluz yo' fren'." (51)

Thus their relationship on the river begins, with Jim genuflecting before Huck, passively pleading for mercy from his young interlocutor.

Following the novel's first gratifying domestic experience ("When breakfast was ready, we lolled on the grass and eat it smoking hot" [52]), Huck's dialogue with Jim indicates the extent to which they both struggle to overcome the mistrust inherent in relations between black and white in the southern society that has made them:

> "How do you come to be here, Jim, and how'd you get here?"
>
>   He looked pretty uneasy, and didn't say nothing for a minute. Then he says:
>
>   "Maybe I better not tell."
>
>   "Why, Jim?"
>
>   "Well, dey's reasons. But you wouldn' tell on me ef I 'uz to tell you, would you, Huck?"
>
>   "Blamed if I would, Jim."
>
>   "Well, I b'lieve you, Huck. I—I *run off.*"
>
>   "Jim!"
>
>   "But mind, you said you wouldn't tell—you know you said you wouldn't tell, Huck."
>
>   "Well, I did. I said I wouldn't, and I'll stick to it. Honest *injun,* I will. People would call me a low-down ablitionist and despise

me for keeping mum—but that don't make no difference. I ain't
agoing to tell, and I ain't agoing back there, anyways. So now, le's
know all about it." (52–53)

Jim places his trust in Huck for the first time, and Huck immediately considers the troubling results of such a bond, tentative
though it may be. Despite his claims to the contrary, of course,
these first pangs of "conscience" will indeed make a difference.

In the course of his narrative, Twain painstakingly traces
Huck's growing sense of Jim's humanity through a series of crisis-
born epiphanies reflecting the anxiety Huck experiences in choosing between wildly divergent moralities. The first of these occurs
when Huck learns that trackers are coming to the island in pursuit
of Jim. Linking his own cause with Jim's, Huck cries out, " 'Git
up and hump yourself, Jim! There ain't a minute to lose. They're
after us!' " (75). Identifying himself with Jim for the first time,
Huck separates further from the cultural mores of St. Petersburg
and moves closer to a kind of multicultural ideal that is ever at the
periphery of the novel, the potential bonding of black and white
that he will never fully accept.

Likewise, the well-known dialogue following the passage in
which Huck and Jim become separated in the fog reveals Huck's
growing awareness of a slave's humanity. He begins here for the
first time to see behind the performance of race, though such
awareness comes only after Huck has first manipulated Jim, in
imitation of his friend Tom Sawyer. When Huck claims that Jim
has only dreamed their separation, Jim is incredulous:

"Huck—Huck Finn, you look me in de eye; look me in de eye.
Hain't you ben gone away?"

"Gone away? Why what in the nation do you mean? *I* hain't
been gone anywheres. Where would I go to?"

"Well, looky here, boss, dey's sumf'n wrong, dey is. Is I *me*, or
who *is* I? Is I heah, or whah *is* I? Now dat's what I wants to know."
(103)

Jim characteristically links his confusion here to his own identity and to his relationship with Huck, questioning not Huck but his own presence on the raft and his self-awareness. Never before in the work of a white writer have we seen so clearly the internal dimension of a black character, but Huck has returned to the duplicitous role he earlier held. As a result, Jim, having already cast his lot with Huck, can no longer determine his own identity: " 'Is I *me*, or who *is* I?' "

As in earlier scenes in which Jim questions Huck's identity, Twain's focus is the separation of the two. Just as Huck will constantly forget his newfound awareness of Jim's humanity and his resultant resolve to set Jim free, they are time and again separated from one another. Ernest D. Mason explains this pattern of digressions in the relationship as a "combination of revulsion and fascination, intimacy and remoteness, attraction and repulsion" in which Huck's frequent failures to achieve moral development are symptomatic of his "desire to worship Jim the child and dominate Jim the man" (36–38).

After Jim realizes that Huck has tricked him, his admonishment leads to Huck's repentance and the passage that Fiedler calls "an apology for all of white America" (*"Huckleberry Finn"* 6):

"When I got all wore out, wid work, en wid de callin' for you, en went to sleep, my heart wuz mos' broke bekase you wuz los', en I didn' k'yer no mo' what become er me en de raf'. En when I wake' up en fine you back agin, all safe en soun', de tears come en I could a got down on my knees en kiss' yo' foot I's so thankful. En all you wuz thinkin' 'bout, wuz how you could make a fool uv ole Jim wid a lie. Dat truck dah is *trash;* en trash is what people is dat puts dirt on de head er dey fren's en makes 'em ashamed."

Then he got up, slow, and walked to the wigwam, and went in there, without saying anything but that. But that was enough. It made me feel so mean I could almost kissed *his* foot to get him to take it back.

It was fifteen minutes before I could work myself up to go and
humble myself to a nigger—but I done it, and I warn't ever sorry
for it afterwards, neither. I didn't do him no more mean tricks, and
I wouldn't done that one if I'd a knowed it would make him feel
that way. (105)

Once again Jim has been calling through darkness, challenging
Huck to identify himself. But when Huck deceives him in the
manner of Tom Sawyer, Jim learns precisely whom he is calling: in Jim's reckoning, Huck is now (white?) "trash" for his
cruel behavior. Cut off from their relationship, Jim himself is
lost. Huck, in turn, becomes emotionally lost upon hearing Jim's
condemnation.

Huck regularly tricks the whites on the river with impunity,
but the result is never the same when he tries to trick Jim. The
reversed genuflection here suggests that finally no true sense of
"equality" is possible in this narrative: the raft, far from being the
placid and just preserve from civilization that so many have declared it to be, is in fact the site for a never-ending series of moral
one-upmanship. If Jim takes the upper hand by demonstrating a
superior moral sensibility, Huck will soon wrest it back from him.
The earnestness in Huck's "apology for all of white America" is
typically short-lived for both boy and nation, and Huck's claim
that he "didn't do [Jim] no more mean tricks" is a laughable lie. If
he learns here that race is enacted and that the human supersedes
the performative, he will shortly come to insist yet again on the
performance with which he is familiar, shunning his brief gaze
behind the curtain.

Shortly after the fog passage, in fact, Huck has already forgotten his newfound resolve. Telling Jim that he is going to look
for news of Cairo, Huck instead sets out to turn Jim in, a pretty
mean trick indeed. Jim calls to Huck as Huck strikes out for shore:
" 'Pooty soon I'll be a-shout'n for joy, en I'll say, it's all on accounts
o' Huck; I's a free man, en I couldn't ever ben free ef it hadn' ben

for Huck; Huck done it. Jim won't ever forgit you, Huck; you's de bes' fren' Jim's ever had; en you's de *only* fren' ole Jim's got, now' " (125). Several critics have suggested that Jim's abundant praise comes because he guesses what Huck has in mind and so senses a need to remind Huck of the obligations they have toward one another, even as his rhetoric recalls the social structure that enslaves him.

Jim, of course, emphasizes the word "friend," a term he uses regularly but one that Huck never once uses in reference to Jim.[10] In the subsequent paragraph (in contrast to the "trash" Jim has associated with Huck in the previous scene), Jim describes Huck as " 'de on'y white genlman dat ever kep' his promise to ole Jim,' " ironically alluding to the very social structure that he is trying to escape. Calling Huck a "genlman," Jim associates Huck with southern gentility, granting his would-be betrayer the same power that Miss Watson holds over him. Jim is yet again performing, balancing Huck's expectations of race with the new and, for Huck, troublesome obligations of friendship.

Gentleman or no, when the slave catchers ask Huck if the man on the raft is white or black, he nearly gives Jim up, "but," he tells us, "the words wouldn't come." The words that *do* come are themselves performative: "I tried, for a second or two, to brace up, and out with it, but I warn't man enough—hadn't the spunk of a rabbit. I see I was weakening; so I just give up trying, and up and says—'He's white' " (125). Huck fails to respond to the social conscience that bothers him so, as he will again when he decides to "go to hell" and free Jim from slavery. Neither in this scene nor in the later one can he find words to express society's desires over his own. His confession that he "warn't man enough" to turn Jim in to the slave catchers demonstrates the extent to which he links his emerging identity to Jim and thus to a growing identification with a marginal identity he associates with blackness. Indeed, in claiming that *his* man is white, Huck the trickster figure reveals a measure of his own blackness.

Drifting Southward

Whatever Twain's intentions in his portrayal of him, Jim loses the only unconstrained power he had as a slave in southern society—his ability to escape his master and earn freedom through the use of his own cunning and physical strength—when the raft passes the mouth of the Ohio River. Thereafter, Jim can no longer attain freedom of his own accord and must depend upon the benevolence of the white boy who accompanies him. And when Huck fails to tell Jim that he has lost his chance to escape up the Ohio, the boy takes active control of Jim's flight, wresting from Jim any autonomy he might have retained. The quintessential black journey of the period—the escape from slavery—loses its narrative power as Huck's story trumps Jim's and he begins his journey back to a white world. In thus taking back the narrative from Jim, Huck likewise compels his companion back to the performance of race that is most fixed in his mind. Huck's ultimate discomfort grows in part from his inability to accept the performance as real.

Having forgotten Jim altogether in his stay with the Granger-fords (and having shown no remorse for what he surely would have taken to be Jim's death), Huck is reunited with Jim only by the efforts of the local slave community. Fishkin notes that Huck reveals his understanding of African American speech when the slave Jack—whom Huck easily accepts as his own slave—suggests that Huck come down to the swamp to see "a whole stack o' water-moccasins" (149). As Fishkin suggests, Huck knows what Jack must be signifying here, and he follows Jack despite the fact that "a body don't love water-moccasins enough to go around hunting for them." Jack, of course, leads Huck to the spot where local slaves have kept Jim in hiding. In describing the slave community's assistance in helping Jim escape, Twain engages his protagonist in a central trope of the slave narrative.

As when he first approached Jim on Jackson's Island, Huck here sees Jim's sleeping form and, upon identifying him, claims a metaphoric possession: "I poked into the place a ways, and come to a little open patch as big as a bedroom, all hung around with vines, and found a man laying there asleep—and by jings it was my old Jim!" (149). This language of possession and domesticity is much the same as that which Huck has used to describe the young slave: "[M]y Jack" (151). On Jackson's Island, Huck identified Jim as "Miss Watson's Jim"; now, despite their journey downriver, Jim still hasn't escaped the slave's designation, though he has changed masters.

The social hierarchy of the raft reestablished, Huck and Jim soon escape the violence of the feud that so sickens Huck and that we come to associate with the white world on the river's banks. Huck maintains that he and Jim are content upon leaving the banks of the river: "We said there warn't no home like a raft, after all. Other places do seem so cramped up and smothery, but a raft don't. You feel mighty free and easy and comfortable on a raft" (155). His comfort has everything to do with a nurturing blackness that contrasts sharply with the dissembling, murderous white world he has left.

But such bliss is predictably fleeting, and, in the next pages, the king and the duke, would-be white trash royalty, arrive to impose their own sense of social order on the raft. In an aside to the reader, Huck claims to know "these warn't real kings and dukes," but as with the news that they have passed the Ohio, he elects not to tell Jim because "[i]t wouldn't a done no good; and besides, it was just as I said; you couldn't tell them from the real kind" (201).

Huck's ironic commentary here serves to emphasize by contrast his increasing emotional kinship with Jim:

> I went to sleep, and Jim didn't call me when it was my turn. He often done that. When I waked up, just at day-break, he was setting there with his head down betwixt his knees, moaning and mourning to himself. I didn't take notice, nor let on. I knowed what it was about. He was thinking about his wife and his children, away up

yonder, and he was low and homesick; because he hadn't ever been
away from home before in his life; and I do believe he cared just
as much for his people as white folks does for theirn. It don't seem
natural, but I reckon it's so. He was often moaning and mourning,
that way, nights, when he judged I was asleep, and saying, "Po' little 'Lizabeth! po' little Johnny! it mighty hard; I spec' I ain't ever
gwyne to see you no mo', no mo'!" He was a mighty good nigger,
Jim was. (201)

Though he uses the essentialist language he will never escape,
Huck is coming to see Jim's goodness beyond type. And if he
takes a paternal role in withholding his knowledge of the king
and the duke from Jim, Huck is also capable of understanding
Jim as a paternal figure, though he never relates to him as such.
Lionel Trilling famously wrote that, in Jim, Huck "finds his true
father. . . . The boy and the Negro form a family, a primitive
community—and it is a community of saints" (108). But whatever
we might hope for the relationship, their communion never leads
to any lasting recognition on Huck's part of Jim's superior moral
sense and certainly not of Jim's role as surrogate father. Instead,
Huck constantly seeks the high ground for himself: to gain it, he
must reject the kinship with Jim he has begun to feel.

The reader surely finds a large degree of irony in Huck's denial
of a sense of connection with blackness itself: of all the characters
he is closest in demeanor to Jim, and, as we have seen, he has
been drawing his truest sense of himself from the black world
throughout the novel. Even in his ultimate rejection of the king
and the duke, we see a concomitant rejection of blackness. When
he sees the two crying over Peter Wilks's death to gain advantage for themselves, he exclaims: "Both of them took on about
that dead tanner like they'd lost the twelve disciples. Well, if ever
I struck anything like it, I'm a nigger. It was enough to make
a body ashamed of the human race" (210). Huck's metaphor, of
course, is anything but innocent: throughout the text he contrasts

the hypocrisy and greed of white southern culture with Jim's sim-
plicity. In condemning the immoral acts of the king and the duke,
Huck ironically distances himself from the "nigger" in whom he
has repeatedly discovered a profound humanity. In the terms of
the novel, what better identity could he adapt?

Leaving the king and the duke to a lynch mob, Huck runs
straight to Jim, once again returning to his companion's arms.
But he finds Jim's nurturing presence masked in a moment of
surprise that is, for the reader at least, comic:

> "Out with you Jim, and set her loose! Glory be to goodness, we're
> shut of them!"
>
> Jim lit out, and was a coming for me with both arms spread, he
> was so full of joy, but when I glimpsed him in the lightning, my
> heart shot up in my mouth, and I went overboard backwards; for
> I forgot he was old King Lear and a drowned A-rab all in one, and
> it most scared the livers and lights out of me. But Jim fished me
> out, and was going to hug me and bless me, and so on, he was so
> glad I was back and we was shut of the king and the duke, but I
> says:
>
> "Not now—have it for breakfast, have it for breakfast! Cut loose
> and let her slide!" (258–59)

Huck's return to Jim—and to his central narrative—reveals the
metaphoric trepidation with which he inevitably approaches Jim:
costumed so dramatically as a sick Arab, Jim terrifies his young
companion. Huck's efforts to reclaim the interracial union we had
seen earlier will be thwarted through the remainder of the text.

For all of his vacillation, Huck comes closest to an acceptance
of a marginalized identity, of blackness as he has come to identify
it, in the novel's best-known passage, when he decides to "go to
hell." On completing his letter to the Widow Douglas, Huck is re-
lieved of the guilt pressing upon him: "I felt good and all washed
clean of sin for the first time I had ever felt so in my life, and I
knowed I could pray, now" (269). He uses language decidedly not

his own in describing his relief, language he has learned from his white community: from Miss Watson and from the Widow Douglas surely, and especially from the revival he has witnessed on the river's shore. Yet it is no surprise that Huck's hedonistic personality gravitates toward language that gives him more pleasure and requires less Christian ardor. "Feeling good" may be a credo for Huck Finn, but he has surely never before felt good from being "all washed clean of sin."

And his thoughts quickly return to the river life with Jim, a life he recalls in language that contrasts starkly with that of the revival:

> [I] got to thinking over our trip down the river; and I see Jim before me, all the time, in the day, and in the night-time, sometimes moonlight, sometimes storms, and we a floating along, talking, and singing, and laughing. But somehow I couldn't seem to strike no places to harden me against him, but only the other kind. I'd see him standing my watch on top of his'n, stead of calling me—so I could go on sleeping; and see him how glad he was when I come back out of the fog; and when I come to him again in the swamp, up there where the feud was; and such-like times; and would always call me honey, and pet me, and do everything he could think of for me, and how good he always was; and at last I struck the time I saved him by telling the men we had small-pox aboard, and he was so grateful, and said I was the best friend old Jim ever had in the world, and the *only* one he's got now; and then I happened to look around, and see that paper [the note to Miss Watson].
>
> It was a close place. I took it up, and held it in my hand. I was a trembling, because I'd got to decide, forever, betwixt two things, and I knowed it. I studied a minute, sort of holding my breath, and then says to myself:
>
> "All right, then, I'll *go* to hell"—and tore it up. (269–71)

The moral language he had discovered earlier pales in comparison with the river poetry we find here, language that he adapts whenever he is with Jim. It is the language of Huck's own journey toward the margins. For Stephen Railton, Huck's recollection of the river journey defines "with great human clarity exactly what is lost when you call a person a 'nigger'—by showing us what you see instead when you call him by his right name" (397). Huck, who sees Jim only in the context of their relationship, for the first time sees Jim completely outside of the multiple stereotypes southern society places upon African Americans. Just as important, he sees himself outside of southern society: going to hell, for Huck, is entering into a compelling yet terrifying blackness. And because, for the moment at least, Huck's catalyst is no action of Jim's, as in the fog sequence, but rather his own sense of goodness, Twain would have the reader believe that Huck's decision, unlike earlier epiphanies, reflects genuine moral development.

Yet Huck's innate sense of goodness—that "sound heart" Twain spoke of years later—matches exactly his sense of the comfortable. However much trust he may have as he enters into a compact that could confirm his identity within a black world, he quickly reverses himself in the ensuing pages. As in the earlier moments on the raft, for all the ceremony of this moment, Huck finally does what is easiest for him. When he "see[s] Jim," he sees mostly a fawning domestic: Jim stands Huck's watch, calls him "honey," and pets him. It is apparent that Huck's moral growth finally represents no deeper resolve than we have seen earlier when he apologizes to Jim at the conclusion of one chapter and sets out to return him to slavery at the beginning of the next.

Huck among the Crickits

The final section contributes to what Robinson calls the novel's "endless rage for diversion . . . an oblique manifestation of the culture's submerged discomfort with itself, most especially with the inhumanity of its treatment of black people" (*In Bad Faith* 133). Tom's evasion—and Huck Finn's participation in it—denies

Jim the humanity he has so lately gained in Huck's estimation as the boys reduce his plight to a succession of raucous exploits. Huck, in his capitulation to Tom Sawyer's elaborate plan to free Jim, loses what resolve he had found in this section, a failure Twain acknowledges with a wink in having Huck assume the identity of Tom Sawyer as his final alias. Huck plays Tom with a pious zeal, remarking, "[I]t was like being born again, I was so glad to find out who I was" (282). Just this quickly he has returned to the language of salvation, and salvation now comes in his resumption of a white identity. Having anxiously borne an increasing awareness of the part played by otherness in his own identity, Huck now returns joyfully to white society as Tom Sawyer himself. Jim has asked Huck time and again to identify himself, and Huck has on occasion come close to accepting an identity at the very margins of society with which he associates blackness. Now Huck fairly leaps at the opportunity to redefine himself within the white world.

Huck's adventures as Tom Sawyer resemble the boyhood pranks and misdeeds that typify the first three chapters of his book and the whole of Tom's. At the end, he has returned to a childhood in which he revered Tom, so he is more awed than horrified when Tom manipulates Jim in the name of the romance novel (and, one might argue, the New South). In the troubling final third of the novel, Tom plays the Southern Redeemer, a mock emancipator intent upon reestablishing a lost social order of old, which for Huck Finn means a return to whiteness itself. If his flirtations with a black identity were chaotic, uncertain, and fraught with peril, Huck finds whiteness by contrast ordered, sure, and safe. He is "born again" indeed.

Huck appears to emphasize his acceptance of the ideology of white culture upon his return to the banks of the river. When Aunt Sally asks if anyone was hurt in the steamboat accident, Huck responds, " 'No'm. Killed a nigger' " (279). We do see here, as Fishkin argues, Twain's satirical critique of the "vicious underpinnings" of the white southern world in this text (64). But if we are tempted to read Huck's swift acceptance of white ideology as a necessary manipulation designed to free Jim the quicker, we need only look to the following chapters to see how readily Huck postpones his plans once Tom Sawyer makes his meddling return to the novel. Twain's slight satire in the whole of the evasion hardly accounts for the enormity of Huck's reversal.

It is surprising that critics have so often found the ending of Twain's novel out of balance with the remainder of the text, for, as Victor Doyno notes, we should expect Huck's return to society: throughout the text we have seen constant ambivalence in Huck's response to Jim and, ultimately, to the recognition of the place of black culture in his own identity. And it would surely have been very unlike Mark Twain the comedian-author to end the book with a sober assessment of the tragedy of slavery; he could no more avoid the evasion than could Tom.

The inevitability of the evasion is but one of many critical points Seelye makes in his "revision," *The True Adventures of Huckleberry Finn*, in which Huck fully realizes his tragic potential: in Seelye's conclusion, Huck Finn never encounters Tom Sawyer again and can only watch in silent anguish as Jim drowns, pursued by slave catchers and weighed down by chains. At the end, Seelye's Huck continues downriver in darkness, with the weight of his experiences near as heavy as Jim's chains: "[D]ark as it was and lonesome as it was," he says, "I didn't have no wish for daylight to come. In fact, I didn't much care if the goddamn sun never come up again" (*The True Adventures* 339). Seelye demonstrates that such an ending could never be in the fiction of Mark Twain, even if we would have it so: as Seelye's Huck says of the "crickits," echoing Twain's own admonition to his readers, "[N]ow that they've got *their* book, maybe they'll leave that other one alone" (*The True Adventures* xii). That we can't suggests something of our desperation to rationalize the novel in the face of its transformation at the end.

But if Mark Twain could find no alternative way to end the book, little evidence supports the suggestion, made often enough in recent years, that he was consciously making a damning critique of society with the evasion of the sort he would indeed later make with *Pudd'nhead Wilson*. As we will see, his public readings of the novel belie such a possibility. As Howells noted, Twain's penchant for travesty and burlesque was a self-destructive obsession.

We find the blueprints for Tom's evasion in the novel that bears his name; the romantic fictions that guide Tom's thinking also warp Huck's. Mark Twain brought Tom Sawyer back onstage precisely because the irrepressible Tom enabled Twain to evade completely the social union of black and white that the book had been moving toward before the king and the duke came aboard the raft. It was, of course, not the quicksandlike territory of race that had helped to make Samuel Clemens a successful writer—and "Mark Twain" a famous pseudonym—but instead the far safer childhood adventures of Tom Sawyer.[11] As Robinson argues, *Tom Sawyer* is a book in which race is persistently ignored. We could no more ignore the presence of race in *Huckleberry Finn* than we could ignore the wide and rolling river.

Through his passive acceptance of Tom's chicanery, Huck aligns himself with the white world that Tom has always represented for Twain. Tom, for his part, specifically endeavors to remove the threat of otherness altogether from the novel.[12] Neil Schmitz argues that Tom, in this last section, is engaged in altering Jim from a black slave—which he, of course, knows that Jim is not—to a "fugitive courier." For Schmitz, it is a "skillful caricature of the process which ennobles the black man by expunging his negritude. In order to rise from the degradation of slavery the black man must first become a white European" through the vehicle of romance fiction (62). Huck's willing participation in the process emphasizes his final movement away from the vision of racial union that has dominated the text and, indeed, from otherness itself.

According to Cox, Huck's return to Tom and to childhood, like Jim's corresponding return to stereotype, represents a burlesque that undermines the position of the reader: "If the reader sees in Tom's performance a rather shabby and safe bit of play, he is seeing no more than the exposure of the approval with which he watched Huck operate. For if Tom is rather contemptibly setting a free slave free, what after all is the reader doing, who begins the book after the *fact* of the Civil War? This is the 'joke' of the book— the moment when, in outrageous burlesque, it attacks the sentiment which its style has at once evoked and exploited" (175). The narrative's conclusion—in Cox's reading—implicates the reader in Huck's failure to act immediately upon his resolve to set Jim free. And yet, if this is the case, it is also true that Twain participates in this same process of "setting a free slave free" in developing Huck's narrative.

As Huck, Tom, and Jim step onto the raft following their escape, Huck heralds Jim's return to freedom: " '*Now*, old Jim, you're a free man *again*, and I bet you won't ever be a slave no more' " (340). It's hardly a safe bet, of course, and Huck's reduction of Jim's plight to wager reveals the extent to which he has aligned himself with Tom. If he has accomplished his goal of setting Jim free, he has also, in the process, forgotten the urgency with which he made his decision to "go to hell." In forgetting, he has lost the resolve to "take up wickedness" that we so admired earlier.

But Huck's satisfaction at his success in obtaining Jim's freedom is cut short when he and Jim realize that Tom has been shot in the calf during the escape. Despite Tom's insistence that they "man the sweeps" and head the raft downriver, Jim refuses: " 'Well, den, dis is de way it look to me, Huck. Ef it wuz *him* dat 'uz bein' sot free, en one er de boys wuz to git shot, would he say, "Go on en save me, nemmine 'bout a doctor f'r to save dis one?" Is dat like mars Tom Sawyer? Would he say dat? You *bet* he wouldn't! *Well* den— is *Jim* gwyne to say it? No, sah—I doan' budge a step out'n dis place, 'dout a *doctor*; not ef it's forty year!' " (340–41). The speech represents an ironic and ill-fated transcendence for Jim because in it he equates himself with the roguish boy who has "helped" him to escape, a posturing central to the formulaics of sentimental fiction. Jim, of course, holds himself to moral standards that surely don't exist in his would-be savior: Tom Sawyer has thoroughly demonstrated the very sort of solipsism that Jim forgoes here. Having delayed Jim's rightful freedom in order to indulge his romantic fantasy, Tom has been "saving" his own narrative from the fugitive sequel all along.

If earlier Huck demonstrated benevolence sufficient to consider Jim's humanity before his own, he has apparently lost that ability at this late point. "I knowed he was white inside" (341), Huck decides after Jim's sublime speech, as if any remaining trepidation he may have had in taking Jim out of slavery disappears with the revelation. Huck's ability to see Jim in moral terms as "white"— his society's metaphor for goodness—rather than acknowledge Jim's humanity delivers him from the fleeting remorse he has felt all along. Thus he bases his later assertion that Jim "had a good heart in him and was a good man" (354) largely on the racial dogma that he had symbolically rejected earlier. If Huck has been moving toward an awareness of the role of otherness in his view of himself, he now repudiates that journey in attempting to see Jim as white. Of course, Twain's satire suggests that he is very much aware of Huck's moral failings, but such moments, frequent as they were in earlier sections of the novel, are rare at its ending.

The reader leaves with the same feelings of ambivalence and doubt that Huck himself possesses. Huck, for his part, cedes all control of events, if not quite his narrative, to Tom Sawyer. We know that Tom has taken over when he reimburses Jim for his trouble: Tom gives Jim forty dollars "for being a prisoner for us so patient" (360). We can read Tom's gesture as a reference to the failed Radical Reconstruction of the South. Southern Redeemer in miniature, Tom mocks the promise made to freed slaves of "forty acres and a mule." Indeed, among the acts leading up to the Compromise of 1877 was the repeal of the Southern Homestead Act, which had offered freedmen the land in the first place. [13] In return for Tom's charity, Jim gives abundant thanks: " '*Dah*, now, Huck, what I tell you?—what I tell you up dah on Jackson islan'? I *tole* you I got a hairy breas', en what's de sign un it; en I *tole* you I ben rich wunst, en gwineter be rich *agin;* en it's come true; en heah she *is*! *Dah*, now! doan' talk to *me*—signs is *signs*, mine I tell you; en I knowed jis' 's well 'at I 'uz gwineter be rich agin as I's a stannin' heah dis minute!' " (360–61). [14] Jim has thus made the full circle back to a minstrel's portrayal of blackness as Twain once again emphasizes the superstitious and comic in his character. Huck, for his part, has traded black superstitions for Tom's white romantic games. And though Jim, like Tom, is to follow Huck to the Territory after the novel's end "for howling adventures amongst the Injuns" (361), they will not return to the river or to Huck's briefly shared sense of Jim's marginal identity.

At the end, Huck's decision "to light out for the Territory ahead of the rest" (362) tacitly acknowledges his own need to escape a society in which he cannot help but be corrupted by the predominant ideology. In this there is hope for Huck; he has experienced clear moral development through his relationship with Jim, returned to white society to shun that development, and finally, perhaps, sensed that he must attempt to recover what he had attained on the river. In this way, the Territory for which Huck lights out is the "hell" to which he had earlier resigned himself. He has been to hell and back and would, at narrative's end, return without the mentor who enabled his passage.

But if there *is* hope for Huck here, there is precious little for those slaves not so lucky as Jim. Through his relationship with Jim, Huck has sensed something within himself that cannot accept the hypocrisy of his society, yet finally, he can pursue this elusive identity only by using Jim as a springboard for his own escape. Ever isolated, Huck escapes the very society for which his growth might have held some consequence. With his failure to follow his own resolve, his narrative devolves into a pattern of black sacrifice for white gain that will become as familiar to readers of the southern novel as it will to students of American culture.

Indeed, in "lighting out for the Territory," Huck Finn has returned the antebellum United States to the point at which he found it. As the nation slowed the coming conflict over slavery by employing the territories to deflate passions on both sides, Huck Finn takes off for the Territory too, leaving behind the vexing questions his narrative has raised. If we expected a savior, we won't get one in Huck Finn.

Twain's Blackface

Mark Twain's working notes for his novel adequately demonstrate that in the years between writing the two major portions of the manuscript he planned to focus in some detail on African American folk culture. In the Group A notes, for instance, written between mid-November 1879 and mid-June 1880, we find four references that place African American culture in the planned text to follow: "Negro camp meeting & sermon—'See dat sinner how he run.' Swell Sunday costumes of negros"; "[d]escribe aunt Patsy's house. & Uncle Dan, aunt Hanner, & the 90-year blind negress"; "Negro Sermons"; and "po' $22-nigger will set in Heaven wid de $1500 niggers" (Blair and Fischer 725, 728, 730).[15] Likewise, in the Group B notes, written during the same period as the Group A notes, we find a reference to "Negro sermons— & the shouts" (Blair and Fischer 735). None of these notations, of course, emerges as a part of the final text. While Twain makes these notes alongside many others that do appear in the text in one form or another ("[d]runken man rides in the circus" [Blair and Fischer 729], for instance) and many that did not ("[r]uffian burnt up in Calaboose" [Blair and Fischer 727]), they surely demonstrate that, at this point in the development of his manuscript, Mark Twain intended that the Africanist presence—to use Toni

Morrison's term—would be much more evident in the second half of the book than it came to be.

To solve the dilemma of what to do with Huck and Jim, and in place of Huck's further movement toward African American culture, Twain focused upon the social satire of the South in his portrayal of the king and the duke and in Huck and Tom's evasion. Thus he avoided a portrayal of black culture that might have provided the satire with a stronger undercurrent of protest as he moved toward a narrative focused upon any aspect of the South but slavery: for example the skewed notions of honor to be found in the South, the gullibility of its citizens, their simplistic faith.

A consideration of Twain's African American characters other than Jim demonstrates his development of a minstrel show atmosphere in the novel. Critical treatment of Twain's minor black characters is relatively rare, yet we find that Twain employs them in much the same way that he employs Jim and that they serve to illuminate Jim's plight in startling ways. Prior to the evasion section, we see sympathetic characters derived largely from the slave narratives with which Twain was familiar, for example, in the slave family at the Wilks home, crying as they are sold in different directions, and in Jack, the Grangerfords' slave who directs Huck to Jim without committing himself and risking censure.[16] Indeed, rather than merely portraying stereotyped African American characters in the background of the novel, we find that Mark Twain has in fact worked carefully within the tradition of the slave narrative in his portrayal of the slaves other than Jim, drawing from the central tropes of the family divided by sale and the trickster figure who undermines white authority.

By the end of the novel, however, Twain has instead moved toward the minstrel show in his portrayal of minor black characters as in his portrayal of Jim. The slave Nat, for instance, emerges as a clear minstrel figure, played for comic effect principally by Tom but also by Huck through his narration of the scenes. Huck,

who came to Jim in earnest to determine what would become of
Pap, now mocks African American spirituality by laughing with
Tom—and, of course, the reader—at Nat's superstitions. For example, when Nat sees the dogs running into Jim's shed through
the hole that Tom and Huck have dug, he believes they must be
witches, and Tom explains that he must make a "witch pie" to
ward them off:

> "But my lan', mars Sid, howe's *I* gwyne to make 'm a witch pie?
> I doan know how to make it. I hain't ever hearn er sich a thing
> b'fo'."
>
> "Well, then, I'll have to make it myself."
>
> "Will you do it, honey?—will you? I'll wusshup de groun' und'
> yo' foot, I will!" (311)

Traditional social order in the South thus established, Huck leaves
his moral cause behind. It was Huck, of course, who earlier said he
could have "almost kissed" Jim's foot after he pretended that the
fog sequence was only a dream. In returning Tom to the narrative
and in forgetting Huck's moral obligation to Jim, Twain restores
the traditional balance of southern society. Thus, on the stage of
the Phelps farm we've returned to the minstrel show that Sam
Clemens himself so enjoyed.

Free and Easy

Adventures of Huckleberry Finn represents a way of thinking
about race relations that Americans have embraced and imitated
often, perhaps because, as Huck would have it, it is so "free and
easy" (128): Huck's hard-won resolve finally amounts to little. Yet
Huck's reversal comes at great cost, to Huck Finn as to us, for in
it he loses the self-recognition for which we so admire him. Huck
Finn may well be black, to use Fishkin's description, but we leave
his book with his denial of that blackness, and Huck's denial is an
echo of our own. The fog on the Mississippi River in which Huck

and Jim pass Cairo parallels Twain's own navigational difficulties in the course of his novel, considering that he left off its composition soon after he completed that section. Twain intended to depict Huck's moral growth through the boy's relationship with Jim and his increasing awareness of the participation of otherness in the formation of his own identity. But emerging from the fog of his own work, he passed his intended story and found himself drifting swiftly southward.

Given the extant notes on his readings of the text, I find little support for the argument that suggests Twain was conscious of the parallels to Reconstruction, that he was in fact placing Jim in this position as part of a larger social critique. In fact, Twain was playing this final section for laughs, as evidenced by his readings on the "Twins of Genius" tour with George Washington Cable. For example, the scene from the novel in which Jim is set "free" by Huck and Tom (called "A Dazzling Achievement" by Twain for his public readings) swiftly became his favorite for public performance. Shortly after trying it out for the first time, Twain wrote his wife that it "went a-booming," and, later in the tour, he described it as a "triumph" (Blair and Fischer 767).

In looking at the revisions Twain made for his readings, we find anything but an emphasis upon the effect of the boys' evasion on Jim. Indeed, Twain cuts the scene leading up to Huck's famous ironic declaration that Jim is, after all, "white inside" (Blair and Fischer 803), thus reducing Jim to minstrel figure more fully than he had in the published version and confirming his own debt to the minstrel show in his public performances.[17] In the few moments during Twain's public reading in which he represents Huck's former companion, Jim is solely the object of humor, complaining of the "circus" of animals that Tom and Huck have brought to the shed where he is held captive and concluding that "if he ever got out, this time, he wouldn't be a prisoner again, not for a salary" (Blair and Fischer 796). The minstrel's humor is evident here, and we see in Twain's usage of the minstrel show's basic elements the contradictory impulses that run throughout his novel. As Eric Lott writes, "[T]he contradiction between the book's overt politics and its indebtedness to the minstrel show was much less cumbrous in the nineteenth century" (31–32). Twain emphasizes Tom's mock heroics over the drama of race out of marketing necessity: he knew his readers, like his listeners, would be expecting a narrative rather like *Tom Sawyer* in form and tone. This is just the dilemma he faced in the conclusion of the novel.

Just as Twain continued to enjoy minstrel shows throughout his life despite his awareness that they failed to represent the humanity of African Americans, he chose to devote the last third of his novel to Tom Sawyer's outrageous burlesque despite the declaration of independence that was Huck's decision to "go to hell." Even if Twain knew that Tom was a fraud and that all the hope of the novel lay in the relationship of Huck and Jim, we nevertheless see that he uses Tom's deceit to great comic advantage, both in the novel and onstage. Wayne Booth points out that the vast majority of Twain's audience since the book's publication have found in his ending little more than innocent fun, and Twain surely knew this would be the case, as he demonstrated in his stage performances of the novel.

Eric Sundquist observes that "in their opposition to radical racists, liberal politicians and writers were likewise compelled toward fantasy or, in any event, toward significant accommodation of racism" (249). We find just such accommodation in *Huckleberry Finn*. Though we admire Twain's liberal outlook on American race relations, it seems plain that he chose to profit at Jim's expense by appealing to the dominant racial ideology of the culture in the novel's final section. As Robinson notes, the failure of Twain's original reviewers—and of so many literary critics and readers throughout the twentieth century—to remark on the book's obsession with race as well as the evasion of that central theme in the ending reflects on the nation's failures in regard to race.

In *The Company We Keep*, Booth proposes an assessment of Twain's treatment of race in the novel that balances the narrow with the transcendent:

> [T]hough Twain's racial liberalism was inevitably limited, though he failed to imagine the "good Negro" with anything like the power of his portrait of good and bad whites, though in effect he simply wipes out Jim as a character in the final pages, he has still, by his honest effort to create the first full literary friendship between a white character and a slave, permanently opened up this conversation we are engaged in. We would not be talking about what it might mean to cope adequately with the heritage of slavery, in literary form, had he not intervened in our conversation. (474)

Booth himself immediately calls into question such a strained vindication and concludes that the novel's merits in regard to its treatment of race are equivocal at best.

Strained or not, such a vindication of the novel has led numerous liberal southern writers after Twain to engage in conversations that propose little beyond Twain's opening remarks. Recasting literary relationships closely resembling that of Huck and Jim, southern writers have time and again entered a conversation about race that leads to the same denouement, in which a black character formerly redeemed from stereotype is promptly returned to it. Intending to go to hell, white characters like Huck Finn often return before they get there. We go with them on this journey to hell and back, hoping to pass by the racial guilt we feel so keenly and find in its place a transcendence through which we might at long last obtain racial innocence. Wrestling with the racial ghosts that haunt us in the literature that helps to produce our conception of race, we return to the dissonance on which our nation was founded, and in this particular, Mark Twain's most distinctly southern novel continues to speak for all America.

✳2✳
DIRTY BOOKS FOR YANKEES
William Faulkner and Elizabeth Spencer
Respond to Southern Unrest

> Mark Twain's Mississippi River ultimately drains off
> into William Faulkner's county of Yoknapatawpha, where
> the tradition of comic (and cosmic) violence as a southern way
> of life is continued. Starting with the humourists who founded
> the tradition in which Mark Twain wrote, the southern writer
> posits a world reflecting a deep division which, like the
> bond between black and white, is an inseparable knot
> binding love and loathing, affection and hatred,
> mutual dependence and a desire to part.
>
> JOHN SEELYE

Almost since the publication of *Huckleberry Finn* American novelists have looked to it as an archetypal model of fictional race relations.[1] Some southern writers in the years after Twain published
his novel, for example, tried to re-create the relationship with
varying success. Writing six years after Twain published *Huck
Finn*, Louis Beauregard Pendleton, for instance, set his *King Tom
and the Runaways* in southern Georgia in 1855 and centered his
narrative on two adolescent boys—"King" Tom and Albert—and
a runaway slave named Jim. In contrast with what we find in
Twain's work, the novel's impulses are largely conservative, reflecting the ideology of the plantation romance while attempting
to assess the uncertain nature of blackness. The conservative slant
means that many of the essential tensions of *Huck* and later southern novels are absent.

Writers as distinct as H. L. Mencken, Ralph Ellison, and Toni Morrison have praised the novel's contributions to American literary culture. But for some American writers it was a decidedly off-and-on affair: William Faulkner dismissed Twain as a "hack writer" but also called him "the first truly American writer" and ordered both *Tom Sawyer* and *Huckleberry Finn* when forming his library in Charlottesville (Blotner 672). When speaking on the subject of American writers late in life, Faulkner called Twain "our grandfather" (Chakovsky 236). Ultimately, for Faulkner more than most, the significance of Twain and his novel has as much to do with the vision of interracial union found at the center of *Huckleberry Finn*. Seeking to ease the moral complexities of racial relationships, southern writers have looked back to the "free and easy" moral arrangement of *Huck Finn*, which allows for the profession of high ideals while requiring no definitive action.

The union of a white protagonist with a black guide emerges as a central trope of the southern novel just at the time when the southern novel came to be celebrated as a unique American art form, and just as the consciousness of civil rights developed in the South. Thus a fascinating parallel to the transformation of the South during the civil rights era is the national celebration of a body of southern fiction that offers a conservative response to these transformative events. The white southern novelists I consider in this and subsequent chapters recast the elemental American relationship between white and black. If they often portray a new Eden in the pairing, just as often they return the black character to the essentialized position from which he or she had been so lately rescued.

If these mostly modernist writers respond in part to an emerging awareness of civil rights, they respond as well to the affirmation of the association of whiteness with an American cultural identity that Walter Benn Michaels describes as a persistent movement within modernism itself. For Michaels, the movement to oppose racial and cultural minorities within modernism "made Americanness into a racial inheritance and culture into a set of beliefs and practices dependent on race" (141). White southern writers in the middle years of the twentieth century, for all their emphasis on region, affirmed a white American identity, often by portraying a journey toward an otherness paralleling Huck's.

Numerous southern novels at mid–twentieth century—many of them largely forgotten works such as Robert Lewis Taylor's *A Journey to Mattecumbe* and Reuben Davis's *Shim*—engaged characters in transracial transgressions. In *Shim*, Davis describes rural Mississippi in the days just after Henry Grady announced the coming New South, and his work recalls the tradition of the plantation novel. Fourteen-year-old Shim comes to see himself standing outside his white culture through his relationship with Henry, a servant on the farm owned by Shim's family. Shim and Henry finally split because Henry cannot bear the coming of the new and wanders off into the wilderness, bearing himself back in time.[2]

In this chapter, I assess two mid-twentieth-century works by William Faulkner, *Go Down, Moses* and *Intruder in the Dust,* and another by Elizabeth Spencer, *A Voice at the Back Door,* each of which confronts and assesses the question of race at the moment in the nation's history when the relationship between black and white was being radically reformed. These two writers, in examining the political and cultural transformations of the period, incorporate, on the one hand, the voice of racially liberal southerners conscious of the coming of civil rights for African Americans and, on the other, the more conservative voice of their southern forebears.

Faulkner and the Myths of Race

Throughout his career, William Faulkner returned to the examination of a southern mythology bound up in race, often by portraying black characters as central moral figures in his novels. Such characters—like Dilsey in *The Sound and the Fury* and, in vastly different fashion, Joe Christmas in *Light in August*—gauge the moral character of white southern society, compelling that society to confront racial identity so as to know itself.

If the moral lives of white characters intertwine with those of black characters throughout Faulkner's fiction, nowhere is that bond so apparent as in the two works in which Faulkner is most indebted to *Huck Finn*: *Go Down, Moses* and *Intruder in the Dust*.[5] In these works, Faulkner portrays characters of mixed race as moral guides for his protagonists, Ike McCaslin in the former, Chick Mallison in the latter. In both, Faulkner revises the relationship between white adolescent and black mentor for a South and a United States poised for the civil rights era that each book anticipates. Faulkner's black characters are complex and autonomous, informed by his reading of Twain, surely, but by his modernist sensibility as well, by his need to portray black characters largely removed from the minstrel tradition to which Twain remained faithful.

Cursed Land: Go Down, Moses

While the antecedents for the work are many, critics have long pointed out the indebtedness of *Go Down, Moses* to Twain, particularly in Faulkner's portrayal of race. R. W. B. Lewis, for instance, argues that "the most significant prototype of *The Bear* [is] *Huckleberry Finn*" (197). For Lewis, the relationship between the two is most evident "in their common sense of friendship between black and white, in their common identification of slavery as a kind of original sin, in their common reversal of the conventional morality that legitimizes social injustice" (197). Likewise, for James Nagel, "The Bear" and *Huckleberry Finn* "seem to say that what is important in life is the capacity to rise above imposed values to affirm a code based on fundamental truth" (63).

Faulkner arrives at such truth through his portrayal of Ike Mc-Caslin's relationship with Sam Fathers, a former slave of both Native American and African ancestries. Faulkner consciously portrays an ultimate disavowal of the relationship between his twinned characters: Faulkner's Ike McCaslin attains a sense of independence from white culture through his relationship with Sam Fathers, yet Ike cannot finally bring himself to accept the debt that comes with his development, as we shall see in the concluding story of the book, "Delta Autumn."

The central narrative of *Go Down, Moses* turns upon Ike's renunciation of the patriarchy of Yoknapatawpha and of his inheritance and his heritage. The seeds of his renunciation grow in the warm embrace of Sam Fathers, represented by Faulkner as a noble savage: "[T]he wild man not even one generation from the woods" acts as both inspiration and catalyst for Ike's development (236). In coming to understand Sam Fathers, Ike shares in Sam's marginal identity and moves toward a new vision of himself, free of the moral and material dictates of white society. His abhorrence of his ancestors' abuses of their slaves is a direct corollary of his acceptance of Sam Fathers as a moral guide.[4]

Sam Fathers appears in *Go Down, Moses* at the beginning of "The Old People" when Ike first joins the men who go each November to the wilderness to hunt. In teaching Ike to become a hunter, Sam leads Ike toward a respect for the wilderness much different from that held by the white hunters in whom Ike for the first time begins to see white duplicity and for whom the wilderness is a place not for spiritual growth but instead for instruction in the rituals of white patriarchy. When Sam shows Ike his first buck, for instance, the boy immediately understands its symbolic value in a way that other white hunters do not: "He did not come into sight; he was just there, looking not like a ghost but as if all of light were condensed in him and he were the source of it" (157). In the course of his relationship with Sam, Ike comes to see the wilderness, like the buck, as a symbol of freedom from society. But freedom for a white protagonist contrasts with the relative lack of it for the character at the margins of this southern society, and Ike struggles throughout the narrative against a white society he comes to view as corrupt and hypocritical. Ike's relationship with Sam Fathers draws him toward the margins of his southern society, from which vantage point he can see what he will come to view as the failings of whiteness itself.

As Ike stands waiting for the buck, we sense keenly his isolation from white culture, indeed, from any culture: "At first there was nothing," the story begins, stressing Ike's detachment in the "gray and constant light of the late November dawn." Out of the abyss come the voices of the approaching dogs and, with them, Sam Fathers, "standing just behind the boy as he had been standing when the boy shot his first running rabbit with his first gun and almost with the first load it ever carried, touched his shoulder and he began to shake, not with any cold" (157). Out of nothingness comes Sam Fathers, alone able to fill the void left by the white world from which Ike has now been separated for the first time. Faulkner emphasizes the primacy of the scene in his repetition of the word "first," establishing in the relationship of white seeker and black acolyte a familiar American Eden. Sam ushers Ike into his early manhood just as Jim accompanies Huck into adolescence: surrogate fathers both, they supplant inadequate or absent parental models for their literary children. For Ike, a marginal identity will come to seem a natural remove from southern society, and in the first pages of the book, Sam Fathers guides his charge to these new places.

The ritual that bonds Ike with Sam symbolically removes Ike from his white culture. When the boy shoots his first deer, Sam leads him through an Indian rite of passage that marks Ike "forever one with the wilderness" (171). The lines are familiar but merit examination here:

The boy did that—drew the head back and the throat taut and drew Sam Fathers' knife across the throat and Sam stooped and dipped his hands in the hot smoking blood and wiped them back and forth across the boy's face. Then Sam's horn rang in the wet gray woods and again and again; there was a boiling wave of dogs about them, with Tennie's Jim and Boon Hogganbeck whipping them back after each had had a taste of the blood, then the men, the true hunters—Walter Ewell whose rifle never missed, and Major de Spain and old General Compson and the boy's cousin, McCaslin Edmonds . . . sitting their horses and looking down at them: at the old man of seventy who had been a negro for two generations now but whose face and bearing were still those of the Chickasaw chief who had been his father; and the white boy of twelve with the prints of the bloody hands on his face, who had nothing to do now but stand straight and not let the trembling show. (158–59)

Sam's horn here blazons Ike's initiation into the hunters' culture, but, ironically, it announces as well the union of the two outside of white culture. For the first time, a rift forms between Ike and his own white culture after he joins with Sam through Native American ritual: as the "true hunters" look down upon the two of them, Ike is excluded from the white society to which he had aspired. And even as he feels himself distinct from his kinsmen, the "bloody hands on his face" mark the bond that now forms between himself and Sam Fathers. Ike and Sam adopt a like posture here as Ike aligns himself with Sam against his own kin. Later he will realize that it was in this moment, in which he first rescinded his white heritage, that "he had ceased forever to be the child he was yesterday" (175). For Faulkner such growth emerges inevitably from the relationship that Ike develops with Sam Fathers.

Faulkner observes the shifting, arbitrary nature of race, suggesting that a component of Ike's development may be a new comprehension of race itself. In describing Sam as "a negro for

two generations," Faulkner compels the reader to confront the
vagaries of racial identity even as Ike does so. Yet even as he
acknowledges the complexities of race, Faulkner celebrates the
primitive within Sam Fathers as well: "They were the white boy,
marked forever, and the old dark man sired on both sides by savage kings, who had marked him" (159). The blood on Ike's face,
"joining him and the man forever," suggests both defilement and
honor. Faulkner describes the moment with religious imagery,
and Ike sheds his white identity in this baptism in favor of an
allegiance to the "savage kings" who sired Sam. Faulkner bluntly
portrays the union of the two as a rejection of Western values:
the sacrament is of the wilderness, and Sam is its priest. Such
autonomy is unimaginable in Twain's Jim, for Faulkner with his
modernist sensibility cannot make the same negative assumptions
of race as Mark Twain.

Ike witnesses Sam's insistence on autonomy when he sees Sam
bear himself "with gravity and dignity and without servility or
recourse to that impenetrable wall of ready and easy mirth which
negroes sustain between themselves and white men" (164). But if
such recognition moves Ike toward transformation, he nevertheless continues to view Sam through the narrow filter of the white
community's essentializing stereotypes of African Americans, at-
tributing, for instance, Sam's sense of autonomy not to his individual strengths but to the "chief's blood in him" that overcomes
the black and white blood with which it is mixed (162). Ike cannot
wholly remove Sam from an essentialized view of race. Faulkner
seems to recognize the extent to which African American identity
is socially created, but he asserts that Native American identity is
reducible to essential qualities.

In "The Bear," Faulkner frequently underscores Ike's bond
with Sam through his use of sexual imagery. If Ike has been initiated into the wilderness in "The Old People," he comes to sexual
maturity in his union with Sam in "The Bear": as they ride on
a wagon "wrapped in the damp, warm, negro-rank quilt" (187),

the wilderness opens for them briefly, then closes a moment later. Sam's embrace marks both the boy's entry into his "novitiate" and the loss of his innocence.[5]

From the "infinite waste of the ocean" that Ike associates with the surrey and with white culture, he penetrates the "true wilderness" secure in his bond with Sam under the "negro-rank quilt."[6] In the subsequent paragraph, the sexual nature of Ike's bonding with Sam has the usual result, and it occurs to Ike that he is "witnessing his own birth." Born outside the ideology of white cultural hegemony and within the marginalized wilderness of interracial relations, Ike discovers in Sam Fathers both lover and mother. It is a view of the other idealized in the extreme: exotic and erotic, matronly and maternal, Sam, in these moments, offers every necessary comfort to the white adolescent who is his charge.

But Ike's relationship with Sam leads to a sense of purpose from which Ike will not immediately retreat. If, in the wilderness, Ike decides to "go to hell," rejecting the oppressive and hypocritical values of his white society, he does not recoil from acting upon this decision. His eventual repudiation of his inheritance results directly from the moral guidance he has gained from Sam Fathers. If, in contrast to Huck Finn, Ike takes certain action in response to the wrongs he encounters, we will nevertheless see by the end of the novel that he cannot maintain his stance invariably.

When Ike discovers the ledgers that reveal to him the atrocities of slavery under his grandfather, Old McCaslin, he realizes that they "contained a chronological and much more comprehensive though doubtless tedious record than he would ever get from any other source" (256). Ike comes to believe that the ledgers document the history of "his people," by which he means both his white and his black forebears; he thus acknowledges the participation of otherness in the formation of his own identity. In no small part, of course, this awareness comes as a result of his relationship with Sam Fathers. With his new knowledge, Ike now believes that Old McCaslin has betrayed the land by claiming ownership over it and by maintaining sexual relations with the slaves. Ike's rejection of McCaslin's patriarchal role, which he associates with white identity, is underscored by his recognition of the land's ability to subdue racial differences: the ledgers are the record of "the land which they had all held and used in common and fed from and on and would continue to use in common without regard to color or titular ownership" (256). Ike's repudiation ostensibly causes the final break with his white culture, and he endeavors to repay money owed the black descendants of Old McCaslin as recognition of the common blood he shares with them. In repudiating his white culture, he comes to accept a shared identity with African Americans.

Ike's grave doubts about his white society lead him to attempt to right the wrongs of that society, yet, toward the end of *Go Down, Moses*, he expresses the same deeply felt ambivalence over race that we found in *Huck Finn* and that we will see in later southern novels. When Ike travels to Alabama to return money to his (and Old McCaslin's) relatives, Tennie's husband rebuffs him. Though Ike attempts to convince the man to take the money so that the couple can leave the South forever, his efforts reveal his ultimate reservations concerning racial parity:

> "Dont you see?" he cried. "Dont you see? This whole land, the whole South, is cursed, and all of us who derive from it, whom it ever suckled, white and black both, lie under the curse? Granted that my people brought the curse onto the land: maybe for that reason their descendants alone can—not resist it, not combat it— maybe just endure and outlast it until the curse is lifted. Then your peoples' turn will come because we have forfeited ours. But not now. Not yet. Dont you see?" (266)

Such passages typify Faulkner's response in his fiction, as in his life, to proposals for civil rights for African Americans. And each time Faulkner's white characters come to recognize the justice of racial equality, that recognition serves only to make them more keenly aware of the impossibility of any such equality in the present South, a position closely resembling that which Faulkner himself asserted. "Go slow, now," Faulkner wrote of efforts toward integration in the South ("A Letter to the North" 78).

In "Delta Autumn," the final story of *Go Down, Moses* in which Ike figures, he completes his symbolic rejection of Sam Fathers through a return to a patriarchal position within Yoknapatawpha society. Fragile and aging, Ike returns to the woods to hunt with his cousin Roth and others. Too feeble to go out on the hunt one morning, he meets Roth's black mistress, who comes looking for Roth because she is pregnant with his child. In the course of their conversation, Ike slowly realizes that she is not white: "*Maybe in a thousand or two thousand years in America,* he thought. *But not now! Not now!* He cried, not loud, in a voice of amazement, pity, and outrage: 'You're a nigger!' " (344).

Faulkner's sad point is that Ike, at the end of the book, is but another bigot, for all that he has learned through his relationship with Sam Fathers. Ike has, at the end of the book, recoiled from the possibilities of interracial accord with which his story began. The symbolic exchange of identities we find in his relationship with Sam Fathers bears no relevance for Ike here: he is once again in the woods, but where earlier we had seen trust and rebirth, Faulkner's imagery now suggests death and deception. Unable to accept Roth's mistress in white society, Ike sends the woman away: " 'Then go,' he said. Then he cried again in that thin not loud grieving voice: 'Get out of here! I can do nothing for you! Cant nobody do nothing for you!' " (344). Yet he cannot allow her to leave with nothing more than that between them: " 'Wait,' he said. She paused again, obediently still, turning. He took up the sheaf of banknotes and laid it on the blanket at the foot of the cot and drew his hand back beneath the blanket. 'There,' he said" (344). Ike's act constitutes apology for his guilt; the irony is that Ike, who has rejected materialism throughout his life in large part because of his relationship with Sam Fathers, can finally offer no more than money.

Unable to conceive of the sort of interracial relationship she proposes, Ike would send the woman away from the South. Marriage to a black man can be her "only salvation," and in this assessment we find the relationship between white protagonist and alienated other turned on its head: where Ike had earlier found salvation in his relationship with Sam Fathers, salvation for Roth's mistress can come only by her rejection of her relationship with Roth and by marrying a black man. If as a young man he had been closer to Sam Fathers than anyone else, he now rejects the possibility for such rapport across racial lines. In doing so, of course, he stands within the southern patriarchy, rejecting as well the possibility of a romantic relationship between Roth and his black mistress. But he is duplicitous even in this: as he sends the woman away, he claims for himself an enlightened perspective. " 'We will have to wait,' " he says, as though his waiting entails a grieving similar to hers (346). We see Faulkner's irony in Ike's use of "we." Roth's mistress admonishes Ike's hypocrisy: " 'Old man,' she said, 'have you lived so long and forgotten so much that you dont remember anything you ever knew or felt or even heard about love?' " (346). Through her rebuke, Faulkner implicitly critiques the return to essentialism we find in Twain and thus in American culture itself.

For a second time in Ike's life, his moral guide is black, yet he is unable to respond as he had earlier to Sam Fathers. Where his relationship with Sam Fathers was paternal and male—albeit fraught with sexual allusions—and thus concerned with no issue save Ike's freedom, the sexual joining he encounters here has specific implications for his southern culture that he cannot ignore. He rejects the lessons the woman would teach him and sends her off. If, as he claimed earlier in the text, " 'Sam Fathers set me free,' " Ike has at the end of the novel returned to the white society from which Sam freed him (286). While he sheds whiteness through his relationship with Sam Fathers, he reclaims it in sending Roth's mistress north, assuming, as he had earlier with Tennie, a paternal authority that she rejects.

Intruders and Betrayers

Six years after the publication of *Go Down, Moses*, a period during which the nation became increasingly aware of the abuses of the Jim Crow South, Faulkner in *Intruder in the Dust* directly addresses the plight of blacks in the modern South.[7] The narrative emerges as allegory for the relationship of black and white in the South at mid-twentieth century; in Faulkner's telling of it, he draws on the component parts of a familiar story that will begin to look like an American myth.

In Faulkner's *Intruder in the Dust*, two boys—Charles Mallison junior (Chick), Faulkner's white protagonist, and his black friend, Aleck Sander—work to free a black man, Lucas Beauchamp, whom they discover to have been wrongly imprisoned for murder. The protagonist's companion is no practical joker like Tom Sawyer; Aleck Sander is instead very much immersed in Lucas's plight, fearing he may be punished by a white lynch mob simply for being on the streets. Rather than granting his black character a freedom gained at the hands of playful adolescents, however, Faulkner grants Lucas agency by portraying his autonomy within an oppressive white culture. Initially skeptical of Lucas's professed innocence, Chick questions the older man's autonomy throughout. The result is an uneasy ambivalence at the end in which neither character can fully trust the other. Even so, each dimly recognizes the bonds between them.

At the outset, all of Yoknapatawpha County believes that Lucas Beauchamp—like Sam Fathers, a character of both Indian and African blood—has killed Vinson Gowrie. Gowrie, a white man, comes from Beat Four, a section of the county into which the only stranger to enter "with impunity was God and He only by daylight and on Sunday" (35). Nearly everyone in the county also believes that Beauchamp—an uncomfortable anomaly in Yoknapatawpha because of his refusal to accept the meaning all Yoknapatawpha assigns to blackness—will soon be lynched by Gowrie's

rough-hewn kin, since this is the certain fate of a black man accused of murdering a white man in Jim Crow Mississippi.

Chick's previous knowledge of Lucas shapes his early thinking
of the older man's arrest: when Chick fell into a frozen creek as
a young boy, Lucas rescued him with an indifference maddening
to Chick. And as he now watches Lucas being taken into the town
jail, Chick remembers crawling up the bank of the creek

> until he saw two feet in gum boots which were neither Edmonds'
> boy's nor Aleck Sander's and then the legs, the overalls rising out of
> them and he climbed on and stood up and saw a Negro man with
> an axe on his shoulder, in a heavy sheep-lined coat and a broad
> pale felt hat such as his grandfather had used to wear, looking at
> him and that was when he saw Lucas Beauchamp for the first time
> that he remembered or rather for the first time because you didn't
> forget Lucas Beauchamp; gasping, shaking and only now feeling
> the shock of the cold water, he looked up at the face which was
> just watching him without pity commiseration or anything else,
> not even surprise. (6–7)

The woodsman-priest Lucas, like Sam Fathers in relation to his
young charge, placidly welcomes Chick into the relationship of
black and white, baptizing the boy with a new identity that will
bring him to a self-conception removed from his genteel southern society. As Ike had been, Chick is reborn with the onset of the
relationship between himself and the marginalized black culture
represented by Lucas. Lucas compels Chick toward self-awareness
by bringing the boy to see within himself a multifaceted American identity that white southerners around him reject and that
makes him exceedingly uncomfortable.

Early in their relationship, Lucas undermines Chick's essentialist assumptions of blacks by refusing to play the role expected of
him, and Chick in turn attempts to compel Lucas to take a subservient role in their relationship, insisting, for instance, on pay-

ing the older man after the rescue at the creek. But Chick's efforts are to no avail, as Lucas maintains the autonomous stance that will eventually land him in jail. Chick can only accept Lucas's autonomy when he separates himself from a white identity symbolized by Gowrie, on the one hand, and by Chick's patrician uncle, Gavin Stevens, on the other. In this initial encounter, the ritual of rebirth—emerging as a central moment in the mythos of interracial harmony in the southern novel—prepares us for Chick's eventual separation from white society.

Watching the jail from across the street, Chick recalls his encounters with Lucas since that winter day. Their meetings were convivial until once when "Lucas looked straight at him, straight into his eyes from five feet away and passed him and he [Chick] thought *He has forgotten me. He doesn't even remember me anymore*" (24). When Chick learns from his uncle that Lucas's wife, Molly, had died just before their encounter, Chick sees Lucas in human terms for the first time: "*That was why he didn't see me . . .* thinking with a kind of amazement: *He was grieving. You dont have to not be a nigger in order to grieve*" (25). Chick's recognition that his black mentor possesses an emotional existence beyond their experience together marks his first step toward moral growth.

Yet if Chick has thus removed Lucas from the narrow gaze of white culture, he also demonstrates a vengeful desire, shortly after seeing Lucas taken into the jail, to return him to that essentialized position. Of Lucas's prospects, Chick says to his uncle Gavin, " 'They're going to make a nigger out of him once in his life anyway' " (31). Having been humbled when Lucas steadfastly refused to take money for rescuing him, Chick covets revenge as the novel opens. And coming with his uncle to the jail, Chick is surprised to see Lucas asleep in the cell, concluding, "*He's just a nigger after all for all his high nose and his stiff neck and his gold watch-chain and refusing to mean mister to anybody even when he says it. Only a nigger could kill a man, let alone shoot him in the back, and then sleep like a baby as soon as he found something flat enough to lie down on"* (57). Despite his desire to return Lucas to an essentialized racial identity (a desire that will remain largely intact throughout the novel), Chick is never fully able to do so. Chick's smug tone reveals the satisfaction he takes in seeing Lucas forcibly returned to a position from which he cannot help but accept the expectations of a white audience, gazing through the bars of the jail cell. Lucas, however, a performer of racial identities, is able throughout the novel to undermine the expectations of a white audience.

In jail, Lucas immediately assumes agency rather than passivity: recalling the favor that the boy owes him, Lucas asks Chick to dig up Vinson Gowrie's body to prove that he did not murder Gowrie. After Chick's initial objections, he agrees to Lucas's demands: *Intruder in the Dust* develops as a detective story laced with race consciousness. Despite Lucas's cool detachment and authoritative stance against all people of the county, black and white, Chick gains respect for Lucas in the course of his investigations. In discovering Lucas's innocence, Chick will uncover something of his own guilt.

Gavin Stevens, Faulkner's portrait of the southern racial liberal, emerges as the one character who speaks lucidly and at length about racial conflict in the South, yet his views, like Faulkner's, consistently reassert the southern hegemony of days past.[8] Stevens is in large part a mouthpiece for Faulkner's own views on the burgeoning civil rights movement and the resistance the movement encountered among white southerners. Faulkner himself claimed that Stevens's voice was that of "the best type of liberal southerner" (qtd. in Blotner 499). Stevens expects Chick to adopt the same patriarchal status, and the same essentializing view of African Americans, that he himself holds.[9]

Stevens, whose pronouncements on race center the novel in the debate over civil rights, maintains a significant remove from Lucas, yet he nevertheless does what he can to save him from the hands of an angry lynch mob. Upon his arrival at the jail, Stevens confronts Lucas with both advice and a reprimand: " 'Lucas,' he

said, 'has it ever occurred to you that if you just said mister to
white people and said it like you meant it, you might not be sitting
here now?' " (60). Lucas's ironic response reflects the independence that he maintains throughout the novel: " 'So I'm to com-
mence now,' Lucas said. 'I can start off by saying mister to the folks
that drags me out of here and builds a fire under me' " (61). In his
irony—a characteristic tone for Lucas utterly absent in Twain's
Jim—Lucas rejects the hypocritical nature of Stevens's southern
liberalism and the notion of genuflecting before the lynch mob.

Chick vacillates between the figures of his uncle and Lucas
Beauchamp throughout the novel, caught as he is between the
white and black worlds they represent. Listening to his uncle,
Chick takes in a view of southern race relations that he must balance against his own practical experience. Stevens maintains that
white southerners "must resist the North" to retain the right to set
blacks ("Sambo") free in their own time. "It will have to be us,"
he claims, to free blacks so that "someday Lucas Beauchamp can
shoot a white man in the back with the same impunity to lynch-
rope or gasoline as a white man" and vote wherever he likes and
send his children to any school he chooses. "But it wont be next
Tuesday," he concludes, despite what northerners might think.
They have forgotten that "Lucas Beauchamp's master was not
merely beaten to his knees but trampled for ten years on his face in
the dust to make him swallow it" (189). Stevens claims the same
power for southern whites that unreconstructed white southerners claimed in order to maintain postbellum cultural hegemony,
under which southern blacks were obligated to whites for any
freedoms they obtained. Stevens is thus a modern Southern Redeemer, seeking an older order.

Swayed by both his uncle and Lucas Beauchamp, Chick develops a measure of ambivalence over the issue of race. As an
"intruder in the dust," Chick intrudes not only into Gowrie's
grave but also into the burden of southern history and American race relations. And if Stevens speaks in large measure for the

author, Faulkner nonetheless creates Chick, who finally cannot bring himself to accept fully the patriarchal beliefs his uncle espouses.

At the conclusion, Lucas asserts his autonomous position relative to white society by insisting on paying for Gavin and Chick's services, a gesture that recalls his earlier refusal to accept money from Chick for assisting him after he fell into the creek.[10] Lucas's payment is political claim, asserting as it does his equality in this southern society. Lucas acknowledges the connection between the present scene and the earlier one by teasing Chick about their earlier meeting: " 'You aint fell in no more creeks lately, have you?' " (235). Chick responds merrily to Lucas's inquiry (" 'I'm saving that until you get some more ice on yours' " [235]) and then watches passively as his uncle and Lucas banter over the money. For Chick, the novel thus ends in stasis: given a choice between serving as a white patriarch in his society or rejecting the white community's essentialist ideology, he finally cannot act. Chick remains a passive observer, his development stunted by the intractable problem of race in the South.

The stasis we find at the end of the novel reflects upon the southern society in which Faulkner wrote: the novel is replete with the ambivalence and anxiety over race felt throughout the South and, indeed, the nation preceding the civil rights movement of the 1950s and 1960s. In Elizabeth Spencer's *A Voice at the Back Door*, we find a novel rich in this same ambivalence and anxiety and one that plainly looks back to both the tradition of Twain and the revisionism of Faulkner in its assessment of interracial accord.

Unheard Voices

"Going North, there is a discriminatory tariff on the heart," Elizabeth Spencer writes in her introduction to a 1965 edition of *The Voice at the Back Door* (xxi). Outside the South, she suggests, one feels the absence of African Americans, adding that, while living in Italy (as she was when writing the novel), she found it "very exciting to write about the South" because, from that distance, "the outlines of [the issue of race] stood out very clearly in my mind" (xviii). She claims that her "black" characters filled a void created by the absence of African Americans in Italy:

> I missed Negroes. If you have always lived where half the popula-
> tion is black (at least half, for I knew far more Negroes than white
> people until I got sent to school), then when you leave that, you
> feel the world is lacking something, and then you know you are
> wishing to see black skins around. Somehow one never imagined
> that there would come a time when they wouldn't be there. To
> write in this book about as many Negroes as I thought I could con-
> vincingly imagine was a way of being with them. I liked writing
> those parts. (xviii)

Spencer celebrates the union of black and white even as that union limits the role of African Americans to a prop in the larger drama. And her sentimental language reveals the essentialism implicit in her novel: she misses not particular individuals but "Negroes," a mass of men and women cast in an inferior position in the South Spencer memorializes.

Like *Intruder in the Dust, Voice* considers the role of race in a small southern town. In the early pages, we find Travis Brevard, sheriff of Lacey, Mississippi, dying in Duncan Harper's grocery store because he is as unwilling to have his wife " 'spread me out on a pink bedspread and stick a thermometer in my mouth' " (9) as he is to embarrass Ida Belle, his "nigger woman," by leav-ing her to deal with his corpse. Brevard exemplifies the old or-der of the South, as we see in his illicit relationship with Ida Belle and in his quiet acceptance of protection money from the local bootleggers. Brevard's last wish is that Harper, a former star running back, take over the duties of the sheriff's office. When Brevard's death exposes the hidden hypocrisies of Lacey's racial identity, Harper immediately begins a campaign for sheriff, running largely on the promise of racial equality.

Set in the early 1950s, the novel's plot centers upon the tensions of racial conflict in the rural South, symbolized by the two men who vie to succeed Brevard: Harper, who as acting sheriff finds himself embroiled in a bitter fight to rid Winfield County of the bootlegging operation owned in part by his friend Jimmy Tallant, and his opponent in the race for sheriff, Willard Follansbee. The latter blindly supports the bootlegging operation and fervently embraces segregation. A fierce rivalry between Harper and Tallant develops during Harper's campaign for sheriff against Follansbee: Harper's benign attitude toward blacks, in combination with his opposition to bootlegging, threatens to cost him the election. In the midst of the controversy is Beckwith Dozer, a black man whose autonomy enflames the racial consciousness of Lacey and who serves as a catalyst for each of the principal events of the novel.

Beckwith Dozer guides Duncan Harper toward a new awareness of moral responsibility, compelling Harper to read race in new ways. Indeed, in the course of the novel, Harper comes to judge himself in part through his relationship with Dozer. In their first encounter after Brevard's death, Dozer asks Harper to see that his son, W.B., will not lose his job carrying groceries at Harper's store because he ran from the store as Sheriff Brevard was dying. Just as important to Dozer, though, is determining whether Harper intends to run for sheriff himself. " 'It's no business of yours,' " Harper replies, uncomfortable with the implication that African Americans have any public role whatever (18). Not so easily put off, Dozer responds that his " 'acquaintance is not cultivated' " because, as a black man in the South, he lacks a vote. As the two stand in the county courthouse, Harper encounters the issue of racial equality not as an abstraction but, for the first time, in the form of a living man. Despite his own like sentiments, he attempts to evade Dozer by evoking a familiar response: " 'That kind of talk's no good,' he seemed to be merely remarking. 'On your way, boy' " (19). Harper employs language that returns Dozer to the accepted, passive role for blacks in the South, yet Dozer will not be denied. He compels Harper to view him as an individual by declaring his own name and tying it to his father's murder:

> The Negro withdrew from the shadow of the big white man, but he was still erect when he stopped in the door and said, "My name is Beckwith Dozer, Mister Harper. When I was a small child, my father was shot to death upstairs in this courthouse. I never been inside here before tonight."
>
> "Oh, I see." Their eyes met and though they were alone in an empty building, and no one knew they were there, it seemed that the world listened, that a new way of speaking was about to form in an old place. They were a little helpless, too, like children waiting to be prompted. What should the words be? (19)

Spencer presents the scene as a nascent American Eden, where the vision America has always held of itself can be fully realized: "[A] new way of speaking was about to form in an old place." But, unable to find the words for this new identity, the two part, with Dozer wishing Harper luck in the campaign for sheriff. Harper is left savoring Dozer's words "like the taste of something new, trying to decide if they mocked him, or spoke sincerely, but he could not" (19). For Spencer, the interracial relationship at the center of the novel implies not only individual but cultural rebirth ("it seemed that the whole world listened"), yet the possibility of such renewal is checked by the same mistrust that has characterized all the relationships we have encountered.

Writing on the precipice of momentous change to a South trapped in the very stasis to which her portrait of Harper and Dozer alludes, Spencer conceived of her text as a political commentary on the relationship between black and white in the South. She develops the confrontation between black and white as a negotiation formed equally of enmity and dependency in which any relationship across the color line can advance only through an elaborate structure of deception and manipulation. The pair cannot gain even an outward sense of accommodation, and the novel turns upon their mistrust. Like Faulkner, Spencer is careful not to mystify the relationship with sentiment, the rhetorical technique taboo to mainstream modernist writers though hardly absent from the southern novels of the period: in *Intruder* and *The Voice at the Back Door*, the reader shares in the anxiety and dread within the relationship between black and white characters.

In their next meeting, Dozer asserts his rightful place in the polity of the town, even as he admits his dependence upon Harper. Dozer comes to Harper's back door and asks Harper to protect him from the white man he claims to have been fighting: "The Negro had not knocked, but had stood saying, 'Mister Harper? Mister Harper?' over and over, and now that they [Harper and his wife] saw him it seemed they had heard him for certain all the time, for no telling how long, for it is part of the consciousness of a Southern household that a Negro is calling at the back door in the night" (90). One recalls Jim's query at the beginning of Twain's novel (" 'Who dah?' "): the southern novels we are reading suggest that a black voice has ever been calling for the white South to identify itself. To answer is to be drawn into the very conversation of race that the white southerner has grown up avoiding.

Dozer reports that he has been fighting with Bud Grantham, a local bootlegger. Harper suggests that Dozer should leave immediately, considering Grantham's violent disposition, but Dozer plays upon Harper's liberal sentiments so that the white man will instead agree to custody protection: " 'If a Negro never takes advantage of what legal rights are open to him, he can't hope to enjoy those that ought to be open and ain't. You are the law, Mister Harper. I have come to you' " (93). Dozer's appeal convinces Harper to take him into custody in the small jail downtown, risking his election as sheriff, since he will be perceived as offering protection to a fugitive from the county's rough form of justice.

That Kerney Woolbright reassures Harper that Dozer will not be lynched undermines literary representations of race employed by white southern writers such as Faulkner and Erskine Caldwell:

> "It's raining too hard to lynch a nigger. It's too cold."
>
> "It's what?"
>
> "It's the wrong time of year, too. These things are supposed to happen in the middle of September after it hasn't rained for forty weeks, after all the cattle have died of thirst and their stench rolls in from the country and there's so much dust the sun looks bloody all day long. Isn't that right?"
>
> "I don't know," said Duncan. "I never saw a lynching."
>
> "I never did either," said Kerney. "All I know is what I read in William Faulkner." (100–101)

Woolbright's ironic tone undercuts the gravity of the predicament that he and Dozer face. For Peggy Whitman Prenshaw, the scene exemplifies the manner in which Spencer "co-opts the Faulkner presence by dramatizing it as a force within the novel itself" (64). Spencer thus employs the motifs of southern literature in the scene even as she maintains an ironic distance from them. Through her irony she undermines the ground of southern literary essentializing, deliberately upsetting her reader's expectations of the literary relationship of black and white.[11]

As the two men wait in the jail cell, Dozer tells Harper that he is either "the only white man around with principles, or everybody else is stitching their principles together out of a different bolt of goods," and Dozer's apparent faith in Harper arouses sympathy in both Harper and the reader (111). Yet we soon find that the situation is not at all what we had thought: Dozer's dilemma is actually a trick played on Harper so that Jimmy Tallant can photograph him defending Dozer in the jail. Harper's political opponents then plan to portray him publicly as an advocate of equal rights for blacks, a stance sure to cost him the election. Dozer, it turns out, has been paid to act out this scene with Harper, and so it happens that *his* voice at the back door cannot be trusted. Dozer performs the role of the black supplicant only for pay. [12] And if Harper has been tricked into the condescending stance of the white southern gentry, the reader, too, has been duped by a faith in the paradigmatic literary relationship of Huck and Jim. Dozer's unreliability exposes the fluidity of what we had taken to be fixed southern racial identities. In the course of the novel, Spencer thus parodies our expectations of racial conflict, finally emphasizing not Dozer's dependence upon the white community but rather his ability to manipulate it successfully.

In Spencer's novel, the gaze of white authority no longer establishes the racial identities with certainty. This shift in authorial view takes place in the nascent period of the civil rights movement, and, indeed, Spencer composed the novel even as the Supreme Court, in *Brown v. Board of Education of Topeka, Kansas,* was preparing to outlaw a system of segregation that had purported to permanently fix southern racial identities. In this context, Dozer's request for protection and the consequent confrontation with a faux lynch mob emphasize the precarious nature of white southern liberalism with the rise of black consciousness in the South.

After the jailhouse photographs appear in northern newspapers sympathetic to civil rights, Duncan Harper's campaign for sheriff seems all but lost, but he attempts to salvage it by enticing Dozer to admit publicly to his participation in the ruse. Dozer initially rejects Harper's plea despite the white man's ostensibly liberal agenda:

> "You've seen a light these days," Duncan went on. "All of you have. You keep casting around for the best way. You want to deal equally with white men but you don't know who to trust. You'd rather have Mr. Willard Follansbee in office instead of me?"
>
> "To be honest with you, Mister Harper, I prefer the status quo. You can climb the status quo like a step ladder with two feet on

the floor, but trying to trail along behind a white man of good will
is like following along behind somebody on a tightrope. As he gets
along towards the middle his problems are likely to increase, and
soon he gots to turn loose of me to help himself." (137)

Spencer acknowledges the ephemeral nature of the relationship
between black and white in the South in Dozer's refusal to dis-
regard the personal investment that Harper has in attempting to
gain his assistance. Harper and Dozer ultimately do come to an
agreement, but only after fully recognizing the extent to which
their association is leveraged by need.

Having acknowledged the contrived nature of their bond, however, both men find comfort in a shared sense of dependence, as
we see in their examination of the Latin texts Dozer's father in-
herited from Senator Upinshaw, the first white man in Lacey to
demonstrate a genuine concern for blacks. They enter the library
declaring their openness to one another: " 'You are the first white
man I ever showed the inside to,' " Dozer says, and Harper replies
that Dozer is " 'the first Negro I ever invited to my house' " (139).
Yet for all of the apparent sentiment of the moment, Dozer remains reluctant to help Harper expose how Jimmy Tallant got
the picture in the jail. Dozer asserts that he is better off yoked to
Jimmy Tallant, since " '[t]here isn't anything one of us thinks that
the other hasn't thought too. They say a nigger's got to belong to
some white man' " (139). But Harper brings Dozer to admit that
he doesn't believe in such dubious sentiments. When Harper argues that he is as much at risk because of their union as is Dozer,
the latter agrees to reveal Tallant's ploy. They stand facing one another over a gate, and Dozer inquires once again into the nature
of Harper's character:

> "Why you wants to act like this, Mister Harper?" and one of his
> dark cheeks gleamed wet, smeared down from the gold rim of his
> glasses lens.

"No reason," Duncan returned. "I want to do what's right, I guess. That's all." (140)

Harper offers Dozer his "freedom" from Jimmy Tallant, and the passage recalls Huck's decision to "go to hell" and set Jim free from slavery, but the hell to which Harper resigns himself is a murky, uncertain future promising no transcendence but the possibility of survival. And where Huck's compensation is psychological, Harper's is material and political: he has no other option if he wishes to be elected sheriff. Spencer carefully portrays Dozer's own agency in the relationship: " 'All right then. I'll come,' " he says in agreeing to Harper's proposal (140). In Spencer's fiction, the black guide is no passive bondsman awaiting his freedom but a complex character who enters the relationship on his own terms. Events in the South compelled white southerners to grant their black characters an agency absent in earlier southern novels.

Yet traditions have a way of maintaining themselves: just prior to this shared unburdening of guilt, Spencer describes Beckwith Dozer's son as a "savage." The essentializing ideology of the description undermines her attempt to rid this scene of the irony that pervaded the earlier scene in the jailhouse; likewise, her choice of language anticipates an insistent motif in the novel that counters the portrayal of the transcendent relationship of Harper and Dozer. The central pattern in the novel, in which Harper and Dozer come to see each other as individuals caught in an essentializing society, is frequently subverted in the final third of the novel by the essentialist ideology that Spencer draws upon in creating her African American characters. She makes further reference in the latter parts of the novel, for example, to the "savage" nature of blackness itself: for Spencer, blacks struggle yet fail to overcome a savagery that she ostensibly views as romantic even as she attempts to demonstrate the ways in which whites and blacks can benefit from interdependence. The impulse to set free carries with it the impulse to restrain, and we find the liberal southern novelist often moving from the former to the latter.

Ironically, the savagery the narrative ascribes to blacks becomes most apparent following the brutal act of a white man. When Willard Follansbee, the candidate opposing Harper in the race for sheriff, rapes Dozer's wife, Lucy, Spencer writes only of Lucy's "savage instinct" (232) and not of any such instinct on Follansbee's part: "Lucy turned her head aside. She was conscious of the white man's slack jaw where the stiff black hair roots were visible like punctures and the breath moved in and out. She went dull all over, animal, African, obedient to the forcing whip" (230). As Lucy returns to her home immediately afterward, Spencer addresses the reader in a lengthy aside in which she links Lucy (and the rape) to the experience of all blacks in the South. She suggests that Follansbee's brutality develops concomitantly with the white man's "will to survive" and that Lucy's savagery enables her to survive as "a night creature, alive in the dark" (235). [13]

This narrative aside reveals the depths of the novel's primitivist and essentializing ideology, a position that places Spencer much more within the culture she critiques than outside it. In her description of African Americans, Spencer appears to be informed more by Thomas Dixon Jr. than by Mark Twain, and, in addressing "the instinctive motion of their strange society," Spencer links her narrative to the very prejudices she had ostensibly set out to expose. We are finally unable to enter the perspective of the black characters she portrays, and they remain largely figments of a white imagination eager to apologize for the South and rationalize its past.

While Duncan Harper is linked to Beckwith Dozer through a vague sense of guilt and moral responsibility, Jimmy Tallant is inextricably tied to Dozer for more explicit reasons. It was Tallant's father who brutally murdered Dozer's father, Robinson Dozer, along with eleven other black citizens of Lacey, in the county courthouse thirty years before the action of the novel takes place. This event weighs on the consciousness of Lacey, and the bond between Dozer and Tallant, like that between Dozer and Harper, is bound up in both resentment and need. Dozer recognizes the significance of the bond in telling Harper: " 'Mister Tallant and I are tied together on account of what his daddy did to mine. He wouldn't lose me, nor let me come to harm for anything in this world. He's my main protection in this life' " (136). The link between the two men exemplifies the relationship of the white community to the black in the modern South: Tallant provides "protection" for Dozer against the ill will of other white men in order to expiate past sins.

Not long after the ruse at the jailhouse, Beckwith Dozer finds himself in a predicament much more dire: he is wrongfully accused of shooting Tallant, and he has no alternative but to flee. As the election draws near, frustration in the county runs high because Harper has failed to apprehend Dozer, and Willard Follansbee exploits Harper's inability to capture him. As the candidates give their campaign speeches on the eve of the election, Harper gets word that Dozer is ready to come in to jail, and Harper races away to get Dozer before a lynch mob can reach him. In the process, Harper defends Dozer against two men who want "to scare the hell out of him" to prove that "blacks are not equal to whites" (334). When Harper defends Dozer, the men turn the brunt of their anger on him:

> The two men did not want to give ground.
> "I hear you're against segregation, want to let the niggers vote," said the tall one. "Is that right?"
> Duncan flushed. "Why don't you go to the speaking and hear what I've got to say?"
> "Why should I if you can tell me yes or no right now? Do you or don't you?"
> "I haven't got time to waste on you," Duncan said.

"*Waste* on us? You don't talk much like a politician to me. You ask for our vote and you're talking like that?"

"You can vote for whoever you want to," said Duncan. "The way you're talking, I wouldn't want to claim you on my side." (334)

Having defended Dozer earlier when he was never truly in danger, Harper proves himself an ally yet again when the danger is real. Ultimately, though, he is a martyr for the cause: he dies when he wrecks his car while being pursued by the lynch mob on the way to town.

Though Harper has symbolically sacrificed himself for the cause of racial equality at the novel's conclusion, the empty act will apparently effect no change. Jimmy Tallant leads Dozer through the angry mob surrounding the wreck near the end of the novel, but this is just what he has always done: Tallant is once again Dozer's "main protection in life." Stagnation rather than growth is the likely outcome of movements toward social change in Spencer's portrayal.

Books for Yankees

When asked if he was the model for the character of Gavin Stevens, Faulkner's uncle, John Falkner, replied, "Me that nig-gerlovin' Stevens? Naw, I don't read Billy's books much. But he can write them if he wants to. I guess he makes money at it— writing those dirty books for Yankees!" (qtd. in Blotner 493). The comment suggests the role the South has come to play in the American imagination: when Americans look to the South we expect to find the unwashed, the rude Snopeses of our literary imaginations, remote from our own experience; instead, we find a discomfiting reflection of ourselves. Thus the South, as John Falkner's comment unwittingly suggests, is not just for southerners: indeed, it is the mirror that reflects the national drama in which we all participate.

If Faulkner and Spencer employ Twain's model ironically, variously parodying Twain, they nevertheless also reflect the reversal of moral perspective at the center of his novel. We see in the next chapter two writers at mid–twentieth century, Carson McCullers and Harper Lee, who are more faithful to a southern mythology that Twain established.

❊3❊

DIVIDED HEARTS

*Carson McCullers and Harper Lee
Explore Racial Uncertainty*

> There was a stage, when we were about thirteen, in which we
> "went Negro." We tried to broaden our accents to sound like
> Negroes, as if there were not enough similarity already. We
> consciously walked like young Negroes, mocking their swinging
> gait, moving our arms the way they did, cracking our
> knuckles and whistling between our teeth.
>
> WILLIE MORRIS

> I hardly let characters speak unless they are Southern.
> Wolfe wrote brilliantly of Brooklyn, but more brilliantly of
> the Southern cadence and ways of speech. This is particularly
> true of Southern writers because it is not only their speech and
> the foliage, but their entire culture—which makes it a homeland
> within a homeland. No matter what the politics, the degree
> or non-degree of liberalism in a Southern writer, he is still
> bound to this particular regionalism of language and
> voices and foliage and memory.
>
> CARSON MCCULLERS

Popular narratives of race in the South appeared more frequently
in the wake of World War Two. The pattern of initiation and reversal I have traced took hold in the popular imagination in post-
war America, even as civil unrest among African Americans in
the Jim Crow South was beginning. In the two decades following
the war, racial certainties spun apart in popular culture as in the
southern novel. When Elvis Presley recalled his turbulent first

days as a rock singer, he remembered what it meant to sound black for a white audience: "[W]hen the record came out a lot of people liked it and you could hear folks around town saying, 'Is he, is he?' and I'm going, 'Am I, am I?' " (qtd. in Marcus, *Mystery Train* 152).

The potential of racial uncertainty characterizes Carson Mc-Cullers's *The Member of the Wedding* and Harper Lee's *To Kill a Mockingbird*, both of which repeat the pattern of inversion we have been tracing thus far—an emerging American mythos pertaining to race—in narratives that focus upon the development of adolescent characters through their relationships with marginalized and exotic African American characters. While both novels portray white girls whose mothers are absent and who look to their black servants for counsel, McCullers equips Frankie Addams's black mentor, Berenice, with a degree of autonomy comparable to that of Faulkner's Lucas Beauchamp. Lee, by contrast, portrays African American characters wholly dependent upon the white community.

A Sad and Ugly Room

Frankie Addams of Carson McCullers's *The Member of the Wedding* discovers her identity in moving back and forth between black and white worlds, a theme alluded to by her recurrent name and costume changes. Because her mother has died and she is increasingly alienated from her father, Frankie looks to Berenice, her family's black cook, as moral guide and as model for self-discovery. She vacillates between conflicting desires to remain in the exoticized black world of Berenice's kitchen—territory owned by Frankie's father but ruled by Berenice alone—and to escape to a white one symbolized by her brother's imminent wedding. She fears discovering a marginalized black identity within herself as she moves into adolescence, a time when she will feel compelled to shed all association with blackness. Frankie's attempts to escape the black world that Berenice represents as well as her repeated efforts to return to that world give shape and focus to the broken identity she forms. Frankie perceives Berenice in a series of familiar stereotypes: as Margaret McDowell writes, for Frankie, Berenice is variously "affectionate or stern mother, the primitive seer, and the black queen who once lived with her dream lover" (81). Frankie sees her mentor through the prism of white society's gaze; Berenice, however, persistently attempts to compel Frankie to view her as an individual outside of the socially enforced constructs of self and other.

For Frankie, the black world dominated by Berenice is fractured and incomplete and thus an accurate reflection of her own state of mind. In her romantic notions of joining her older brother and his new wife on their honeymoon, she believes that she has found a path that will lead her to the wholeness she associates with whiteness and away from the childhood world inextricably tied to Berenice and to a marginalized black identity. When Berenice cautiously tries to dissuade Frankie from her plan, Frankie suspects her of jealousy.

From the opening pages of the novel, Frankie feels ill at ease in Berenice's kitchen, for it is a "sad and ugly room" in which the walls are covered with Frankie's cousin John Henry's "queer, child drawings, as far up as his arm would reach" (4). In her longing to escape childhood, she likewise wishes to grow out of her relationship with Berenice: the kitchen soon looks to her "like that of a room in the crazy-house. And now the old kitchen made Frankie sick. The name for what had happened to her Frankie did not know, but she could feel her squeezed heart beating against the table edge" (4). In her departures from the kitchen, Frankie escapes all guilt: it is a place from which Frankie wishes she could "just light out," yet her dependence upon Berenice leaves her unable to do so (6).

Yet Frankie persistently returns to that kitchen, for if she experiences guilt there, she also finds solace. Berenice recognizes Frankie's dilemma throughout, insisting that Frankie confront her own identity. " 'You jealous [of the wedding],' said Berenice. 'Go and behold yourself in the mirror. I can see from the color in your eye' " (2). Frankie attempts to understand her own experience through the filter of Berenice's perspective. Immediately after her brother and his fiancée come to visit, Frankie asks Berenice to recount the visit for her once again:

"Tell me," she said. "Tell me exactly how it was."

"You know!" said Berenice. "You seen them."

"But tell me," Frankie said. (26)

Frankie validates her experiences by channeling them through Berenice, and, while she struggles throughout the novel to achieve an identity independent of her mammy, she never quite achieves the goal. " 'Tell me,' " Frankie says again. " 'Exactly what did they look like?' " Frankie says once Berenice has interpreted the visit for her (27). Winthrop Jordan writes of the need westerners have always felt to see themselves through the experience of the colonized other; for Jordan, the English used "peoples overseas as social mirrors" that reflected the very traits the English feared in themselves (40). Here Frankie reifies her own experience through that of her black companion, reflecting a like dependence in American culture in which the dominant society has always defined itself by the margin, by what it claims not to be.

Despite her stated desire to become a "member of the wedding" and leave with her brother when he marries, Frankie remains entranced by the mysterious blackness she associates with Berenice. When Berenice's son, Honey, and her suitor, T.T., interrupt a discussion between Frankie and Berenice one evening, Honey perplexes Frankie. " 'That sure is a cute suit you got on, Honey,' " Berenice says. " 'Where'd you get it?' " Honey's response initially troubles Frankie: "Honey could talk like a white school-teacher; his lavender lips could move as quick and light as butterflies. But he only answered with a colored word, a dark sound from the throat that can mean anything. 'Ahhnnh,' he said" (36). Already forbidden and unknown, blackness becomes more fascinating to Frankie as it becomes less articulate.

Honey's contradictions attract Frankie, for he is, like herself and like Berenice, caught between a white world and a black one. Frankie feels a strong communion with Berenice and the two men: when the three patiently wait for Frankie to leave so that they can drink whiskey, "[s]he stood in the door and looked at them. She did not want to go away" (36). And yet once Frankie leaves, she suspects Berenice will betray her plan to join the wedding party. "She closed the door, but behind her she could hear their voices. With her head against the kitchen door she could hear the murmuring dark sounds that rose and fell in a gentle way. Ayee—ayee" (36). McCullers emphasizes Frankie's curiosity with black dialect and black culture while further establishing the maternal bond between Frankie and Berenice. The words of the three—"murmuring dark sounds"—nurture rather than threaten Frankie as she eavesdrops. The marginal identity they share provides Frankie what sense of self she has, and if she aspires to join the white world symbolized by the wedding, she nevertheless takes comfort in the black one she has discovered in the kitchen. The nurturing Frankie receives is of course limited: she hears the sounds as she does only because she *is* eavesdropping. When Honey asks Berenice what she and Frankie had been discussing, to Frankie's surprise Berenice does not betray the girl's confidence: " 'Just foolishness,' " she says (36).

Frankie's awareness of Berenice's othered status throughout the novel draws her to the older woman: she thinks that "nobody human" (3) would ever know why Berenice chooses to have a blue glass eye, and yet as "a member of nothing in the world" and "an unjoined person" (1), Frankie identifies with precisely this sense of alienation; ultimately, it is Berenice's blackness with which Frankie claims empathy. The black world to which Berenice is a kind of envoy offers Frankie a definition of her present self, since, like her, it is incomplete and abstract; by contrast, the white world, associated strongly with the wedding, gives her hope for future wholeness.

Later in the novel, Berenice attempts to ease Frankie's distress by pointing to the similarities between them: " 'We all of us somehow caught. We born this way or that way and we don't know why. But we caught anyhow' " (113). But Berenice refuses to allow Frankie, who has adopted the name "F. Jasmine," to yoke their troubles too closely, asserting,

> "I'm caught worse than you is. . . . Because I am colored. Everybody is caught one way or another. But they done drawn completely extra bounds around all colored people. They done squeezed us off in one corner by ourselves. So we caught that firstway I was telling, as all human beings is caught. And we caught as colored people also. Sometimes a boy like Honey feel like he just can't breathe no more. He feel like he got to break something or break himself. Sometimes it just about more than we can stand." (113–14)

McCullers thus engages the nation's anxieties over race, explicitly referencing the Jim Crow era, allowing Berenice a critical voice free of irony that contrasts sharply with Frankie's juvenile longings. Frankie expresses a desire "to break something, too," so as to share in Berenice's sense of being cast out despite Berenice's attempts to isolate the black experience (114). Yet Berenice's assertion that " 'they done squeezed us off in one corner' " only draws Frankie closer, for she herself has a "squeezed heart" (4). In delineating the terms of her own life, Frankie appropriates Berenice's blackness, attempting to explain her alienation from white society through Berenice's explanation of racial oppression.

Berenice rejects any such yoking: though willing to act as a maternal figure to both Frankie and John Henry, she will not allow either of them authority over her own experience: " 'I am black . . . I am colored' " (113). Later, Berenice observes Frankie's inability to "pass" as black, ironically proposing a reversal of

racial identity as Frankie attempts to understand why she cannot change her name as she sees fit. " 'Why is it against the law
to change your name?' " Frankie asks. Berenice responds with
pointed mockery: " 'Suppose I would suddenly up and call myself
Mrs. Eleanor Roosevelt. And you would begin naming yourself
Joe Louis. And John Henry would try to pass off as Henry Ford.
Now what kind of confusion do you think that would cause?' "
(107). Berenice's levity is hardly innocent: Frankie's proposal of a
shared racial identity threatens Berenice's authority over her own
identity, so Berenice insists that no such exchange can take place.
She claims her suffering—and her identity—as her own.

Despite Berenice's objections, Frankie persists in associating
her own alienation with that of Berenice and so with the black
community. And, having latched on to blackness as key to her
own development, Frankie cannot now remove it from her understanding of herself, for all of Berenice's objections. We sense her
alienation when later, left behind by Berenice, Frankie wanders
to John Henry's house, where she tries to communicate with her
cousin to no avail.[1] With dusk falling, she stands apart from John
Henry, watching him as a blues horn—"the sad horn of some colored boy"—begins to play from "somewhere in the town" (41).
Despite the fact that she does not know the player, Frankie immediately feels a kinship with him that she does not feel with her
cousin: "Frankie stood stiff, her head bent and her eyes closed,
listening. There was something about the tune that brought back
to her all of the spring: flowers, the eyes of strangers, rain" (41).
The horn player acts as muse to Frankie's alienation, his music
reflecting the tangle of her consciousness and drawing her into
herself even as she strains to hear. She believes the player, like
Berenice, speaks to her in a fragmented form of communication
her cousin cannot comprehend. Blackness thus becomes metaphor
for Frankie's alienation. The expression that the "colored boy"
gives to his blues brings Frankie to reminisce—her own blues—
about the spring, a time before she felt cast out of childhood, a
time before her present "long season of trouble" (41).

And yet, like Berenice, the horn player stops short of offering anything beyond mere association: "Just at the time when the tune should be laid, the music finished, the horn broke off" (41). Frankie awaits guidance that will not come, and in place of finding her own direction she mimics the black blues that she has heard: in her own blues, she "began to talk aloud" but pays no attention to her own words (42). Her improvisation leads her not toward the black world that inspired it but toward a white world in which blackness itself is suppressed:

> For it was just at that moment that Frankie understood. She knew who she was and how she was going into the world. Her squeezed heart suddenly opened and divided. Her heart divided like two wings. And when she spoke her voice was sure.
> "I know where I'm going," she said. (42)

Embrace and repulse, unite and betray. In the literary union of black and white, the one follows the other. Frankie decides to go to the wedding, toward what she believes will be an enveloping whiteness that will take her away from the ambivalence and frustration of Berenice's black world. Her evasion of darkness, of the place of blackness in her nascent identity, comes to constitute the major conflict in the novel, yet Frankie's resolution yields no definitive action. Because she has decided to set her sights on a white identity and to escape Berenice, her heart is no longer "squeezed," as it had been, but after her decision to become a member of the wedding, she momentarily retreats into childhood and her dependence upon Berenice. She ventures to the shores of a white world only to return to the comforting waters of a black one. In the end, however, what growth she does attain comes as a result of her rejection of any connection she might feel to a black identity.

Back in Berenice's kitchen, Frankie remains uncomfortable with the remnants of her participation in a black world and with the extent to which her desires and tastes are shaped by that world. Frankie questions Berenice about the name of her favorite food, hopping-john; she is reluctant to call it by its southern name now that she plans to join the white world that the wedding has come to represent. Southern food, of course, like southern identity, emerges out of the conflation of black and white cultures, and Frankie demonstrates deep discomfort with this multicultural reality.

> "Tell me. Is it just us who call this hopping-john? Or is it known by that name through all the country. It seems a strange name somehow."
>
> " . . . Well, I have heard it called peas and rice. Or rice and peas and pot-liquor. Or hopping-john. You can vary and take your pick."
>
> "But I'm not talking about this town," F. Jasmine said. "I mean in other places. I mean through all the world. I wonder what the French call it."
>
> "Oh," said Berenice. "Well, you ask me a question I cannot answer." (80–81)

Berenice, who knows a thing or two about signifiers, dismisses the importance of such transformations of language in much the same way that she has tried to dissuade Frankie from changing her name to F. Jasmine. Berenice dismisses Frankie's longing for a different name for hopping-john that is less southern, and less black, while Frankie ponders: " 'I wonder what the French call it.' " In slighting the name "hopping-john," Frankie symbolically rejects the black and southern experience of which Berenice is a constant reminder; likewise, she refuses to see the contributions of this racial blending to her own tastes and desires. Hopping-john is, after all, her preferred dish: "Now hopping-john was F. Jasmine's very favorite food. She had always warned them to wave a plate of rice and peas before her nose when she was in her coffin, to make certain there was no mistake" (76). Once again she aims to overcome her discomfort by embracing whiteness. " 'I know where I'm going,' " Frankie tells us, and her chosen destination is her brother's wedding, the refined ritual in which she finds a purity that contrasts with the mongrel identity she has taken on in Berenice's kitchen (42).

Frankie's distress at her present circumstance increases when Berenice tells her that her change of names is just as illogical as would be a change of race. Frankie reacts by circling the kitchen table with a knife in her hand, frustrated that she cannot bring herself to tell Berenice of her plans to go dancing, plans that also represent for her an escape from the black world of Berenice's kitchen. Berenice finally stops her: " 'Set here in my lap . . . [a]nd rest a minute.' "

> F. Jasmine put the knife on the table and settled down on Berenice's lap. She leaned back and put her face against Berenice's neck; her face was sweaty and Berenice's neck was sweaty also, and they both smelled salty and sour and sharp. Her right leg was flung across Berenice's knee, and it was trembling—but when she steadied her toes on the floor, her leg did not tremble any more. . . .
>
> F. Jasmine rolled her head and rested her face against Berenice's shoulder. She could feel Berenice's soft big ninnas against her back, and her soft wide stomach, her warm solid legs. She had been breathing very fast, but after a minute her breath slowed down so that she breathed in time with Berenice; the two of them were close together as one body, and Berenice's stiffened hands were clasped around F. Jasmine's chest. (112–13)

The passage reveals the two embraced "as one body," a nurturing in which Frankie momentarily accepts Berenice as mother, something she has been reluctant to do throughout the novel. And for this one moment Berenice's compassion, even forgiveness, overcomes Frankie's ambivalence over her association with blackness. Frankie will turn yet again from Berenice, but she finds momentary solace amid the confusion of racial identity that confronts her just as she nears adolescence. While McCullers described John Henry as "Frankie's inverted double" (qtd. in Carr 235), we know, of course, that her true double, or "twin," to use

Arnold Rampersad's term, is Berenice, and their bond encompasses all of the characteristics of these literary unions so unique to American culture: fraternity, maternity, sexuality. At the conclusion of the novel, once Frankie has found that she will not be accepted as a member of the wedding, she lashes out at Berenice, who sits next to her on the long bus ride home: "She was sitting next to Berenice, back with the colored people, and when she thought of it she used the mean word she had never used before, nigger—for now she hated everyone and wanted only to spite and shame" (135). Frankie, now sensing the power to form an identity through betrayal, recalls the stereotypes of her southern culture in order to end their relationship.

If Frankie's rejection of Berenice is purely symbolic, she soon achieves a final break from her mentor when she and her father move out of their house, leaving Berenice behind. For her part, Berenice "had given quit notice and said that she might as well marry T.T." The Addamses' decision to move to "the new suburb of town" anticipates the white flight that would change the racial dynamic of every southern town and city in the later years of the century and marks the beginning of Frankie's final break with Berenice (149). The two gather in the kitchen a final time (and "the first time in a long while"), and Frankie recognizes the transformation of their world and of their relationship: "It was not the same kitchen of the summer that now seemed so long ago. The pencil pictures had disappeared beneath a coat of calcimine, and new linoleum covered the splintery floor. Even the table had been moved, pushed back against the wall, since now there was nobody to take meals with Berenice" (149).

The alteration of the kitchen signals the loss of the black world that Frankie, now Frances, associates with her childhood: John Henry's manic pencil drawings are painted over, covered in white just as Frankie vehemently cuts off her own association with the black world those drawings represented. McCullers further emphasizes Frankie's symbolic rejection of Berenice as Frankie makes sandwiches (thus supplanting Berenice's role as sustenance provider) for Mary Littlejohn, a new friend who is coming to see her: "Frances glanced at Berenice, who was sitting idle in a chair, wearing an old raveled sweater, her limp arms hanging at her sides" (150). Berenice has served her purpose for Frankie, who at the conclusion of the narrative has made a final break from the black world she has alternately embraced and rejected.

Frankie's view of herself depends on the contribution of otherness to her identity, yet she finally represses that knowledge in a bitter recoiling. Berenice's arms hang limp at her sides, her authority in the kitchen having been usurped and, so, her connection to Frankie breached. The literary relationship between black and white can only be maintained when forces outside of it exert little pressure upon the white character: Huck views Jim as an individual only when they are on the river. In like manner, Frankie abandons Berenice—and blackness—upon finding her own Tom Sawyer in Mary. McCullers sets her black character apart from Twain's in that Berenice lacks Jim's remarkable patience. While Jim reacts with only mild displeasure as he watches Huck and Tom fritter away the possibility of easy escape, Berenice reacts with the vitriol of a spurned lover when Frankie announces that she and Mary Littlejohn will "travel around the world together" after she moves:

"Mary Littlejohn," said Berenice, in a tinged voice. "Mary Littlejohn."

Berenice could not appreciate Michelangelo or poetry, let alone Mary Littlejohn. There had at first been words between them on the subject. Berenice had spoken of Mary as being lumpy and marshmallow-white, and Frances had defended fiercely. . . .

"There's no use our discussing a certain party. You could not possibly understand her. It's just not in you." She had said that once before to Berenice, and from the sudden faded stillness in her eye she knew that the words had hurt. (150–51)

For the first time in the novel, Frankie prepares her own food, and, not coincidentally, the meal is for her and Mary Littlejohn, who has supplanted Berenice. Mary's surname (perhaps Frankie has found her new name for hopping-john?) associates both girls at the end of the novel with whiteness, for it was little John Henry who, as we've seen, was associated throughout the text with white identity. Berenice's conspicuous dislike for Mary further under-scores her distance from Frankie at the end of the novel.

In particular, it is Mary Littlejohn's whiteness that offends: Frankie "had defended [Mary] fiercely" against Berenice's asser-tion that Mary was "lumpy and marshmallow-white." Berenice seems to object to the rejection of the black world that Frankie's new friendship represents. Frankie's assertion that Berenice "could not possibly understand" Mary Littlejohn ironically sym-bolizes Frankie's growth in the course of the novel, a growth that will register only after she forsakes her relationship with Berenice.

The final lines of the novel reveal the extent to which Frankie's identity remains fragmented, yet she has redirected her search for wholeness to the white world exclusive of Berenice: " 'I am simply mad about—' But the sentence was left unfinished for the hush was shattered when, with an instant shock of happiness, she heard the ringing of the bell" (153). Frankie no longer associates her fragmentation with Berenice; rather, at the conclusion of the novel she has rejected her union with her mammy in favor of a possible wholeness in her relationship with Mary Littlejohn. At the end, we find Berenice at the margins of Frankie's conscious-ness and, as ever, at the margins of southern society. No longer romanced by an exoticized black world, Frankie participates in Berenice's marginalization at the novel's conclusion and gains a white identity as a result. The process reflects the reality of south-ern childhood for middle- and upper-class whites through the end of Jim Crow who almost invariably grew up to leave black mam-mies behind, reflecting the reality of the larger American culture.

Double Lives

Like *The Member of the Wedding,* Harper Lee's *To Kill a Mockingbird* confronts the oppression of blacks in the modern South;
with Spencer's *Voice* and Shirley Anne Grau's *The Keepers of the
House,* it comments upon the civil rights movement from an ostensibly liberal position within southern society. Atticus Finch's
legal defense of Tom Robinson, a local black man wrongly accused
of raping a white woman, parallels his daughter Scout's growing understanding of their mysterious neighbor, Arthur Radley.
The didactic imperatives of the novel emerge from the interwork-
ings of the two narratives: Lee ties Scout's curiosity about Radley
(whom Scout calls "Boo") to Atticus's defense of Robinson. Scout's
moral development in the course of the novel comes largely from
Atticus, whom Lee depicts as a modern and enlightened southern
gentleman. Atticus instructs through his interactions with black
culture and in particular through his pro bono defense of Robinson. Lee portrays Tom Robinson, the namesake of Harriet Beecher
Stowe's Tom, as the maligned victim who can only be saved by
Atticus, pater familias in this southern society.

While Scout initially assumes Boo to be a lascivious demon
haunting her neighborhood, by the end of the novel she has removed him from this essentialized position and come to see him
outside such confines. Just as the townspeople type Tom Robinson
as a menace, Scout, her brother, Jem, and their friend Dill view
Boo Radley as a bogeyman, at one point daring one another to go
as close as possible to his house. In the end, Boo becomes an ironic
metaphor for white understanding of blacks in the novel, given
the whiteness with which he is so strongly associated.

The children initially understand Boo only through the stories they have been told: like Tom Robinson, Boo is suspected of
aberrant sexual behavior and blamed for Maycomb's more bizarre
crimes. When the citizens of the town begin to find their chickens
and pets mutilated, they blame Boo, and though the actual culprit

is later found, "people still looked at the Radley Place, unwilling to discard their initial suspicions" (9). Such suspicions, of course, mirror those whites have of the black community, and Lee demonstrates the ways in which Scout learns to overcome her baseless fears of Boo even as her father demonstrates Tom's innocence to all Maycomb.

Scout comes to understand blackness through her relationship with her black mammy, Calpurnia. Like Frankie Addams, Scout seeks solace and self-definition in her mammy, who, like Berenice, serves as a maternal figure in the absence of a biological mother. Black mammies fill the absences in their domestic spaces, but the protagonists come to associate blackness with a passivity that hardly threatens the stasis of the white domestic space. Calpurnia is moral guide for Scout, but her guidance largely reaffirms the white social order within which she is employed. When, for instance, Scout is rude to Walter Cunningham, a poor white boy whom she has invited to eat with the family, Calpurnia sets her charge straight: " 'Yo' folks might be better'n the Cunninghams but it don't count for nothin' the way you're disgracin' 'em—if you can't act fit to eat at the table you can just set here and eat in the kitchen!' " (27). Calpurnia's sense of propriety falls safely within the parameters of patriarchal white culture; in this, she contrasts with McCullers's Berenice, whose matriarchal refuge offers an exotic model of feminine sexuality.

In Scout's superstitions, we find a movement toward a black world that Calpurnia would disallow. When, for example, Scout and Jem discuss the superstitions surrounding "Hot Steams," the warm spaces in the air that are reputed to be spirits who can't get to heaven, Scout remembers that Calpurnia dismissed the idea as "nigger-talk" (41). The idea appeals to the children nonetheless, just as blackness and the possibility of interracial union intrigues them. If we encounter Jem spending his days reading the speeches of Henry Grady, the New South he envisions will be rather different from that of the editor of the *Atlanta Constitution:* for Lee, as for McCullers, blackness emerges as the catalyst for the moral growth of a white protagonist. Lee, however, defines that identity within the narrow confines of white perception.

Still, the novel's multiple voices allow the reader to glimpse the broader possibilities. When Calpurnia takes Scout and Jem to her church, the narrative momentarily escapes a white perspective and the concomitant rejection of black identity. Because of the controversy surrounding Tom Robinson's arrest, some of the church members are reluctant to accept the white children:

> I felt Calpurnia's hand dig into my shoulder. "What you want, Lula?" she asked, in tones I had never heard her use. She spoke quietly, contemptuously.
>
> "I wants to know why you bringin' white chillun to nigger church."
>
> "They's my comp'ny," said Calpurnia. Again I thought her voice strange: she was talking like the rest of them.
>
> "Yeah, an' I reckon you's comp'ny at the Finch house durin' the week." (135)

Lula's challenge to the children and Calpurnia reflects black resentment of the white community in Maycomb and perhaps as well the condescension inherent in the role Atticus Finch has made for himself. Lula points to the inescapable fact that Calpurnia forgets: though Cal earlier calls Scout and Jem "my children," theirs is primarily an economic arrangement (134). Scout's surprise at Calpurnia's "strange" voice, now inflected with her African American dialect, represents her remove from this black world. The special welcome the children receive from the pastor only serves to isolate them further from the congregation.

Still, the children come to recognize the members of the black community as individuals outside of the essentializing gaze of whites. Scout and Jem express their surprise when the town garbage collector, Zeebo, leads the congregation in a hymn. For the Finch children, Zeebo thus emerges as an individual capable of a complexity they could not have imagined earlier. As they leave the church, Scout yearns to "stay and explore," her curiosity having been piqued by this encounter with blackness, but Calpurnia won't allow it (140). Scout remains entranced: " 'Why do you talk nigger-talk to the—to your folks when you know it's not right?' " (143). Scout's curiosity and surprise at Calpurnia's "modest double life" leads her to desire a bond with Calpurnia outside the white world in which they have functioned previously, much like the bond she will ultimately form with Boo Radley (143). For Scout there is an enthralling mystery in blackness itself that she will return to throughout the novel, and the doubleness she now perceives is American life itself, always characterized by a multilayered racial identity, Calpurnia's denials notwithstanding.

Scout interrogates race as the novel unfolds, seeking to understand the mystery of the black world at the edges of Maycomb. As she becomes increasingly aware of her father's role in the mediation between black and white in Maycomb, she questions him in the language she has adopted from her schoolmates, asking: " 'Do you defend niggers, Atticus?' " The explanation Atticus offers Scout for his decision to represent Tom Robinson reveals his role as white patriarch. " 'Of course I do,' " he replies. " 'Don't say nigger, Scout. That's common' " (85). Atticus's initial acceptance of the word points to the position he takes in regard to Tom, whereas his insistence that Scout not use the term because it is "common" demonstrates his link to the traditional southern fictional representations of race and class. He forbids Scout to use the word not because it is degrading to blacks but because it reflects poorly upon the Finch family, which Atticus holds up as a bastion of southern pride. While class is the primary motivating force for Atticus, race will remain Scout's obsession.

Lee relies heavily upon numerous conventions of southern literature that characterize the white South's confrontation with blackness. Repeatedly in these southern novels we encounter scenes of beset justice in which a white character rescues an unjustly accused black man from certain death at the hands of an angry mob. As we have seen, Elizabeth Spencer employs irony in just such a scene in *The Voice at the Back Door* to reveal the complexity of both her white and black characters as they resist the essentializing stereotypes that the culture forces upon them. Lee, on the other hand, delivers the scene straight to the reader, inflating the traditional clichés with pathos. Her approach anticipates the pattern we find in popular southern novels following her own.

After Atticus takes a defensive position in front of the Maycomb jail where Tom Robinson is being held, an angry mob confronts him, intending to lynch the prisoner. When the mob demands to know if Tom is in the jail, Atticus coolly responds that he is, " 'and he's asleep. Don't wake him up' " (172). Not to be put off by this paternal warning, the mob presses on, but Scout ultimately thwarts their intentions when she quietly asks after the son of one member of the mob. Her innocence amidst this racially charged scene leads him to call the lynching off, yet Lee's heavy sentiment undermines the intended weight of the scene. After the mob has left, Tom calls to them on the street:

> "Mr. Finch?"
>
> A soft husky voice came from the darkness above: "They gone?"
>
> Atticus stepped back and looked up. "They've gone," he said.
>
> "Get some sleep, Tom. They won't bother you any more." (176)

Atticus maintains his willingness to sacrifice himself for Tom Robinson, yet he has plainly established a distance between himself and Tom which he makes no effort to bridge: " 'Get some sleep, Tom,' " he says. And when Jem worries that the mob might easily have killed his father, Atticus responds in the manner of Twain's Colonel Sherburn: " 'Every mob in every little Southern town is always made up of people you know—doesn't say much for them, does it?' " (180). The emotional distance that Atticus establishes through his condescension is precisely the same as that which Scout will establish between herself and Boo Radley at the end of the novel. Having taken her lesson from her father, Scout will speak to Boo, twenty years her senior, as if he were a child.

Tom's trial underscores the theme of interracial union even as it reasserts white hegemony in Maycomb. Secretly watching the proceedings from among the blacks sitting in the courtroom balcony, Jem and Scout have become like Mr. Dolphus Raymond, the white man who so fascinates Scout because he chooses to live among blacks. When Jem explains to Scout that Raymond's children are to be considered "Negroes" in the terms of their southern culture, Scout recognizes the absurdity of racial categories: " 'Well how do you know we ain't Negroes?' " she asks (185). It is a question he can't conclusively answer, since race under such terms is inherently fluid. We will see Atticus's two children moving toward knowledge of the absurdity of racial terms as they witness their father's defense of Tom Robinson from the black gallery.

Scout evaluates Tom from her perch in the balcony: "He seemed to be a respectable Negro, and a respectable Negro would never go up into somebody's yard of his own volition," as Mayella Ewell has accused him of doing (220). And Scout likewise finds Tom attractive: "Tom was a black-velvet Negro, not shiny, but soft black velvet. . . . If he had been whole, he would have been a fine specimen of a man" (220). Lee conveys Scout's ability to see the human traits that Tom possesses, even as her language contradicts such a view: Tom is no man on equal footing with other men but rather a sort of laboratory animal, and a damaged one at that, given his limp arm. Even as her protagonist moves closer to a recognition of the place of blackness in the formation of her own identity, Lee removes her black characters from the realm of humanity. In the end, the marginal identity that so fascinates will remain only as a moral measure of the white characters of Maycomb.

Like Stowe's Tom, Tom Robinson reacts with indifference to the harsh treatment he receives. He is unable to speak out in the face of bitter injustice throughout the courtroom scenes, in which we discover him to have been utterly passive during the events that led to the crime of which he stands accused.[2]

Upon hearing Tom's description of the events, Scout decides that "in their own way, Tom Robinson's manners were as good as Atticus's," a sensible enough conclusion, for Tom Robinson is Atticus Finch's black ideal (222). Lame, docile, victimized, he represents the black man that white liberals prop up time and again in novels that ostensibly call for better treatment of African Americans: he is foil to the novel's central figure of masculinity, Atticus. For Atticus, a feminine or polite masculinity is an expression of his role in southern gentility; by contrast, these same characteristics in Tom demonstrate his passivity and his status as victim. " 'Why were you scared?' " Atticus Finch asks after Tom has testified. " 'Mr. Finch, if you was a nigger like me, you'd be scared, too' " (223). Tom, it seems, has fantasies of his own about white identity.

In his summation, Atticus Finch debunks Maycomb's essentialized perception of blacks, arguing that the state's testimony against Tom Robinson has been designed to play upon the white jury's stereotypes of black behavior "in the cynical confidence" that the jury would assume that "*all* Negroes lie, that *all* Negroes are basically immoral beings, that *all* Negro men are not to be trusted around our women" (233). Atticus associates such manipulation on the part of the state "with minds of their caliber," suggesting again that the likes of Bob Ewell are to blame for racism in the South (233).

Atticus reminds the jury that this stereotype of blacks is unfounded, " 'a lie as black as Tom Robinson's skin, a lie I do not have to point out to you. You know the truth, and the truth is this: some Negroes lie, some Negroes are immoral, some Negro men are not to be trusted around women—black or white. But this is a truth that applies to the human race and to no particular race of men. There is not a person in this courtroom who has never told a lie, who has never done an immoral thing' " (233). The summation confirms Atticus as the white patriarch we have always suspected him to be; he attempts to develop and complicate the white community's view of African Americans by denying the predominant stereotype. Yet we see here the seeds of stereotype as well: Atticus asserts that the lie is "as black as Tom Robinson's skin," ironically linking Tom with the very stereotype from which he ostensibly attempts to free him. And though surely Atticus speaks for Lee, she creates in Tom Robinson an affable, compliant victim to symbolize the predicaments of southern blacks. Like both Stowe and Twain in the previous century, Lee creates a character who poses no threat to the dominant paradigm, allowing one stereotype to replace another.

The jury acts in a more straightforward manner. For all of Atticus's pleading, they find Tom guilty of rape. When the black community nevertheless reveres Atticus for his efforts to help Tom, we see the final valuation of white identity over black that the novel has been moving toward throughout. The contemporary reader may well share Scout's astonishment that the loss of Tom Robinson's case results not in black protest but in black adulation of the white lawyer. Sitting quietly in the balcony in the moments after the announcement of the verdict, Scout marvels when the African American men and women around her stand to honor her father as he leaves the courtroom: "I looked around. They were standing. All around us and in the balcony on the opposite wall, the Negroes were getting to their feet. Reverend Syke's voice was as distant as Judge Taylor's: 'Miss Jean Louise, stand up. Your father's passin' '" (242). Maycomb's black community shares Tom Robinson's docile nature as well as his reverence for white identity; we find that only rarely in the novel does a black character break free from the sort of essentialized view of race that Atticus so eloquently denounces. The courtroom scene is a white fantasy of black behavior, in which the black community pays homage to the failed but noble efforts of a liberal white southerner, much as generations of readers of

Huckleberry Finn have paid homage to Huck in celebrating his decision to go to hell and overlooking his failure to take up residence there.

When, at the end of the novel, Scout's teacher announces a pageant for the schoolchildren, she chooses Scout to portray an exceedingly appropriate Maycomb County agricultural product: a ham. Lee is a bit of a ham, too, particularly in this final section, in which she completes the link between Boo Radley's plight and Tom Robinson's.

Bob Ewell emerges as a sort of white trash sacrifice for middle-class guilt. When Ewell attacks Jem and Scout on their way home from the pageant, Boo Radley comes upon the scene and kills him. Scout later sees her savior in detail, in contrast to the stereotypes she had assigned to him earlier in the novel.

Like Tom Robinson, Boo Radley is an outcast impaired: his "sickly white hands" (310) and the "delicate indentations at his temples" (311) distinguish him from the Finches, and these characteristics also lead Scout to take a benevolent and finally paternalistic attitude toward him. Scout's aversion to Boo's whiteness—his "sickly white hands" that "stood out garishly against the dull cream wall" (310) remind us of Pap's "fish-belly white"—reflects on her discomfort with her own white identity, given what she has witnessed in the course of the novel. But the condescension inherent in her paternal stance at the end of the novel belies any such anxiety. At the end, Scout has returned to a white world she could never fully escape. The control she assumes over Boo Radley parallels that which Atticus takes over Tom Robinson in court, and if both Atticus and Scout are protective of their charges, they also limit them with their condescension.

Figures in Black

Carson McCullers and Harper Lee employ familiar parameters of the relationship between black and white in developing their white protagonists through relationships with African Americans. While McCullers portrays Berenice as an autonomous and complex figure, Lee portrays Calpurnia as a figure ever tied to the patriarchal world headed by Atticus Finch. Like Tom Robinson, Calpurnia merely reaffirms her charge's white identity, whereas Berenice endeavors in vain to encourage Frankie to confirm an identity within the black world.

In the contemporary period, the pattern has become commonplace, and we find it in the work of southern writers of nonfiction like Anne Moody (*Coming of Age in Mississippi*) and Erskine Caldwell (*In Search of Bisco*) as well as in the work of a wealth of southern novelists. In the following chapter, I consider two contemporary writers, Sara Flanigan and Kaye Gibbons, who work very much within the tradition of McCullers and Lee as they characterize the development of teenaged girls nurtured by black communities.

❈4❈
PASSING THROUGH DARKNESS

Sara Flanigan and Kaye Gibbons
Search for Hope

> The American South has often provided the
> metaphorical and actual settings, the playgrounds
> of the American racial drama, the locations of American
> racial meanings. The region has been central to the erasure
> of the whiteness of American identity precisely because its
> dramas have been so graphic, so violent, so perversely pleasing.
> White Americans generally have failed to see the ways they
> imaginatively "live" in a metaphorical South, even as
> their relationship to the region has danced between
> the poles of attraction and revulsion.
>
> GRACE ELIZABETH HALE

Contemporary white writers in the South focus upon racial identity as much as any group of southern writers has since 1865, and
we see elements of the pattern of cross-racial companionship and
betrayal in novels as diverse as Harry Crews's *All We Need of Hell,*
Clyde Edgerton's *Raney,* and Shirley Ann Grau's *The Keepers of
the House.* Novels that take as central theme the cross-racial relationship include Carol Dawson's *Body of Knowledge* and Lane
von Herzen's *Copper Crown* as well as John Ehle's *The Journey of
August King* and John Hyman's *The Relationship,* among dozens
of others.[1] Jesse Hill Ford's *The Liberation of Lord Byron Jones*
places a cross-racial relationship at the center of social unrest and,
as Martha Cook notes, emphasizes the violence that is "an un-
fortunate but inevitable consequence of the rapid social changes

occurring in the South" (531). If our understanding of southern literature has ever been linked to race, in the contemporary era the South often takes form and meaning for readers through the relationship we can trace back to Huck and Jim.[2]

Following the civil rights era, the pattern in which a white protagonist attains moral growth through a relationship with a black character became so commonplace as to be reduced to cliché, especially on television and in films.[3] We see it on stage as well: Alfred Uhry's *Driving Miss Daisy* directly parallels Twain's narrative, both in its initial portrayal of a union of black and white and in a subsequent return of the black character to type. In Uhry's play, the characters are different in age and ethnicity (the elderly Daisy is Jewish; Hoke is her African American driver), but they resemble Huck and Jim in that the African American character is acolyte to the white character's growth and healing. If Daisy teaches Hoke to read, Hoke teaches Daisy to embrace humanity. The play may well be for the author a remembrance of a past South, but it is surely for its largely white audience also a fantasy of black behavior. Here we have Hoke, who is, in the midst of the civil rights movement, far less interested in rights of any sort than was even Twain's Jim. It's an updating of the plantation novel as the writer references racial behaviors of an earlier day.

In this chapter, I consider two popular novels by contemporary writers—Sara Flanigan's *Sudie* and Kaye Gibbons's *Ellen Foster*—that portray young girls responding to changes in the South wrought by the civil rights movement. Each writer narrates a southern society enmeshed in racial enmities, and both see hope for that society in the interracial relationships at the center of their narratives.

Liars

Sara Flanigan's *Sudie*, set in the 1940s in the all-white southern town of Linlow, Georgia, tells the story of the developing relationship between two girls and a black man, Simpson, who lives in the woods on the outskirts of town. Through much of the novel, the narrator, Mary Agnes, refuses to see Simpson in other than essentialized terms, while Sudie, Mary Agnes's best friend, accepts Simpson from the beginning despite her initial fears. Following Harper Lee's portrayal of Bob Ewell, Flanigan represents the racial sins of the white community with a white rapist who contrasts with the wholly benevolent if utterly passive Simpson. Like Harper Lee in her portrayal of Tom Robinson, Flanigan develops Simpson as a charitable and passive primitive, willing to endure nobly the insults of white society.

We learn from Mary Agnes that Simpson shocks Sudie in her first encounter with him, when she comes upon him standing on the railroad tracks leading out of town, holding a bleeding rabbit, and she responds with inert terror: "She said she jest couldn't git her legs to move or her arms or nothing" (64). Such jarring moments of initial contact repeat themselves in countless scenes in American literature. We continue to relive these miniatures of the drama of Columbus as if trying finally to get it right. As Sudie stands watching Simpson "all she could think about was them stories we'd heard all our life about niggers being boogers that would git us and eat us alive. She said it was jest spooky" (64).

Simpson immediately assumes a passive position relative to Sudie, however, one he will maintain throughout the novel: " 'Don't be scared, miss. . . . All I'm gonna do is take this little rabbit and doctor him. Somebody's dogs was about to make a meal out of him' " (64). If it is a wonder that a man living in a broken-down shack beside the railroad tracks would heal a rabbit rather than stew it, it is less surprising that Sudie would accept Simpson on the terms he establishes here. The nurturing disposition he exhibits toward her (and the rabbit) in telling her not to be afraid allows Sudie to accept him, but if she overcomes one stereotype of African Americans, she accepts another in the process. No longer the cruel and inhuman "booger man," Simpson is instead a compassionate and docile black angel, a first cousin of Tom Robinson and thus another discovery in our genealogical work on the family of Harriet Beecher Stowe's Tom, whose good deeds are surpassed only by his patience and sagacity.

In the American race narratives we've examined, the black character often figures as hero for tolerating the afflictions heaped upon him by whites (Faulkner spoke of the nobility of the capacity of African Americans to "endure"); these white writers thus resurrect the role of the "good nigger," a delimiting if insistent portrayal in American literature. In my next chapter, I show how African American southerners challenge this representation; here, we see Flanigan swapping one essentializing structure for another in her portrayal of white perceptions of black identity.

In parallel to Sudie's relationship with Simpson, the novel traces Mary Agnes's emergent appreciation for him, which grows from a background of extreme prejudice. Her father and grandfather have helped to keep blacks out of Linlow—" 'Daddy says he wouldn't raise no younguns in a town full of niggers' " (6)—to the extent that most of the children living there have never seen a black person. When Mary Agnes learns that Sudie has a black friend, she exclaims: ' "But, Sudie! Niggers is boogers! They kill folks!' " (46). Sudie, having already debunked Linlow's mythology of black identity, replies that he doesn't kill folks, but Mary Agnes's questions reveal the bitter stereotypes she has learned from her family and from the citizens of Linlow (" 'Does he have a name?' " [47] and ' "Does he act like a real man acts?' " [48]); like Sudie, she eventually acknowledges the hypocrisy of the white world in which she has been raised. By the novel's conclusion, Mary Agnes recognizes that nearly everyone in Linlow manipulates and deceives in order to maintain southern myths of racial identity. Ultimately, she spurns her white world as a result of her indirect relationship with Simpson.

Sudie turns upon a series of epiphanies arising from the girls' increasing awareness of the American cultural dissonance over race. When Sudie realizes that she has been duped by her white elders into believing that blacks are cruel, she tears down the signs at the outskirts of Linlow, altering one to read, "NIGGER, PLEASE LET THE SUN SHINE ON YOU IN LINLOW." When she brings the revised sign to Simpson, their pleasure over her prank leads to an exchange in which they willfully attempt to undermine traditional southern gentility:

> He put her down and she said, "Mr. Nigger, sir?"
>
> And he said, "Yes, Miss White Lady?"
>
> She pulled the sides of her dress out and curtsied. Then she said, "You're most welcome to let the sun set on you in Linlow, Georgia, of the United States." (81)

The passage suggests the extent to which Flanigan cannot finally escape the stereotypes of the Old South, even as she attempts to subvert them. Sudie's ironic use of "nigger" here and Simpson's ironic, minstrel-like reply parallel the position in which we find Simpson throughout the novel: a fantasy of white author and white audience, Simpson venerates the white child with whom he is linked. If irony distances Flanigan's characters from the Old South, the relative positions of the characters suggest they have not gotten far.

Flanigan presents her theme through the classic opposition of sentimental literature: Simpson's opposite is Bob Rice, a child molester who pays the girls of Linlow nickels to keep them from revealing his deeds. Sudie and Mary Agnes contrast Simpson with Rice, associating blackness with humanity and whiteness with manipulation, violence, and deceit. After she begins her relationship with Simpson, Sudie tells Rice that she won't have anything to do with him. Rice will not allow her to escape and assaults her sexually: "She was crying harder than ever and it seemed like now he really liked her crying. He started giggling and saying lots of dirty words and cuss words. Then he really got crazy" (98–99). Like Twain's Pap and Lee's Ewell, Bob Rice is a diabolical figure,

Claggart with a drawl. Flanigan juxtaposes the rape with a med-
itative scene in which Simpson attempts to save Sudie's sick rabbit, and her aim is clear, if none too subtle. Like Twain and Lee,
she demonstrates the affirmative aspects of the black world while
exposing the white world as southern Sodom, though surely the
manipulation of melodrama here is more evident than in *Huckleberry Finn.*

As in earlier works, the African American character's individual identity emerges slowly from the morass of stereotypes. When
Sudie asks Simpson about his wife, who has died, she sees him for
the first time as a man capable of emotion. Simpson tells Sudie
that his wife had tried to help him attain his high school diploma
by bringing books home for him to study, "but she died 'fore he
got it. When he told Sudie that, he broke down and cried like a
baby, and Sudie cried too this time, and she patted his shoulder
and his arm and his hand" (144). Through her narration, Mary
Agnes begins to see Simpson in the human terms that Sudie has
earlier accepted.

We know by now that Sudie's newfound awareness is a main-
stay of the genre, and, in order to fully sympathize with her companion, she must first experience white oppression of the black
world. Thus it is that she sets out with Simpson to a town near
Linlow one afternoon. Sudie goes disguised as a black girl, and
she swiftly discovers the realities of segregation when she asks
Simpson why they cannot go into a drugstore to cool off: " 'Chile,
white folks don't let niggers set down in public places where they
set down' " (165). Though wildly improbable (that a white child in
Georgia in the 1940s would be wholly unaware of segregation is,
to use Huck Finn's word, a "stretcher"), the scene enables Sudie to
learn firsthand Simpson's moral imperative that Sudie shouldn't
" 'make fun of nobody that's different' " (119). When Sudie demands to be served ice cream at the lunch counter, however, her
"passing" ends in failure, as the proprietor agrees to serve her only
after he understands that Sudie is white. Try though she might,

she fails to escape her white identity. For Sudie the scene suggests the illogic of racial identity in the South, and her failed disguise ironically enables her to see her own link with an African American identity.

Simpson, unfazed by their encounter with racism but moved by Sudie's reaction to it, immediately apologizes, but Sudie's growing awareness of the oppression of blacks in the South leads her to reject Simpson's attempt to make amends for the white community:

> "Quit saying you're sorry Simpson! Quit saying it, you hear!"
>
> "Alright, Miss Sudie."
>
> "And jest call me Sudie! Jest Sudie! Not *Miss* Sudie. I can't stand you to call me that. Not no more." (167)

Simpson ironically becomes an apologist for southern racism even as he inspires Sudie to reject the hypocrisy that informs such racism. When she insists she can't understand the customs of Jim Crow that compel Simpson to treat her as his better, he replies, " 'Well, you will,' he said and patted her arm. 'One of these days you will. You'll understand it all when you get grown' " (168). Flanigan willfully places Simpson further into an accommodating position here as he accepts the offenses of white society and attempts to persuade Sudie to accept them.

Toward the end of the novel, men searching for an elderly white resident of Linlow, Lillian Graham, discover Simpson's house among the thick kudzu vines in the forest outside of town. A manhunt ensues when all Linlow assumes that the unknown black man must have killed Graham. Sudie falls into a state of shock when she realizes that her friend has left town in order to survive. For her part, Mary Agnes receives harsh punishment after her parents realize that she has known about Simpson all along. She tries but fails to persuade her parents of Simpson's humanity: "Well you'd of thought I was a-talking to myself to hear myself talk. They didn't listen to one single word I said, and while Daddy was switching my legs so hard I thought I'd die, and I was screaming and jumping 'round to try to miss the switch, I thought to myself, You are liars. That's all y'all are. Liars! Jest like Sudie said. This whole day and this whole crazy thing is one big fat bald-faced lie! The worst lie I ever heard of in my life—and I've heard some lies, that's for sure!" (243). Mary Agnes's renunciation of her white society leads to an acceptance of black identity she could not have anticipated. But if blackness here comes to represent an escape from an immoral white society, it is the passive blackness associated with Jim in the final third of Twain's novel. We never encounter anything resembling Jim's moral rebuke of Huck following the fog sequence or Lucas Beauchamp's steadfast autonomy.

Such renunciation leads to Mary Agnes's further development in which she vows her continuing allegiance to Sudie and to the racial awareness her friend has come to stand for. "I was gonna be Sudie's friend," she decides, no matter what her parents might do. She accepts the risk that accompanies such a decision because she sees that her parents' position is unjust: "They was wrong on this thing. Horrible wrong, and I couldn't do one thing about that. Not one thing" (243). Like Huck, she rejects the predominant morality of her society in making her decision to befriend Sudie, and she does so at considerable risk.

In the end, Mary Agnes's final commitment is not to Simpson but to her white friend, Sudie. If this sounds fairly well removed from sympathy for African Americans, it was not an unfamiliar theme in the second half of the twentieth century: John Howard Griffin in *Black Like Me* proposes that his white readers sympathize not directly with oppressed southern blacks, but with him— a white man who in passing as black has also been victimized by the southern racial hierarchy. And of course this is just what the southern writers we have encountered have asked of their readers: the reader sympathizes not with the escaping slave or his descendants living in the Jim Crow South but with his (or her) white companion. The pattern thus ultimately contains the seeds of the essentialist thought it ostensibly rejects.

At the conclusion of Flanigan's novel, we learn that Simpson's presence has had a beneficial effect on the town of Linlow: Sudie's parents allow her to wear the yellow dress that Simpson left for her as a token of his love, and Preacher Miller, who had so often supported segregation in his sermons, no longer preaches "as scarey as he use to" (279). Mary Agnes even sees some development in her parents: "Mama and Daddy snorted and humph'ed for a while and I reckon Daddy would die 'fore he'd say he was wrong about niggers, but at least him and Mama said, Well, okay, I could be Sudie's friend" (279). Mary Agnes, for her part, notes: "I reckon that from now on I'm gonna have to keep on thinking on it myself 'cause I sure don't like what I seen happen in this town about Simpson" (274). Mary Agnes comes to an awareness of the need to question continually the dictates of her white society: "I learned lots of things from her that set me to wondering about people, white folks and niggers both" (274). Such knowledge enables her to distance herself from white society.

Thus Simpson, who has escaped the mob unscathed, has set to right the moral inequities of Linlow and changed nearly everyone for the better. In the process he has recovered from his own melancholia through his love for Sudie. He quietly leaves Linlow and, in so doing, returns Sudie and Mary Agnes to their white world. But as we see in the final pages of the novel, even the previously reserved Mary Agnes now actively fights injustice when she tears down the last of her elders' bitter signs warning blacks away from Linlow.

If this moral restructuring appears proper to Sudie and Mary Agnes, for Huck Finn it would be so much "soul-butter and hogwash" (213). In Simpson's adulation of the childhood world of his white friend, we see in him much of Twain's Jim but more of Stowe's Tom: the type has long been a white ideal, as much for

Stowe before the Civil War as for contemporary liberal writers in the South. The character type emerged in the nineteenth-century race novel by white writers that countered the slave narrative. Simpson, like so many black characters in novels by southern liberals, remains enslaved in the white imagination. Free of slavery and Jim Crow, the docile black character still restricts himself to the world of innocent white children and thus represents no threat to the dominant culture: for Simpson this means moving to the woods where he's safely out of the way, busy protecting the lame rabbits of the world and offering companionship and love to forlorn white children.

Foster Homes

The cross-racial childhood friendship is an increasingly common narrative pattern in southern fiction. Dorothy Allison's *Bastard out of Carolina*, Nanci Kincaid's *Crossing Blood*, and Elizabeth Cox's *Night Talk* portray such relationships as components in a white character's growth. As Sharon Monteith observes, however, the relationships in such novels do not endure. In Kaye Gibbons's *Ellen Foster*, the central place of the relationship suggests the dim possibility that the cross-racial relationship might be sustained beyond childhood, although the threats to that possibility are many.

Like Sudie, Ellen, the protagonist of Kaye Gibbons's first novel, *Ellen Foster*, wavers between her own flawed white world and the black world she encounters as she endeavors to gain a sense of her own identity. Typical of her white, southern community, Ellen initially views her African American friend Starletta and her family with disdain, but her experiences with them cause her to identify with the black community even as she comes to reject her own family. Like Sudie, Ellen fantasizes her participation in a black world. By the end of the novel, though, Ellen finds a white foster home, and the patrician air she assumes in regard to Starletta, even as she declares her indebtedness to her friend, is another instance of the betrayal of cross-racial bonding so persistent in the southern novel.

When her mother dies, Ellen finds herself living alone with her abusive, drunken father, who assumes authoritarian control over his child and in the process becomes the most apparent cause for her rejection of white society. When he brings a group of black men home to drink with him, Ellen overhears one of the men suggesting that Ellen "is just about ripe [because] you gots to git em when they is still soff when you mashum" (37). Ellen crawls into her closet in terror: "What else do you do when your house is run over by colored men drinking whiskey and singing and your daddy is worse than all put together?" Gibbons ties Ellen's white world to a black world straight out of type: her father terrifies her all the more because she links blackness with evil; thus, the desperation she feels in her home develops in part from her fear of a black world she does not know. Ellen overcomes such essentialist thinking through her relationship with Starletta's family, which provides her with a means of temporary transcendence from the nightmare of her white home.

When his companions leave her house, Ellen's father stumbles to her room, apparently intent upon raping her. In Ellen's narration of the attack, we see the extent to which she lacks any identity in her own home:

Get away from me he does not listen to me but touches his hands harder on me. That is not me. Oh no that was her name. Do not oh you do not say her name to me. That was her name. You know that now stop no not my name.

I am Ellen.

I am Ellen.

He pulls the evil back into his self and Lord I run. Run down the road to Starletta. Now to the smoke coming out of the chimney against the night sky I run.

> Down the path in darkness I gather my head and all that is
> spinning and flying out from me and wonder oh you just have to
> wonder what the world has come to. (38)

Thus abused by her father (and called by her mother's name),
Ellen must declare her identity outright.[4] The scene reveals the
psychological violence done by a father who comes to represent
the corrupt and debased southern culture that figures so prominently in this novel and in earlier southern novels. Ellen escapes a
violent whiteness in the welcoming embrace of black characters
who ultimately display more concern for the white companion's
well-being than for their own. The exodus from white culture was
as important in Mark Twain's day as it is in our own, suggesting
that the air of guilt and longing that lingered over white America
in the decades following the Civil War lingers there still.

In leaving her father's home Ellen seeks a more nurturing environment, but she soon discovers that her relatives view her as
a burden. By contrast, she finds compassion in Starletta's home,
which "always smells like fried meat but if you visit there a while
you adjust" (29), but she cautiously refuses Starletta's kindnesses
because of her own prejudices. As Huck Finn begins to see Jim's
humanity through Jim's open display of affection for his family
("It don't seem natural, but I reckon it's so" [201]), Ellen sees
Starletta's family interacting with far more warmth than she has
known in her own house. The greeting she receives on entering
Starletta's home suggests the contrast between white and black
worlds:

> Come on in the house is what her daddy says to me and takes my
> package. They pay grown men to do that in more stylish places.
>   Her mama is at the stove boiling and frying and telling the
> daddy not to let all the heat out through the door.
>   He sneaks up behind her and pinches her on the tail.
>   I saw that.
>   They would not carry on like that if they were at the store or

working in the field. They walk up the road and pick cotton and do not speak like they know they go together. People say they do not try to be white.

As fond as I am of all three of them I do not think I could drink after them. I try to see what Starletta leaves on the lip of a bottle but I have never seen anything with the naked eye. If something is that small it is bound to get into your system and do some damage. (29–30)

The language with which Ellen describes Starletta's family exposes the fleeting nature of her own identity. Her abbreviated, disjointed sentences—"They walk up the road and pick cotton and do not speak like they know they go together"—mirror her alienation from her hosts. Despite Ellen's surprise at the affection she witnesses in the house, she cannot overcome the stereotypes of blacks that she has learned from her parents: "As fond as I am of all three of them I do not think I could drink after them." Ellen disregards evidence of the humanity of her black companions for much of the narrative, relying instead upon the essentialized view of race she has held from the beginning.

For all her destitution, Ellen adopts a privileged position in her interaction with Starletta, insisting, for instance, that Starletta "wash before I will play with you" (31). Ellen eventually comes to realize the folly of such condescension (when she refuses to sit down to dinner with Starletta's family, their compassion undermines her segregationist endeavors), and she comes to view Starletta's family as her own. When Starletta's mother offers Ellen a biscuit, Ellen thinks to herself that "no matter how good it looks to you it is still a colored biscuit," but she is forced to question such assumptions when Starletta's parents unexpectedly give her a present for Christmas: "Oh my God it is a sweater. I like it so much. I do not tell a story when I say it does not look colored at all" (32). Ellen begins to adapt to Starletta's family as though it is her own, even if she clings to her narrow conception of African

Americans in the process. The novel suggests that an essentializing ideology of race provides the structure of a white southern
childhood; Ellen is only able to reject that structure when she becomes aware of her own moral kinship with the African Americans she encounters.

Ellen, with her itinerant heart, soon leaves Starletta to stay with
her grandmother ("my mama's mama"), who, in contrast to Starletta's family, forces her to work in the cotton fields for her keep.
Ironically, her forced labor leads Ellen to a new awareness of black
identity that soon brings her closer to her friend Starletta and to
an understanding of the role of blackness in the creation of her
own identity. Working in the fields, she recognizes that she plays
a role in this southern society traditionally reserved for blacks: "I
thought while I chopped from one field to the next how I could
pass for colored now. Somebody riding by here in a car could not
see my face and know I was white. But that is OK now I thought
to myself of how it did not make much of a difference anymore"
(66). Having partially abandoned her white identity in witnessing the utter degradation of white culture, Ellen now passes as
black. Her momentary denial of her white identity enables her to
find solace in black culture, a progression that leads her to a better
conception of her moral self. While black identity and the poverty
she associates with it are initially reprehensible to Ellen, her experience in the cotton field brings her to see the ties between her
white world and the black one she passes through. Black culture
provides Ellen her sole retreat from the torments of her white relatives, and she comes to fully value this refuge only after "passing" through her own white society as though she were black.
Early in the novel, though, African American culture becomes a
refuge from the oppressions of her own white culture, albeit one
Ellen idealizes through a familiar set of primitivist notions. While
her movement toward African American culture initially allows
her a kind of freedom from self, her narrow construction of blackness eventually compels her return to a white world.

Imagining her own participation in a black world, Ellen is no longer much concerned with her lack of a white identity, deciding that "it did not make much of a difference anymore" (66). However, she adds that she finally cannot escape whiteness (she says she is "just this side of colored"; "I was pinky white"), a judgment borne out by the subsequent narrative. Still, her rejection of the white society of her grandmother suggests the extent to which she looks to the black community for her own identity. Ellen's grandmother, like her father, symbolizes white southern society, and Ellen looks to her newfound blackness and to the black laborers with whom she works to replace her own kin. Indeed, she idealizes the sort of community she finds among these laborers:

> After supper each night it was not raining I walked up the colored path and spied on Mavis and her family.
>
> It looked like slavery times with them all hanging out on the porch picking at each other. They fought strong as they played and laughed. (66)

"The colored path" becomes a sort of yellow brick road to moral sensibility for Ellen: through her observations of Mavis's family, Ellen comes to a new understanding of herself. Part of this epiphany, however, is her essentialized view of Mavis's family. Ellen's remark that "they fought strong as they played and laughed" might have come from any postbellum mythologizing plantation novel, and indeed she fantasizes that such bliss is a return to "slavery times." The analogy is not far off the mark: even as Ellen claims to be indignant at their plight ("My mama's mama didn't pay them doodly-squat" [66]), she views them as lacking in motivation and incentive. Ellen cannot release the family from an essentialized conception even as she offers them up as her ideal because, for her, the essential *is* the ideal. In the very moment when she recognizes the place of the marginal in her own identity, Ellen insists that the black characters who nurture and develop her are, in the end, precisely what she is not.

Long after *Brown v. Board of Education*, white freedom inevitably recalls black slavery, and, if Ellen's essentializing here turns on its head the traditional southern stereotype linking blacks with moral failing, the result is as narrow as traditional southern ideology. Indeed, she adopts an equivalent formula that is becoming familiar: blacks are good, simple, and wholesome, and most whites are evil to the core.

Seeing the warmth in Mavis's family, Ellen concludes that she must "get one of them for my own self soon." Her own family, however, would have to be "white and with a little more money," suggesting the conscious distance she feels between herself and Mavis's family (67). Gibbons's irony, of course, detaches her from this imagined return to stereotype; where Flanigan in *Sudie* reflects primarily Twain's sentimental disposition, Gibbons employs his roughshod treatment of character. The ironic distance she creates between herself and Ellen in the latter sections of the novel provides a critique of her character's eventual return to the ideology of white society largely absent in *Sudie*.

When Ellen's grandmother dies, leaving her to find a more suitable home, Ellen settles into the white foster home from which she takes her name and where she can, ironically, be comfortable as she has been nowhere else. But resettled in the white community, she does not forget Starletta (though she does tend to remember her friend in colonizing terms): "Lord sometime I wish I still had Starletta" (83). Ellen's wish that she "still had" Starletta appears innocent enough; her repeated use of the phrase through the end of the novel, however, suggests that the development she attains through her relationship with Starletta can come only at the expense of Starletta's own growth. And, given her earlier fantasy of a return to "slavery times" for Mavis's family, her words suggest the very cultural oppression in which Ellen denies participation. Seeing Starletta in school, Ellen notices that her friend is growing up and thus out of her control. Betraying the extent to which she ultimately values white identity over black, she mourns the past like a Confederate officer come back from Appomattox: "I feel like she grew behind my back and when I think about her now I want to press my hands to her to stop her from growing into a time she will not want to play" (83).

Shortly after describing these longings, Ellen relates her attempt to guide her friend away from the "white boy" on whom Starletta has a crush. Ellen's jealousy exposes her hypocritical stance: "She told me during lunchtime one day she has a crush on a boy and she pointed him out to me and he was a sassy old white boy. And she would not listen to me tell her she would have to pick out another boy to love" (83). Ellen's insistence that Starletta "pick out another boy" reflects the same deeply felt sense of separation between black and white that we saw earlier in the novel, even as she attempts to assert her closeness to her friend. And the illogic that led Ellen to believe Starletta's interest in the boy (Tom) is motivated by economics matches that which led her to imagine her ideal family to be "white and with a little more money." In this southern culture, whiteness is all, even for Ellen, who has so clearly identified with black culture. She rejects a logical extension of the multicultural ideal that is at the center of the novel and assumes that her friend is being manipulative—she's "getting a itch way down deep and low where a colored boy cannot afford to reach to scratch" (84). Ellen jealously guards this white Tom because, like Starletta, she wants for herself a white family "to set [her] up in style" (84).

Ellen acknowledges her debt to Starletta by asking her "new mama" to let Starletta spend a night with her. She recognizes the courage such a proposal requires: "That is brave to think about because I am not sure if it has ever been done before" (85). She also immediately reveals the condescension inherent in her action: "That is something big Starletta would never forget and she would think back on me and how she stayed in the white house all night with Ellen" (85). Ellen recognizes and claims a superior position relative to Starletta even as she maintains that she has attained moral growth through their relationship: "I wonder to myself am I the same girl who would not drink after Starletta two years ago or eat a colored biscuit when I was starved?" (85).

At the end, Starletta emerges as the focus of Ellen's claim to growth: "All I know now is that I want Starletta in my house and if she tells me to I will lick the glass she uses just to show that I love her and her being colored is just the way she is. That is all" (85). Debunking the social myths of the South that support essentializing ideology, Ellen realizes that whites represent a greater threat to her than do blacks; she acknowledges further that there is no inherent value in a white identity. In her assertions that those "made in the same batch" cannot all be trusted and that "I was cut out to be colored" (85), Ellen contemplates a rejection of white culture itself, yet in her claim that she "will lick the glass" that Starletta uses in order to prove her love for her friend, she demonstrates the very stereotype with which she began the novel when she fretted over the "colored biscuit." She is willing to sacrifice hygiene for her friend but not the claim of difference and the condescension that accompanies such a claim. Hence, even as Ellen pronounces her newfound sensibility, she retains her white ideology of race in attempting to repay Starletta for all she has done for Ellen by inviting her to stay over. Caught between white and black worlds, Ellen finally accepts the white world while maintaining that she prefers the black one: without realizing it, Ellen puts Starletta in her place with her invitation to enjoy the splendors of the big house.

Still, at the end of the novel, Ellen is capable of acknowledging the essentializing ideology she retains. She hopes that Starletta "will remember me good when she is old enough to think and sort through her own past to see all the ways I slighted her oh not by selling her down a river or making her wash my clothes but by all the varieties of ways I felt God chose me over her" (100). She thus rejects the literary and cultural stereotypes of the Old South while admitting to the subtler stereotypes of the New. If such an acknowledgment suffers in the face of her inability to recognize the more pernicious stereotypes she retains, it is nevertheless a conscious recognition of the inevitability of a return to essentialist ideology on the part of Gibbons's protagonist.[5] Ellen's moral balancing exposes the guilt over her own white identity that motivates her: she is driven to goodness out of a keen sense of guilt, and her actions likewise eventually expose that guilt as a superficial balm.

At the conclusion of the novel, Gibbons distances herself further from her protagonist in portraying Ellen's superficial awareness of racial prejudice. Ellen clings to her notion of white cultural superiority even as she claims to be done with it. She apologizes outright to Starletta, regretting the class differences that she invariably ties to race in the novel.

> I came a long way to get here but when you think about it real hard you will see that old Starletta came even farther.
>
> And I watch her resting now because soon we'll all be eating supper and maybe some cake tonight and I say low Starletta you sure have a right to rest. (126)

Watching Starletta sleep, Ellen decides that she can surely think of blacks in a new manner if the entire country can fight a war over their plight: "It seems like the decent thing to do" (126). As she comes to this conclusion, however, she denies Starletta the opportunity to reply to the apology she makes ("You just lay there and wait for supper" [125]), and she again asserts metaphoric possession of her friend in referring to her as "my Starletta." Ellen looks upon Starletta, who is well into puberty, as a child, her child, and assumes a maternalistic stance that denies Starletta any real sense of autonomy within the relationship. Indeed, Starletta remains silent at the end of the book as she has throughout. Our sympathy for Starletta's situation emerges only through the understanding we gain from Ellen: "And all this time I thought I had the hardest row to hoe. That will always amaze me" (126). If guilt alone is sufficient remittance for Ellen Foster, it is not so for Starletta, just as it is insufficient for the American culture out of which they emerge.

Fleeting Connection

Duplicity and violence typify the portrait of the white South in the work of many contemporary writers, and the threat their communities hold over these protagonists leads them to escape to a starkly different black world. If these white protagonists come momentarily to share in a black community (and perhaps to recognize the place of that community in the creation of their own identities), they often likewise come to abandon it. Perhaps they do so because it is conceived so narrowly: in these contemporary works we find no Lucas Beauchamps or Beckwith Dozers; instead, the black world posited here is one lashed to an essentializing ideology that can allow that world or the characters who rise from it no autonomy.

African American writers responding to the vision of America we find in the southern novel persistently assert the autonomous role of black characters that the novels here in large measure restrict. In the next chapter, I examine the ways in which Richard Wright, Ralph Ellison, and Alice Walker assess the central tropes employed by white southern writers in portraying relationships between black and white characters.

5

BEAUTIFUL ABSURDITY

*Richard Wright, Ralph Ellison, and Alice Walker
Confront a Mythology of Race*

It behooves us to keep a close eye on this process
of Americanness. My grandparents were slaves. See how
short a time it's been? I grew up reading Twain, and then,
after all those Aunt Jemimah roles, those Stepin Fetchit roles,
roles with their own subtleties, here comes this voice from Mississippi,
William Faulkner. It just goes to show that you can't be Southern
without being black, and you can't be a black Southerner without
being white. Think of L.B.J. Think of Hugo Black. There are a
lot of subtleties based on race that we *will* ourselves
not to perceive, but at our peril. The truth is that
the quality of Americanness, the thing that the kids
invariably give voice to, will always come out.

RALPH ELLISON

Bamboozled, Spike Lee's angry satire on the minstrel image in
television and popular culture, mocks the work of a black television producer, Pierre Delacroix (played by Daman Wayans), who
fails repeatedly to sell his philosophically oriented work featuring
black characters. Pierre's white boss, Dunwitty (Michael Rapa-
port), prides himself upon his own blackness, talking ghetto slang
in contrast to Delacroix, who speaks in a comic Euro-American dialect so unusual that it mystifies his own father. [1] When Dunwitty
orders Delacroix to develop a new black show ("You can do it, my
nigga!"), Delacroix intends to get himself fired by portraying out-
moded stereotypes of black culture. He creates *Mantan, the New
Millennium Minstrel Show,* complete with blackface characters.

To Delacroix's horror, Dunwitty loves the idea and insists on its development.

The setting for the television variety show they create is a southern watermelon patch in which Mantan dances to his heart's content. Lee parodies southern narratives in choosing his southern setting, but he also observes that the appeal of such shows is broader: *Mantan,* it turns out, is a national hit. Each show begins with an emcee asking a live, mostly white audience in blackface "Is you a nigger?" to which they respond enthusiastically in the affirmative. The film ends with a montage of racist collectibles, Lee's heavy-handed means of assuring that the viewer gets his point that popular culture has supplied an endless stream of essentialist icons. Yet if the film lacks subtlety, it points to a primary theme of the African American novel since the Harlem Renaissance: the reassessment of the white character of goodwill. In Lee's reckoning, Dunwitty's supposed goodwill is inherently suspect, since it leads to the resurrection of minstrelsy itself.

In her work on "racechange," Susan Gubar writes of the means through which races come to know one another: "What one's imagination makes of other people is dictated, of course, by the laws of one's own personality and it is one of the ironies of black-white relations that, by means of what the white imagines the black man to be, the black man is enabled to know who the white man is" (2). African American novelists have perceived the relationship between black and white from the vantage point of the subjugated. Since the emergence of the form from its early model of the slave narrative, they have frequently portrayed cross-racial relationships in which a black character guides a white companion toward moral development. A central moral imperative of the African American novel has naturally been an insistence that white Americans come to recognize the dissonance between the nation's professed ideals and its treatment of minorities. While Huck Finn must first travel a thousand miles down the Mississippi

River with Jim before he decides to "go to hell" rather than return Jim to slavery, Bigger Thomas recognizes the moral inequity present in his society from the beginning of Richard Wright's *Native Son*. The ways in which blacks cope with that inequity provide the locus of the African American novel, a genre that, as Arnold Rampersad has argued, looks back time and again to *Huckleberry Finn* as both source and foil.

The language of white culture necessarily brings with it that culture's essentializing structures, and African American writers of the twentieth century attempted to undo such structures even as the language they used expressed them. Henry Louis Gates argues that the struggle black writers have with the very language they use leads them to employ the traditions of an African heritage; these writers, Gates suggests, "speak in standard Romance or Germanic languages and literary structures, but almost always speak with a distinct and resonant accent, an accent that signifies (upon) the various black vernacular literary traditions, which are still being written down" (*The Signifying Monkey* xxiii). It is a duality that frustrates even as it liberates, fractures even as it joins.

Racial identity appears as central theme time and again in the fiction of African American writers from Charles Chesnutt to Randall Kenan, just as we have found it to be central to the work of white writers in the South. African American writers have of course themselves struggled with the stereotypes placed upon blacks by white culture. Jean Toomer and Chesnutt, both of whom could have passed as "white," made conscious choices to "remain" black rather than pass, and they narrate similar experiences in their fiction. Describing the period in which he wrote *Cane*, Toomer asserted that his "need for artistic expression has pulled me deeper and deeper into the Negro group. As my powers of receptivity increased, I found myself loving it in a way that I could never love the other" (Kerman and Eldridge 97). This intriguing consideration—*whiteness* as otherness—emerges powerfully in Toomer's work, and we see African American writers exploring just such possibilities as they adapt the pattern of reversal we've found since Twain.

Here I examine the ways in which three American novelists—Richard Wright, Ralph Ellison, and Alice Walker—respond to, signify upon, and finally rewrite the relationship between Huck Finn and Jim.[2] Their protagonists work against the negative self-definition placed upon them by the white South. In portraying autonomous black characters removed from the essentializing structures of the white southern novel, these writers repudiate not Twain's text, where they plainly find inspiration, but the powerful recoiling from black identity to be found there. If the white characters here rarely resemble Huck Finn in their social standing, they do, like Huck, look to the black protagonists of these novels for either clemency or redemption. These novelists portray the inherent condescension and manipulation of a white character who seeks false refuge in blackness in broad caricature. Having gained the perspective of their black protagonists, these white characters answer in multiple means the question W. E. B. DuBois claimed the "other world," the white world, asked of him indirectly but interminably: "How does it feel to be a problem?" (43).

Protest Novel

Ralph Ellison called *Native Son* "the first philosophical novel by a Negro American" (qtd. in Rowley 192), and as a philosophy, it is a treatise on the ethics of race. Despite the unflinching violence of its portrayal of Bigger Thomas, *Native Son* was a phenomenal commercial success, the first best-seller by an African American writer and a Book-of-the-Month Club selection. Both *Native Son* and Ellison's own *Invisible Man*, published ten years later, were destined to remain at the center of critical controversy for decades, and reaction to the novels centered on the interrelation of black and white.

Native Son laments the plight of black America in its portrait of the immigrants from the South in the first decades of the twentieth century. Bigger Thomas's Chicago tenement building likely would have been populated by more people born in the southern states than in Illinois, and the novel looks back to Twain as to DuBois in its explicit critique of the northern betrayal of African Americans arriving from the South in the first decades of the twentieth century.

Wright claimed that his inspiration for Bigger came from blacks he encountered as a child in Mississippi, each of whom "consistently violated the Jim Crow laws of the South, at least for a sweet brief spell" (xi) in rebellion against an oppressive southern culture. Yet in choosing Chicago for his setting, Wright makes the implicit argument that the desperation of his protagonist results from the central hypocrisies characteristic of American, not just southern, society. In the tradition of Harriet Wilson's *Our Nig, or, Sketches from the Life of a Free Black* (1859), the novel critiques a northern society that held out false hope to African Americans fleeing the South.

From the beginning of the novel, the symbols of white oppression abound in Bigger Thomas's world: the imposing billboard showing the white face of Buckley, the state's attorney who will ultimately prosecute Bigger; the white movie characters whose glamorous lifestyles Bigger envies. Such images contrast sharply with the squalor in Bigger's life, epitomized by his family's threadbare apartment. Bigger's growing resentment of his own blackness arises from the oppressive structures he associates with whiteness. He fantasizes aloud to his friend Gus that he could fly a plane like the white boys who "get a chance to do everything" (19):

Gus pulled down the corners of his lips, stepped out from the wall, squared his shoulders, doffed his cap, bowed low and spoke with mock deference:

"Yessuh."

"You go to hell," Bigger said, smiling.

"Yessuh," Gus said again. (20)

Gus's mock minstrelsy effectively counters Bigger's aspirations, but the scene anticipates Bigger's later rejection of the association of blacks with servility. In telling Gus to "go to hell," Bigger rejects the subordinate role white society offers him. He fully recognizes the real implications of his friend's joke and turns the minstrel's role on its head by suggesting soon after that they "play 'white,'" stressing again his desire for an autonomy he lacks (21).

In playing white, Gus ironically chooses to be J. P. Morgan, a man quite like Mr. Dalton, for whom Bigger will soon be working. "Yessuh, Mr. Morgan," Bigger responds to Gus, mimicking his friend's feigned subservience shortly after he has rejected it (21). Bigger concludes their playacting by remarking bitterly, " 'Every time I get to thinking about me being black and they being white, me being here and they being there, I feel like something awful's going to happen to me' " (23). Overtly contemplating racial difference for the first time in the novel, Bigger sees his future: ultimately he will be brought to prison after a terrifying descent into whiteness (tracked by whites amidst a blinding snowstorm straight out of Edgar Allan Poe), at the end of which he is pursued like the rat he kills at the beginning of the novel. The slave narrative has moved north, focused now on the betrayal of African Americans encountered so often in American history and in the American novel.

Guilt leads many of Wright's white characters to attempt to make reparations for the broken promises of the culture. When the well-heeled Mr. Dalton, part owner of the Thomas family's apartment building, offers Bigger a job as his chauffeur early in the novel, he does so out of a lingering sense of guilt over his own participation in the marginalization of African Americans, for he believes his generosity will allow Bigger and his family to rise out of poverty. As Bigger discovers in the course of the novel, however, Dalton's ownership of the apartment building establishes his ties to the oppression of black America. Bigger comes to reject the hypocrisy and dissembling on the part of white America symbolized by Dalton's act as his sense of an autonomous black identity becomes more distinct.

Wright's portrayal of the Dalton family exposes the duplicity that is ever the underside of white benevolence in the novel: Bigger sees false pity in the charity of both Mr. Dalton and his wife, who is literally and figuratively blind to Bigger. For Bigger, white compassion can never be distinguished from white guilt, and the result is the demeaning condescension that so infuriates him. Dalton's daughter, Mary, perplexes Bigger all the more through her apparent concern for Bigger and for blacks generally. Early in the novel, though, Mary appears to Bigger as a character cut away from her father's brand of benevolence; she surprises Bigger from the moment he meets her because she so upsets his preconceived notions of a white woman. Ironically, Bigger resents Mary precisely for her capacity to undermine his essentialist view of whites. When she asks him in front of her father whether or not he is a union member, Bigger worries that she will upset the balance of sympathy and subservience he has worked to establish with Mr. Dalton: "[W]hat did she mean by talking to him this way in front of Mr. Dalton, who, surely, didn't like unions" (53). Bigger remains confused when Mary leaves: "He had never seen anyone like her before. She was not a bit the way he had imagined she would be" (54).[3]

Although he is hopeful when their relationship begins, Bigger quickly perceives a rigid disdain in Mary's behavior. When Mary introduces Bigger to Jan, her friend in the Communist party, Bigger's frustration and discomfort only increase, and he becomes "very conscious of his black skin" and of his own black identity: "Did not white people despise a black skin?" (67). Bigger's reaction suggests the experience of the black characters we have encountered as they are returned to an essentialized position by their white counterparts: he "felt he had no physical existence at all" (67). As he perceives the condescension in their benevolence, Bigger's animosity for Jan and Mary grows: "[H]e was something he hated, the badge of shame which he knew was attached to a black skin. It was a shadowy region, a No Man's Land, the ground that separated the white world from the black that he stood upon. He felt naked, transparent; he felt that this white man, having helped to put him down, having helped to deform him, held him up now to look at him and be amused. At that moment he felt toward Mary and Jan a dumb, cold, and inarticulate hate" (67–68).

Bigger more keenly senses the limitations placed upon blackness and black identity when he comes up against characters who appear genuinely compassionate than he had in his meeting with Mr. Dalton, during which he slipped easily into the role expected of him. Wright thus repudiates the nature of Huck's ostensible moral development in his portrayal of Bigger's relationship with Jan and Mary: the false assumptions placed upon black identity lead him to a "No Man's Land" in which he feels isolated and threatened, a locale worlds away from the raft Huck shares with Jim. In *Native Son*, we are wholly within the consciousness of the object of the white character's condescension, and this experience of otherness grants white readers a new awareness of the black character's response to the false compassion of whites. In Wright's novel, we see for the first time in American literature an extended treatment of the terror with which African Americans enter into such a union.

Jan's vision of a world in which "there'll be no white and no black; there'll be no rich and no poor" (69) represents for Bigger a fantasy he cannot afford because his lifestyle suffers so in comparison with that of Mary and Jan. Mary immediately attempts to demonstrate her sympathy with Bigger's life when she asks him which restaurant they might go to: " 'We want to go to a

real place,' " she says, meaning they want to go to a restaurant
frequented by blacks. Hence, she ironically reasserts the very di-
visions that Jan has just claimed might someday not exist. Reality,
in Mary's estimation, is blackness (thus she sees a place for blackness in her own identity), and yet Bigger immediately spots the
implied manipulation. Thus we see the ultimate futility of config-
urations such as "blackness" and "whiteness," based as they are
in essentialist dogma. For Bigger, of course, Mary and Jan cannot
possibly understand the world he lives in or his black identity:
Mary thus further reveals the duplicitous nature of her sympathy
for Bigger and unwittingly distances herself from him even as she
attempts to gain his trust.

When they arrive at the restaurant, Jan's attempts to mimic
black speech likewise expose the condescension of his benevolence:

> The waitress brought the beer and chicken.
> "This is simply grand!" Mary exclaimed.
> "You got something there," Jan said, looking at Bigger. "Did I
> say that right, Bigger?"
> Bigger hesitated.
> "That's the way they say it," he spoke flatly. (73)

Mary's regal language—" 'This is simply grand!' "—contrasts
with Jan's mimicry of black speech, with the result that the two
only confirm their distance from Bigger. Sensing Jan's affectation,
Bigger detaches himself with his cool response. Further, he refuses to allow his own experience to be appropriated as Jan would
have it, not counting himself as one who would "say it" that way.
Wright exposes the superficial nature of the familiar appropriation of blackness through which a white character achieves moral
growth in the novels we have read; as important, he exposes the
false logic that leads to the assertion of essential racial qualities
in such novels and in American culture. In *Native Son*, Wright
contests the very notion of "blackness" itself.

Bigger's refusal emphasizes his role as a new black literary figure specifically responding to and undermining the literary representations of blackness to be found in works in the canon of southern and American literature. Wright focuses upon the failings of
white benefactors, especially in Jan and Mary's various attempts
to reduce Bigger to type. Mary's desire to work in the black community, for instance, is based in the same rationale that earlier
had led her to want to go to a "real place" to eat: " 'I want to
work among Negroes. That's where people are needed. It seems
as though they've been pushed out of everything' " (76). It is soon
apparent that Mary's desire emerges out of ignorance: " 'Say, Jan,
do you know many Negroes? I want to meet some.' " And Mary's
essentialist thinking is evident when she tells Jan that she wants
to meet "Negroes": " 'They have so much emotion! What a people! If we could ever get them going' " (76). Her fascination with
African American cultural productions calls into question the nature of white appreciation of black culture: " 'And their songs—
the spirituals! Aren't they marvelous?' Bigger saw her turn to him.
'Say, Bigger, can you sing?' " (76).

Mary's narrow conception of blackness leads to her shallow
compassion, as Wright's irony reveals: both Mary and Jan ignore
Bigger as Mary contemplates working "among Negroes." And as
Mary and Jan unwittingly force blacks into essentialized roles as
entertainers possessed of "so much emotion," Wright deftly portrays the couple as inverted minstrel figures wishing to be black
for whom Bigger plays straight man with his knowing response
to Mary's question: " 'I can't sing' " (76).

Huck Finn comes to see Jim as a human being who deviates
from type in order to free himself of white guilt and retain his
own humanity; in Wright's novel, Bigger Thomas denies Mary
Dalton her humanity in order to gain his own. He murders Mary
and burns her body in the Daltons' furnace, yet he remains cold
after his deeds: "He did not feel sorry for Mary; she was not real to
him, not a human being" (108). In seeking a "real place" through

Bigger, Mary established herself as a fraud; as he tells Boris Max later in the novel, Bigger feels that justice is served through his act. " 'For a little while I was free,' " he says. " 'I was doing something. It was wrong, but I was feeling all right. . . . I been scared and mad all my life and after I killed that first woman, I wasn't scared no more for a little while' " (328). He was "feeling all right," he says, and we are reminded of Huck Finn, for whom feeling right is a guiding principle. Like Huck, Bigger feels right after making a decision to go to a white hell, but unlike Twain's protagonist, he will not evade responsibility for such a decision. His action violently reverses the equation we have found in the southern novel since Twain.

Bigger comes to see his act as a means of attaining the power he so admired earlier in the images of whites surrounding him: "He felt that he had his destiny in his grasp. He was more alive than he could ever remember having been; his mind and attention were pointed, focussed toward a goal" (141). In the wake of the murder he sees his identity in a new light: "His being black and at the bottom of the world was something which he could take with a new-born strength" (141). Bigger's brutal act overpowers the condescension he had confronted early in the novel and so provides him with power, with choices he had previously lacked. In the end, though, Bigger's flight into the black south side of Chicago, with its strong ironic allusions to Poe's *The Narrative of A. Gordon Pym*, demonstrates his inability to escape a black identity as defined by white society.[4]

In jail, after his arrest for killing Mary and his friend Bessie, Bigger objects to lawyer Boris Max's presence for reasons similar to those he gave earlier for objecting to Mary and Jan: "Bigger felt that he was sitting and holding his life helplessly in his hands, waiting for Max to tell him what to do with it; and it made him hate himself" (319). As he earlier disputed the assumptions that Jan and Mary made of him, he now objects to the passive position in which he finds himself relative to Max. Bigger, of course,

typecasts Max in this regard, assuming that Max resembles the
other whites he has known. Max's question, " 'Do you trust me,
Bigger?' " is one that white protagonists have taken for granted
(320). Max immediately sees his client as an individual within a
larger framework. Wright portrays Bigger's decision to trust Max
as an act of faith, underscoring the integral nature of such relationships to American society: "If he expressed belief in Max, if
he acted on that belief, would it not end just as all other commit-
ments of faith had ended? He wanted to believe; but was afraid"
(321). If Bigger cannot immediately make the leap of faith asked
of him, it is because he feels cut off from his own identity as a
black man: "[A]s always, when a white man talked to him, he
was caught out in No Man's Land" (321). Bigger eventually loses
such trepidation, however, when Max recounts Bigger's plight as
Bigger himself has never been able to do.

The courtroom and prison scenes near the conclusion of the
novel compel readers to consider their own positions relative to
the narrative. Max pleads with the judge, reminding him that
the fate of white society is bound up with that of black society:
" 'I ask in the name of all we are and believe, that you spare this
boy's life! . . . I beg this in order that not only may this black boy
live, but that we ourselves may not die!' " (370). Wright does not
rely on the sort of chimerical pattern we have seen in southern
novels in which a black character is unjustly imprisoned, allowing
the reader to valorize both the black character and his white savior with little scrutiny. Through Bigger Thomas, Wright compels
the reader to examine the specific realities of the confrontation of
black and white in the context of actual crime.

Bigger realizes that he has "flung into their faces his feeling of
being black" (289), and Wright, in like manner, forces this feeling
upon the reader: the novel denies the reader the ability to recoil
from black identity or from participation in the oppression that
Bigger faces. And, as if to audit the white reader, we see Bigger
throughout the novel reading his own story in the white Chicago

newspapers, Wright's ironic allusion to his own effort to undermine and repudiate the "white" texts that came before *Native
Son:* "His eyes ran over the paper, looking for some clue that would
tell him something of his fate" (316).

In his conclusion, Wright enables Bigger Thomas to see, as Jim
never can, that he has been abandoned by his white counterpart.
Shortly after Max attempts to gain Bigger's trust, he tries to link
his own cause with Bigger's. Bigger objects to Max that most white
people "hate black folks":

"*Why*, Bigger?"

"I don't know, Mr. Max."

"Bigger, don't you know they hate others, too?"

"Who they hate?"

"They hate trade unions. They hate folks who try to organize.
They hate Jan."

"But they hate black folks more than they hate unions," Bigger
said. "They don't treat union folks like they do me."

"Oh, yes, they do. You think that because your color makes it
easy for them to point you out, segregate you, exploit you. But they
do that to others, too. They hate me because I'm trying to help you.
They're writing me letters, calling me a 'dirty Jew.' " (322)

Here Max attempts to make Bigger's cause his own, and later he
announces to the white faces in the courtroom, " '*I* shall witness
for Bigger Thomas' " (348), using black dialect sincerely as Jan
earlier could not. His impassioned speeches in defense of Bigger
suggest a vision of the possibility of a union of white and black
that we have seen before if never before stated so explicitly. But
in Bigger's point that "they hate black folks more than they hate
unions" he makes his claim for the unique nature of his own experience.[5]

Even Max ultimately returns Bigger to type: at the end of the
novel, the lawyer utterly forgets the extent to which Bigger suffers
after he is sentenced to die. Max can only tell Bigger that "men

die alone," acknowledging that he, too, can no longer sympathize with Bigger. Bigger, however, urgently tries to get Max to understand him—and his crime—as Max had before: " 'I didn't want to kill!' Bigger shouted. 'But what I killed for, I *am*! It must've been pretty deep in me to make me kill! I must have felt it awful hard to murder' " (391–92). If Max had earlier been able to understand Bigger's motives for killing, at the end of the novel he cannot: " 'No; no; no. . . . Bigger, not that' " (392). Wright makes clear that the white character cannot return to the site of his former embrace. Bigger recognizes that Max is but another white man incapable of fully comprehending him: "Max groped for his hat like a blind man" (392). His blindness anticipates the theme of invisibility that we will encounter in the work of Wright's one-time protégé, Ralph Ellison.

Max's denial of Bigger resembles Huck's betrayal of Jim, but the betrayal is the writer's central point. Unlike Jim, Bigger demonstrates a complete awareness of the extent to which white America forsakes him, as we see after Bigger says good-bye to Max in the novel's final sardonic image: "He still held on to the bars. Then he smiled a faint, wry, bitter smile. He heard the ring of steel against steel as a far door clanged shut" (392).

Race Made Visible

The twelve years between the publication of *Native Son* (1940) and Ralph Ellison's *Invisible Man* (1952) saw the end of World War Two and the emergence of a new consciousness among African Americans with the return of black veterans who had not only fought for their country but also witnessed a world beyond the Jim Crow South or the equally segregated North.

Ellison's novel is, like Wright's, a meditation on African American migration but one that takes a wry look at the emergence of labor consciousness and the political movements of the 1930s. While Wright wrote a stark and severe critique of American culture,

Ellison protests that culture with one hand and celebrates it with the other, even turning frequently to mock the nature of protest itself. Ellison's narrator, as Michael Kreyling argues, "sees protest as yet another co-optation into white-determined identity" (86). And Ellison's view of himself as modernist writer, as critic, prevented him from writing out of the tradition of African American protest: "[W]hen we approach contemporary writing from the perspective of segregation, as is commonly done by sociologically-minded thinkers, we automatically limit ourselves to one external aspect of a complex whole, which leaves one little to say concerning its personal, internal elements" (*Shadow and Act* 88).

Ellison casts his nets wide in the novel, and it would be reductive to suggest that his book signifies solely on Mark Twain's *Huck Finn:* Ellison's book is a rich response to the whole of American literature. But Ellison himself described the signal role that Twain's book plays in the culture: "No Huck and Jim, no American novel as we know it" (Ellison, "What America Would Be Like" 109). And thirty years after the publication of *Invisible Man,* he acknowledged that a primary purpose had been to meditate on the rhetorical and intellectual division of black and white:

> So my task was one of revealing the human universals hidden within the plight of one who was both black and American, and not only as a means of conveying my personal vision of possibility, but as a way of dealing with the sheer rhetorical challenge involved in communicating across our barriers of race and religion, class, color and region—barriers which consist of the many strategies of division that were designed, and still function, to prevent what would otherwise have been a more or less natural recognition of the reality of black and white fraternity. . . . Most of all, I would have to approach racial stereotypes as a given fact of the social process and proceed, while gambling with the reader's capacity for fictional truth, to reveal the human complexity which stereotypes are intended to conceal. (Introduction xxvi)

Like Wright, Ellison examines in part the fraudulent nature of white benevolence. Ellison persistently contests the sincerity of professed goodwill on the part of whites toward his black characters. The narrator's repeated encounters with whites who claim generosity as their motivation leave him convinced they are unable to conceive of their relationships with him in anything but essentialized terms. Their generosity emerges as a form of loathing.

In the second chapter of *Invisible Man*, Ellison looks to Twain's paradigm in joining his narrator with Mr. Norton, a benefactor of the college that so closely resembles Ellison's own Tuskeegee Institute. The narrator chauffeurs Norton through the countryside surrounding the college, a role that emphasizes his servility in deference to this white philanthropist. Norton's claim that his own fate is bound together with the narrator's, which comes as he heaps commands upon the narrator, urges reconsideration of Twain's model: " 'So you see, young man, you are involved in my life quite intimately, even though you've never seen me before. You are bound to a great dream and to a beautiful monument. If you become a good farmer, a chef, a preacher, doctor, singer, mechanic—whatever you become, and even if you fail, you are my fate. And you must write me and tell me the outcome' " (43). We have seen before white characters whose "fate" is bound up with a black companion. Ellison parodies the notion that white characters might achieve wholeness through a vision of their own participation in a black world, through their resultant confrontation with the guilt that haunts them and white America. Norton's plea for racial innocence is much like that of Wright's Mr. Dalton, but Ellison renders such a proposition absurd. The "dream" to which the narrator is "bound" is one that has the familiar result of lashing blacks to subservient roles, as we see in the Golden Day, a bar in which Norton and the narrator encounter the "veterans," former black professionals for whom aspiration will always exceed rank. Likewise, the "monument," a campus statue professedly depicting the college founder removing the veil from kneeling students (but that the narrator suspects may instead depict the securing of the veil), calls to mind the national monument for which the narrator will later mix drops of black paint into buckets of white paint, blackness into a sea of white. The narrator eventually sees just how superficial—and outrageous—Norton's claim to moral kinship is. And even as he claims such connection, Norton of course retains his own patriarchal identity and power.

Throughout the text, the narrator points to the irony of Norton's presumptions through his own naive response. " '*You* are important because if you fail *I* have failed by one individual, one defective cog,' " Norton claims (ironically tying the narrator's individuality to a "cog," which has none), to which the narrator thinks in response, "But you don't even know my name" (45). The narrator forms such fleeting relationships with white characters throughout *Invisible Man,* compelling him to see that white American society persistently appropriates what narrow identity it has allowed him. While the narrator cannot see himself as Jim, as a one-dimensional minstrel figure, the white characters around him persist in asking him to assume such a role. In *Invisible Man,* Ellison exposes the failings not only of the social conscience of white America but also of the literary relationships exemplifying that conscience.

Ellison's literary allusions are quite direct in the narrator's relationship with the son of the elusive Mr. Emerson. The narrator seeks a patron in the senior Mr. Emerson, but the younger intervenes, ostensibly to warn the narrator of his college president's duplicity in sending him north with no hope of employment. We soon discover the younger Emerson to be an aspiring Huck to the narrator's Jim, however, and Ellison references Twain's text to demonstrate how flawed the relationship finally is:

> "Look," he said, his face working violently, "I was trying to tell you that I know many things about you—not you personally, but fellows like you. Not much, either, but still more than the average. With us it's still Jim and Huck Finn. . . . Please don't misunder-

stand me; I don't say all this to impress you. Or to give myself some
kind of sadistic catharsis. Truly, I don't. But I do know this world
you're trying to contact—all its virtues and all its unspeakables—
Ha, yes, unspeakables. I'm afraid my father considers *me* one of
the unspeakables. . . . I'm Huckleberry, you see." (184)

Alan Nadel observes that Emerson's declaration—" 'I'm Huckleberry' "—immediately tips off the reader to his duplicity: the only
character in Twain's novel to use Huck's full name is Miss Watson, who represents hypocritical religious fervor and ignorance.
But the narrator will in any case have no such identity put upon
him: "He laughed drily as I tried to make sense of his ramblings.
Huckleberry? Why did he keep talking about that kid's story?"
(184).

The narrator will not allow Emerson to plead "innocence" à la
Huck Finn: " 'Aren't you curious about what lies behind the face
of things?' " Emerson asks. " 'Yes, sir, but I'm mainly interested
in a job,' " the narrator replies (185). The narrator consciously rejects the white liberal's perception of the relationship between
well-meaning whites and destitute blacks. Huck Finn's tale, appealing as it has been to the southern novelist, holds no relevance
for Ralph Ellison's narrator.[6]

Late in the novel, Ellison's portrayal of Sybil, the white woman
who attempts to seduce the narrator, reveals the writer's outright
rejection of white condescension. As in the earlier scenes, Ellison undermines the role of the white benefactor by reducing it to
the absurd. Sybil claims that she wants the narrator to rape her
because she has always heard that this is what black men do to
white women: " 'Well ever since I first heard about it, even when
I was a very little girl, I've wanted it to happen to me' " (511).
The narrator back-pedals from the advance of yet another white
character who has invested in a blackness that never existed. Like
the younger Emerson, Sybil assumes the existence of a trust that
the narrator will not enter into because of the condescension and

stereotype it implies: Sybil imagines a familiar bond with the narrator, but Ellison makes clear that any such bond is based upon an essentialized view of blacks on the part of whites. The narrator rejects Sybil's proposal outright: when he leaves her lying unconscious in her apartment, the narrator scrawls a message on Sybil's body—"SYBIL YOU WERE RAPED BY SANTA CLAUS"—that demonstrates his recognition of the absurdity implicit in Sybil's fantasy of black behavior: the myth she believes is as false as the myth of Santa Claus (514). Like Wright before him, Ellison chooses the ultimate taboo of southern society—sex between a black man and a white woman—to undermine the stereotypes of that society.

In these few encounters, as in his encounters with the many African American characters who expect him to act in keeping with their racial expectations throughout the novel, Ellison's narrator elects to set his own course rather than allow another to set it for him. Neither will he assume the responsibility of being the "fate" of another. At the end, he concludes that he must stake out his own identity, free of the expectations both the white and black communities place upon him: "I had no longer to run for or from the Jacks and the Emersons and the Bledsoes and Nortons, but only from their confusion, impatience, and refusal to recognize the beautiful absurdity of their American identity and mine. . . . I knew that it was better to live out one's own absurdity than to die for that of others, whether for Ras's or Jack's" (550). The narrator asserts a role for blackness in the American identity, a conclusion that white protagonists have arrived at often enough but one from which they have so often retreated. For Ellison's narrator, that identity is not one of racial unity but instead of individualism, much like that which Huck Finn claims for himself at the end of Twain's novel. In the end, the narrator requires no validating presence at all: he has attained the autonomy that Bigger Thomas was striving for and that Jim and his literary descendants never obtain. For Ellison, individual identity comes not directly from external relationships but instead from one's internal response to

them. In claiming an autonomy for his black protagonist beyond
that attained by the black characters in the southern novel, Ellison
repudiates the mythmaking of *Huck Finn*.

Middle Ground

While the white writers I have considered situate the central relationship between black and white characters before a distant
backdrop of cultural change, African American writers situate the
relationship at the heart of movements for cultural transformation. Wright and Ellison place their protagonists within the massive unrest of the Great Migration, the emergence of Communism
as a force for labor, and the empowerment movements within
black culture in the 1930s. In *Meridian* Alice Walker takes for
her central subject a cross-racial relationship that develops in the
midst of the struggle for civil rights in Mississippi. Walker's protagonist, Meridian Hill, evolves through her awareness of the possibility of change in southern race relations. Her friend Lynne
Rabinowitz, a white college student who has come to Mississippi
to help register black voters, attempts a similar evolution when
she tries to cross racial barriers and rescind her white identity. As
with Wright's Dalton and Ellison's Emerson, Lynne's failure is
her inability to escape the condescension that, for Walker, comes
appended to her white identity, and her beneficence is ultimately
self-serving.

Soon after her decision to remain in the South when other
white civil rights workers are returning north, Lynne marries
a black man, Truman Held, with whom Meridian had an earlier
relationship. Lynne finds that she is perfectly comfortable in the
black community, but her comfort emerges largely out of her essentialist thinking of African Americans. Lynne finds a special
grace in that community that for her is lacking among whites:
"[B]lack people had a unique beauty, a kind of last-gasp loveliness,
which, in other races, had already become extinct" (157). It is a

primitivist perspective of African Americans that leads her into conflict with both Meridian and Truman, both of whom know the condescension that accompanies such a broad characterization.

Indeed, from the first time they meet, Meridian suspects Lynne's motivations for participating in the civil rights movement, as Lynne essentializes the blacks whom she claims to be supporting: "To Lynne, the black people of the South were Art. This she begged forgiveness for and tried to hide, but it was no use" (130). Walker reveals the central paradox of Lynne's role as a white benefactor in her contrasting desires to help the black community gain political power even as she idealizes that community as "Art."[7] Wright, Ellison, and Walker all repudiate such an assessment of African American identity, but for white writers before them, blackness is a sort of art, an enticement because of the transformative if transitory growth it provides.[8]

Lynne's compulsive interest in African American culture both attracts and repulses Truman Held. Truman is first drawn to Lynne when he finds that she "longed to put her body on the line for his freedom. How her idealism had warmed him, brought him into the world, made him eager to tuck her under his wing, under himself, sheltering her from her own illusions" (140). But Truman comes to recognize the false nature of Lynne's "idealism" even as he remains attracted to her for just such a viewpoint: her primitivism ironically binds the pair even as it foretells their eventual split. For Walker, it cannot be otherwise, since Lynne's view of Truman is initially shaped by her romantic and limiting portrayal of African Americans.

In the course of the novel, Truman grows to resent Lynne's pitying demeanor, and, like his friend Tommy Odds, he believes that Lynne, by being white, "was guilty of whiteness" (133), a quality he associates with evasiveness and disingenuousness. Tommy Odds eventually convinces Truman that Lynne is nothing more than a "white bitch," and in short order Truman leaves Lynne to spend increasing amounts of time with Meridian.[8]

When, late in the novel, Tommy rapes Lynne, he attempts to compel her to confront the essentializing ideology of white culture that she retains: " 'You *knows* I can't hep myself' " (158), he says, mocking the stereotypes of blacks that he sees in her condescension. Tommy only becomes more angry when Lynne panders to him: when Lynne "knew she could force him from her," she does not choose to do so, "instead thinking of his feelings, of his hardships, of the way he was black and belonged to people without hope" (159). For Walker, Lynne's white identity leads her to accept rape to atone for "her own guilt." The pity that Tommy senses in her guilt enrages him, and he attempts to further humiliate her by bringing three friends to her house the next day.

When they arrive, Lynne continues to think of herself as "a sacrifice to black despair" (161). Yet Tommy's companions are the first to overcome such essentialized assumptions about relationships between black and white: " 'Go on,' said Tommy Odds. 'Have some of it.' " But Altuna Jones replies, " 'What *it* you talking about? That ain't no *it*, that's Lynne.' " In recognizing Lynne as an individual outside of stereotype, Altuna ironically enables her to see Tommy outside of her stereotypes of blacks, and she realizes that her idea of blacks as passive sufferers is mistaken: "[S]he had not been thinking of individual lives, of young men like Tommy Odds whose thin defense against hatred broke down under personal assault" (162). But, like Mary Agnes in Sara Flanigan's *Sudie*, Lynne has merely traded one stereotype for another. Blacks who are no longer wholly passive in Lynne's view become instead sadistic rapists in reaction to white oppression. Walker undermines Lynne's benevolence in portraying her inability to look at blacks free of guilt: Lynne's thinking inevitably ends in the stereotypes to which that guilt leads her. In the end, Lynne's attraction to blacks emerges as an expression of her own self-loathing, and Walker calls into question the nature of white sympathy and white guilt.

Walker emphasizes Lynne's failure to escape essentialized

thinking of African Americans in her desire to return to a world in which blacks are docile and accommodating. In the nights after Tommy Odds rapes her, she sits at her house with local men, inviting Alonzo to sleep with her "for his kindness," a kindness associated with her original stereotypes of "old-time Negroes," and she clings to her notion of African Americans as passive and acquiescent.

When the child born of Lynne's relationship with Truman dies, Meridian comes to Lynne after a long separation. The bond they establish allows them to experience one another free of the petty jealousies they have felt before and free too of the essentializing stereotypes they had previously held: "They waited for the pain of Camara's death to lessen. They waited to ask forgiveness of each other. They waited until they could talk again" (174). In her conversation with Meridian, Lynne rejects her own white identity in accepting Meridian's view of the world. When Meridian declares to Lynne that she " 'tried very hard not to hate you' " (175), Lynne admits that her connection to Meridian is so deeply felt she no longer has the option to return to white society. Through her relationship with Meridian and other blacks in the South, she has come to see the ills of that society: " 'I can't go back home. I don't even have a home. I wouldn't go back if I could. I know white folks are evil and fucked up, I *know* they're doomed. But where does that leave me?' " (175). Ironically, it leaves her the precise counterpart to Twain's Jim in terms of her racial identity. Like Jim, she is completely dependent upon the protagonist of the novel, and she will be swiftly discarded by that protagonist—and by Walker—when her character no longer suits the plot. Lynne's rejection of her white identity parallels Huck Finn's assumption at the end of his novel that Jim is "white inside": as Jim loses his black identity in Twain's novel, Lynne must lose her white identity in order to gain Meridian's favor.

Having cast off her white identity, Lynne is able to see the black community free of her earlier primitivist perspective. She admits her newfound awareness that "black folks aren't so special" (181), and, in making such a recognition, Lynne escapes the literary stereotypes associated with the white characters of earlier southern novels and sees blacks as human beings capable of the full range of human characteristics. As John F. Callahan argues, "From her naive and sinister view of black folks as Art, she comes to regard them as varied, variable human beings whose responses to experience differ from both her dreams and her nightmares" (170). Having voided her white identity, she is now able to see individual African Americans. Walker's portrayal of Lynne reverses Twain's paradigm as Walker reduces the white character to a single dimension. Lynne's denial of her own identity reminds us of Huck's ultimate denial of Jim's black identity; for Walker, such stereotypes are necessary to debunk stereotypes of the past.

In *Meridian*, Alice Walker examines racial essentialism from numerous perspectives, portraying a modern South in which the archetypal literary and racial stereotypes we have seen still exist. Ironically, Lynne becomes a figure much closer to Jim than to Huck, but in the process of this portrayal, Walker undermines the role of the white benefactor so central to the southern novel.

Fountainheads

Arnold Rampersad argues that *Huck Finn* is "nearer than any other work of fiction" to the "fountainhead" of black American literature, DuBois's *The Souls of Black Folk* (52). Rampersad suggests that Twain, "in his depiction of alienation in an American context, prominently including race, anticipates aspects" of the major African American novels of the twentieth century. Twain, like the African American novelists who follow him, exposes "a moral dilemma, or moral inversion . . . at the heart of southern, and, by inference, American society" (51). Twain's influence ironically extends beyond the very racial boundaries his novel does something to establish.

African American novelists since Twain have often defined the black experience in America by portraying the horror of a black individual's existence at the hands of whites, examining largely the same moral dilemma that Mark Twain confronts in *Huckleberry Finn*. Often addressing a specifically white audience, their final question for that audience is much like that of the narrator in *Invisible Man:* "Who knows but that, on the lower frequencies, I speak for you?" (572).

6

"AIN'T NO MOTIF"

Padgett Powell, Ellen Douglas,
and W. Glasgow Phillips
Narrate a Postmodern South

No wonder the white man so often grows cranky,
fanciful, freakish, loony, violent: how else respond to a paradox
which requires, with the full majesty of law behind it, that he deny
the very reality of a people whose multitude approaches and often
exceeds his own; that he disclaim the existence of those whose human
presence has marked every acre of the land, every hamlet and
crossroad and city and town, and whose humanity, however inflexibly
denied, is daily evidenced to him like a heartbeat in loyalty and
wickedness, madness and hilarity and mayhem and pride and love?
The Negro may feel that it is too late to be known, and that the desire
to know him reeks of outrageous condescension. But to break down
the old law, to come to know the Negro, has become the moral
imperative of every white Southerner.

WILLIAM STYRON

[I]n this wedding of the black and the white it was the Negro
who brought the cultural dowry.

NORMAN MAILER

"And besides playing the freak I can jive a little too."
SIMONS EVERSON MANIGAULT in Padgett Powell, *Edisto*

In the film *Bulworth*, Warren Beatty plays an erstwhile liberal
U.S. senator, Jay Billington Bulworth, who has lost his political
resolve and now spends his days bottling up bills in committee

for insurance companies. In the middle of a primary campaign, despondent at the course his career has taken and estranged from his WASP wife, Bulworth takes a kickback from an insurance lobbyist in the form of a ten-million-dollar life insurance policy and promptly has a murder contract taken out on himself. Then his life takes a turn: freed of the political exigencies that pressured him, he is now willing to speak his mind clearly. He tells a black audience that the Democratic party will never care about them but that they have no other alternative, and he tells an audience of movie executives that their product is "lousy." Further, he finds himself in love with a black resident of Compton, Nina, played by Halle Berry.

Blackness becomes for Bulworth a conduit to a better self, a means to return to the spiritual self he had departed. Fascinated by black street language, he begins to rap his reclaimed political themes and takes his political discourse verbatim from both Nina and L.D., a crack dealer played by Don Cheadle. Despite his profanity and gang banger's clothes (or perhaps because of them), Bulworth's newfound honesty resonates with the public, and he wins his primary as well as a significant number of votes for president. When he awakens from a sleep that has lasted through the election, he asks Nina to join him as he goes to meet his now adoring public. She initially declines and then agrees to join him. When Bulworth expresses his dismay that Nina had left him hanging, she looks at him and says, "Come on, Bulworth. You know you my nigga." The line affirms their love even as it affirms Bulworth's ability to negotiate across the treacherous racial divide. If he has returned to a white identity at the end of the film (and he has left behind both rap and the rapper's raiment), he has nevertheless retained the better self that he discovered in becoming black. He recognizes the place of black and white in the formation of his own character, the very recognition that has proved so elusive in the southern novels I have been examining.

The film demonstrates the breadth of the theme I have addressed here. In creating *Bulworth*, Beatty (producer, director, cowriter, and lead actor in the film) looked directly to the tradition that *Adventures of Huckleberry Finn* inspired in the southern novel and in American culture. Referencing myriad films and cultural texts, he suggests that the reversals we so commonly see in textual/performative relationships across the color line are a denial of the nation's truest self. In this, as Henry Louis Gates has noted, Beatty draws on a rich tradition within black culture. W. E. B. DuBois wrote in 1897: "We are that people whose subtle sense of song has given America its only American music, its only American fairy tales, its only touch of pathos and humor amid its mad money-getting plutocracy" (qtd. in Gates, "The White Negro" 63).

At the end of the film, a lobbyist for the insurance industry shoots Bulworth, and the soulful vagrant played by Amiri Baraka wanders the streets outside the hospital urging upon Bulworth and the audience the mantra that he has repeated throughout the film: "Got to be a spirit, Bulworth. Can't be no ghost." The blending of black and white at the heart of the film is finally about the promises of American culture; in contrast to many of the earlier texts we have read, the white protagonist retains the new identity he gained through his movement toward a blackness neither essentialized nor static.

In the present chapter, I consider three contemporary novelists who attempt to move beyond the parameters of race that we find in the southern novel. Padgett Powell's *Edisto*, Ellen Douglas's *Can't Quit You, Baby*, and W. Glasgow Phillips's *Tuscaloosa* subvert and rework the pattern of moral growth by now so familiar, recasting a white protagonist's role in relation to a black mentor by insisting on the autonomous stance of the latter. If we also find here the pattern of reversal that we have seen so often, it is in part because these writers ironize the shift so that the white protagonist's reversal becomes the focus of their work. The essentializing structures of American society become the subject to which these writers remain bound yet which they openly critique.

In the wake of the civil rights era, contemporary, metatextual southern fiction by white writers maintains a heightened consciousness of African American identity. In the title story of Terry Southern's *Red-Dirt Marijuana and Other Tastes,* for instance, a white child, Harold, first learns to smoke marijuana from C.K., a black man who works for Harold's family. Harold turns down C.K.'s offer at first: " 'It feel good,' " C.K. says, to which Harold replies, " 'I aw*ready* feel good!' " (9). But if Harold initially resists C.K., he eventually agrees to turn on, tune in, and drop out. Like the protagonists of the novels I consider in the present chapter, Harold is learning to be hip à la Norman Mailer. After smoking with C.K., Harold sits with his friend in the apparent bliss of their newly transformed relationship instead of returning to his white world, and the narrative concludes with the two characters linked outside a racially divided southern society, a conclusion unlike any in the work of the white writers we have thus far encountered: " 'You wanta go fishin'?' " Harold asks C.K. as the story closes, to which C.K. responds, " 'Shoot, that sound like a *good* idee' " (14).

The novels I consider here portray autonomous black characters who only dimly resemble the minstrel-like characters of earlier southern novels. The work of these white novelists thus responds to the work of African American writers. Powell's inscrutable character Taurus, for instance, has as much in common with Ellison's narrator as with Twain's Jim. At the conclusion of each of these novels, the white protagonists cannot evade knowledge of the distinct character of their black mentors, and if they retreat to the stereotypes that have led earlier protagonists back to a white world they had initially fled, they do so with knowledge of the artifice involved in such a move. And, unlike earlier protagonists, they fully acknowledge the roles their companions have played in the formation of their own identities. If each, to a

differing degree, continues to assert essentialist thinking on the
subject of race, each author likewise maintains a substantial ironic
distance from that belief.

The possibility of interracial accord is ever threatened in these
narratives: indeed, in Southern's companion piece to "Red-Dirt
Marijuana," "Razor-Fight," C.K. and Harold visit a black bar
(ironically called Paradise, a name that suggests the Edenic qualities white protagonists so often aspire to but so rarely attain in
the narratives of black and white in America), where C.K. dies in
a razor fight with his brother. Returning to his parents and so to
his white world, Harold sobs "not the tears he had known before,
but tears of the first bewildering sorrow" (32). The American
Eden—ever a racially charged atmosphere—is always ready for
the fall. Harold lurches violently into adult (which here equates
with "racial") consciousness, and he grieves in part for the broken
vision of racial harmony in his narrative.

Navigating by Raft

In an early manuscript version of Padgett Powell's *Edisto*, Huckleberry Perry, the archly named narrator, encourages the reader to
be mindful of the literary relationship between Powell's novel and
Twain's classic. Powell's Huck attempts to persuade his mother to
introduce him to her latest suitor, another in a wearisome line
of men for whom Huckleberry has established the generic so-
briquet "coroner." Amidst his protagonist's comic interjection,
Powell carefully delineates his literary obligations and conceits,
overtly praising Twain and commenting upon the motifs his novel
shares with Twain's:

> Whether she ever includes the detail that I am her son, I don't
> know. I put my name into the scene so that she might have to men-
> tion the relationship. "Huckleberry Perry" I say to him, stepping
> up like to address a business associate or something, and I know

that she will have to tell her intent on naming me Huck. I don't mind the name once I have read the book twice and see what a marvel he and Clemens really are, and I think sometimes that if the world were still navigable by raft and not obfuscating slavery I could do well to find me a Jim and haul ass. The way it is, though, who can tell who's the slave, who's got faith, who's a homosexual ala Fiedler, so forth, who knows what in God's name is proved by running and who can say what direction any movement would be *in*? (Ms. 1)

Alas for my argument, but perhaps the better for the novel, Powell substantially altered the passage in his published version, omitting reference to Twain or *Huck Finn* and giving his protagonist an ironic and aristocratic appellation, Simons Everson Manigault. Still, we see in this passage an overt recognition of a contemporary writer's debt to Twain: Powell acknowledges the conscious relationship between his novel and Mark Twain's as he suggests the continuing importance of the latter to American literature. And in isolating the relationship between Huck and Jim in his reference to Fiedler's "Come Back to the Raft Ag'in, Huck Honey!" Powell addresses the particular literary stereotypes of the South. Throughout *Edisto*, he confronts racial identity in the South while undermining the literary parameters of the relationship between a white adolescent and a marginalized character established by Twain. When Simons returns in the end to white culture, the new perspective he has gained from his time at the edges of his southern society leaves him the more secure in an identity that develops from both white and black cultures.

In the course of the novel, twelve-year-old Simons (" 'You say it "Simmons." I'm a rare one-*m* Simons' " [4]) must choose between the white world represented by his patrician father and the black world toward which his mother, an English professor, pushes him. At the outset, Simons lives with his mother—he calls her "The Doctor"—in Edisto, a secluded area of the South Carolina coast. While his father wants Simons to play baseball with the other kids, the Doctor encourages him to frequent a local black bar called the Baby Grand to gain experience for what she hopes will be his career as a writer. Caught between his parents' contesting visions, Simons turns to Taurus, a process server of mixed race who quickly becomes a role model and paternal figure. As a result, Simons develops more swiftly than he has through his relationship with either of his parents.

Simons first encounters Taurus immediately after the boy has fallen out of an open emergency door of his school bus, a mishap he blames upon his mother's insistence that he find his material for writing among the blacks in Edisto: "That's what being a 'material' hound will get you: little you who should be up in the front with the nice kids but are in the back listening to Gullah and watching, say, an eight-year-old smoke marijuana like a man in a cell block" (6). His assumptions about black and white identity signal his ambivalence over the assignment his mother has given him, and only Taurus's intervention maintains his interest in the project. Among the "Negroes from nowhere" (6) who stare down at him as he lies prone at the base of the oak tree that stopped his fall, Taurus's "calm light face" (7) peers at him, a beacon of some sort, but whether it invites or warns away he does not yet know. If the Doctor's assignment has led him to his mishap, it has also led him to Taurus, an unexpected companion he comes to appreciate specifically because Taurus knows how to bridge the gap between white and black cultures and maintain an objective distance from both, skills he will teach Simons.

When Simons observes that Theenie—the family's black maid and mother of the woman Taurus seeks—has failed to fold the Doctor's linen properly, he knows something is astir. The oversight leads him to recall the southern traditions that his mother carries on within the house, a "Southern barony" reduced "to a tract of clay roads cut in a feathery herbaceous jungle of deerfly for stock and scrub oak for crop, and the great house is a model beach house resembling a pagoda, and the planter's wife is abandoned by the planter" (9–10). In the midst of such cultural decline (if linguistic abundance), the Doctor commands a moral order reminiscent of the antebellum South in her control of Theenie: "[T]hat vestigial baroness insists that vestigial slave do her one duty right—'the linen,' all that remains of cotton finery. Theenie vacuums the house too, but that doesn't signify as Preserving the South" (10). Simons's concern with his southern heritage burdens him throughout the novel, much as Huck's participation in white southern culture frustrates him, all the more so in his relationship with Taurus, who agrees to become Theenie's stand-in after he chases her off. Taurus, however, is no "vestigial slave": he is, in fact, beyond the pale of Simons's understanding of race and culture. The narrow understanding of race in Simons's white world can't account for Taurus, whose counsel leads Simons to a new comprehension of himself outside of American and, specifically, southern culture, white or black.

The night after his fall from the bus, Simons and his mother are at home when Taurus comes looking for Theenie. Still ailing from his fall, Simons is fearful of Taurus during this, their first extended encounter. It is no small point that Taurus seeks out his young companion, whereas in earlier southern narratives, the black mentors await salvation at the hands of white interlocutors. Here, the initial salvation is that of the white protagonist, an inversion suggesting the revisioning of the familiar relationship at the center of Powell's novel:

Elbows on the drain counter, I am keeping the weight off my ribs and watching the food cook when I see him. You do not know what in hell may be out here on a hoodoo coast and I do not make a move. What follows is not nearly so ominous as I would sound. He don't ax-murder us or anything like that. Yet there is something arresting about this dude the moment you see him. He is shimmery as an islander's god and solid as a butcher. I consider him to be the thing that the Negroes are afraid of when they paint the doors and windows of their shacks purple or yellow. His head is cocked, his hand on the washtub of the Doctor's old wringer, its

old manila rolling pins swung out to the side. When he comes up
to the screen, I know I have seen his face before. (8)

We, too, have seen his face before, of course, in the pages of so
many southern novels addressing race after Twain. Simons first
identifies Taurus in familiar terms: he associates Taurus with the
culture of local blacks ("out here on a hoodoo coast"), already
aligning himself with black culture in Edisto. (We recall that,
when Huck first seeks Jim, he wants his fortune told.) Yet he likewise reveals his fear of that culture in associating it with the more
conventionally European "hell." Simons's description of Taurus
as "shimmery as an islander's god and solid as a butcher" reveals
both the narrow cultural view he takes of Taurus and the trepidation attending such a view. He is initially caught in a stasis ("I do
not make a move") he will not escape through the early sections
of the novel as he comes to know Taurus.

In hanging out at the Baby Grand ("where I am a celebrity
because I'm white" [8]), Simons has come to the conclusion that,
for the black men at the bar, "life is a time when you get pleasure
until somebody get your ass" (9). Such is Simons's perception of
the black world that the Doctor pushes him toward: it is, in fact,
a perception she shares, and it brings her to direct Simons to the
bar in the first place. Simons arrives at a whole system of such
stereotypes for both black and white in the course of the narrative,
asserting difference while acknowledging that, for the writer he
will become, an objective balance from both white and black will
be crucial, since story can turn up in both worlds. Taurus, born of
both races, teaches Simons to negotiate between black and white;
from a vantage point between black and white worlds, Simons
freely observes both cultures with a detached, ironic perspective
akin to that of his friend.

If Taurus, as Powell has wryly suggested, is the fictional child
of Norman Mailer, a mixed-race hipster, then Simons learns to be
hip from the would-be source (personal interview). Taurus guides

Simons in a way that neither his parents nor the men at the Baby Grand are able: "He was somebody you figured knew something. And he was supposed, as Theenie would have put it, to 'rescure' me" (33). Simons concludes that, with his world in turmoil due to his parents' impending divorce and the failing southern barony, "the center of the storm, calm as it was, was Taurus" (102). The marginal character and the margin provide a measure of tranquility for his white companion that had earlier eluded him.

Despite the dropped reference to Huck's river journey, Simons and Taurus don't do much. In Powell's novel, the relationship suffices for narrative. Simons and Taurus spend time in the Baby Grand; they journey to see a Joe Frazier fight in Charleston. Simons gets a kiss and uncovers sexual intrigue. But little need happen, since the relationship brings with it the drama of race. We find in the narrative's latter half a series of failed attempts to conclude properly the relationship between white adolescent and "black" man. And thus it is here as it is with the nation: having latched on to a vision of ourselves in which these interracial unions take on essential symbolic weight, we return to that vision again and again no matter how frequently we fail to obtain what we imagine there. At the novel's end, both characters attain autonomous roles, a development suggesting that the union has finally achieved the balance it has ever idealized.

In fact, before his relationship with Taurus has hardly begun, Simons realizes that he and Taurus must soon part ways. In the first of several parting rituals, Simons invites his companion to go fishing: "Before you go off to the middle of nowhere we better go fishing, to ratify our experience together" (119). The experience they ratify is, of course, their existence as a modern Huck Finn and Jim, and, on their fishing trip, we see that Simons has, like Huck, come to view the world—and particularly his own white culture—with suspicion. Sitting with a group of black women who are fishing for mullet, Simons recognizes the hypocrisy of one would-be white benefactor who, refusing to go after mullet

himself, heaps false praise upon the women for their success:
" 'Lilly, I bleve you gone catch all the fish in the river!' " (123).
Simons bristles at the man's condescension: "It's one thing to nig-
gerize a fish and think little of it but here's an asshole who goes out
into a mullet run and turns up his nose at them in public" (123).

Simons's relationship with Taurus has given him an awareness
of white duplicity he had lacked earlier, and he concludes that
the man would have been named Psoriasis, "[e]xcept somebody
named him Billy. Or Billy Ray. Or Billy Ray Bob. Billy Ray Bob
Wally Pickett" (123). Simons's play on southern identity reveals
his new ability to see the false nature of such white sympathy;
likewise, it reveals the extent to which he has aligned himself and
his own emergent identity with Taurus. Still, he recognizes that
his education is not complete: "There is something to do to this
kind of guy [Psoriasis] but I don't know yet what it is" (124). By
the end of the novel, he knows: he writes about such men with an
ironic remove he learned from Taurus.

Taurus is not moral guide merely but Simons's sexual, intellectual, and historical counselor as well. As the two sit in a Charleston
restaurant one afternoon, Taurus prepares Simons for his first
date. Through a window, Simons sees the famed statue of Calhoun: "John Calhoun's out there in bronze about forty feet tall,
and it seems he's doing something about the Confederacy by
standing up there so very proudly, but I don't know what, because I don't know what he did, if he was a decent Reb or a bad
one or anything" (130). In portraying Simons's repudiation of a
central taboo of his southern heritage as he sits down to eat with
Taurus, Powell spurns the ingress of southern mythology in the
relationship by specifically denying the significance of that southern heritage.

Since Taurus is moral guide, however, it's appropriate that Simons worries more about matters of the heart than about his
southern ancestry: he has fallen in love with the waitress, who
is Taurus's lover. Not to disappoint but neither to accommodate

at his own expense, Taurus has arranged a double date on which Simons is to lose his virginity with a girl his own age. Simons, apprehensive and speculative, questions Taurus as they leave the restaurant:

"What's happening?"

"We're going sailing," he told me. "With a boatful of willing gentlewomen from the low country."

"Holy God."

"Holy God is right."

Suddenly great old patinaed John Calhoun and the green shutters [Simons's symbols of the Old South] all vanished before what I was sure was the dawning of the real, present South, a new land full not of ghosts but of willing gentlewomen. (132)

Simons consciously rejects the racial entanglements of the Old South symbolized by Calhoun, declares them over and done with. Yet even as he makes this declaration, we know that the old issue of the South, if not the peculiar institution then the special problem, is at the forefront of concern in Powell's novel. Indeed, the ironic language here—"willing gentlewomen from the low country"—suggests that the old order of the antebellum South remains in place. Simons cannot dismiss the Old South as easily as he would like, not even for the chance to shed his virginity on a Saturday afternoon sail.

As though to scrutinize further their conflict with southern identity, Taurus and Simons have snapshots made of themselves in Confederate soldiers' uniforms. To his dismay, Simons finds that they look nothing like the heroes of the southern past: "I thought we'd come out looking like J. E. B. Stuart and Nathan Bedford Forrest. Taurus looked like a criminal and I looked like a mole. But we had them photographs" (139–40). For Simons, the record of their own confederation finally becomes more significant than their resemblance to the heroes of the Confederacy. And if they look little like the military heroes of the Old South, they do, of course, look very much like the first of the literary heroes of the New South.

Simons realizes that his relationship with Taurus is finally at its end when he concludes that Taurus and his mother are having an affair, a relationship that stands in the way of his father's return.[1] When Simons is unable to blame Taurus for having an affair with his mother and equally unable to blame her ("Taurus is a sight [and a damn sight] better than ten coroners boiled into one human being if you could do that" [145]), he concludes simply that there is little sense in blaming anyone. Instead, he recognizes that he remains confused over Taurus's ability to manage his (Simons's) life: "He was giving me my mother? And my father? Could he do that? I didn't know" (146). Simons wonders at Taurus's ability to create his own text, at the literary autonomy that Taurus demonstrates by returning his charge to the white world. And Simons recognizes that his newfound identity has emerged in large measure from their relationship. Taurus is at once symbolic brother, mother, and father, and Simons is cognizant of these roles, even as they confound him: "I was a reader turning pages written some time ago, discovering what happened next" (146). Taurus thus gains an autonomy that Jim never possesses: Simons grants him his own authorship. Among the most autonomous of the black characters descending from Jim in the southern novels I've considered, Taurus, like Faulkner's Lucas Beauchamp, is shrouded in mystery throughout the protagonist's narrative.

When Simons learns that his parents have decided to remarry, he leaves Edisto for Hilton Head, where he sips lemonade at the 19th Hole with the golfing set, a far cry from his afternoons at the Baby Grand, and Taurus leaves for Louisiana (the very place Huck and Jim would have arrived had they continued their trip down the Mississippi River). But left behind Simons and Taurus are the black men and women at the Baby Grand. They remain at Edisto because they are, in Simons's assessment, incapable of stepping into the competitive world beyond the bar.[2] Simons has come to an awareness of his own identity that separates him from the black world at the Baby Grand and, ultimately, from Taurus as well:

> Going into the photo parlor, I caught the essence of it. It was that [Taurus] did not know what his life held and so studied it very closely. And I was different: mine held all the plans the Doctor and Daddy would negotiate, a cross-hatching of professional ambitions. I was not going to get to be a two-cylinder syntax dude at the Grand. I was, I am—I have to admit, that because my life is cloyed by practical plans and attainable hopes—I am white. Best thing to do, I figure, is to get on with it. So I said let's go in that joint for commemorative photos, my heart really beating then. I had one of these white hearts that lub-dub this way: *then-next;* and Taurus had one of these that go *now-next;* and the guys at the Grand went *now-now.* And you can't change that with decisions to be cool. You can't get to that *now-now* without a congenital blessing or disease, whichever applies. (176)

Like Huck, Simons finally accepts an essentialist division of race: in Simons's characterization of the men at the Baby Grand we see Norman Mailer's primitivist assessment of African American culture.[3] Simons actively accepts a return to his white identity, which he views as the antithesis of life at the Baby Grand: "I am white." Yet even as Simons makes this return, he recognizes Taurus's significance in his own development and Taurus's unique role as mediator of black and white.

Leaving Edisto for Hilton Head, Simons passes the Baby Grand and concludes that it is "a crummy dive-looking joint you'd never go in if you didn't know" (164). A seeming return to the old order of the South accompanies his return to the white community: "We got into some big oaks finally and then I started seeing pruned trees. Yards with grass in them. Heavy post fences. Private drives. A Mercedes. Negro on a mowing machine cut a swath about eight feet wide. Hilton Head" (164). But even as Simons has begun to accept his white identity and the apparently concomitant white landscapes of Hilton Head, he pulls back: "I got to heave to, hard-to-lee, or I'll get in the same trap I was in. Just because this place looks like a layout on a ping-pong table don't mean it ain't happening right here too. Whatever's happening" (181). Race itself has at the end become a trap, and Taurus has given Simons the ability to transcend it even as he accepts it. His relationship with Taurus has enabled him to maintain a writerly distance from his white society even as he returns to it: Taurus enables the freedom of his white companion. Simons portrays his arrival at Hilton Head as a return of the old "Southern barony": "Theenie hauls in here, finds the vacuum, falls to in a minute" (182). And he begrudgingly acquiesces to his role in the reformed barony—"It's the modern world. I have to accept it. I'm a pioneer"—even as he laments the absence of "mullet or mullet people" (182).

If, like so many of the white protagonists we have seen before, Simons finally returns to his white culture, he distances himself from white society even as he does so. While Huck attempts to leave Jim and the issue of race behind in going to the territory, Simons returns to his white society with a new vision of himself and of that society. Despite his return, however, Simons retains the moral growth he gained in his relationship with Taurus as he views the residents of Hilton Head with deep irony. When he fails to recognize the name of pro golfer Sam Snead, for instance, Simons is jovially belittled by the golf pro at the 19th Hole:

> "This young fella never heard of Slammin' Sammy Snead," he tells [the men at the bar], and I'm a curiosity all over again. Then they tell me about the beautiful, glorious, gone past of golfing greats who were not kids off scholarship college golf teams but gentlemen who honed themselves on the grindstone of caddying

for two bits a round. You never see these guys fold their arms
and smoke and look for hours at a wall, knowing they don't know
the whole alphabet of success, have all the pieces. They know the
whole alphabet of worldly maneuver.

And how, I have to find out, did they ever come to think they
know that? (182–83)

The men at the golf club assume a superiority that Simons will
not allow them: Simons retains moral growth here in his refusal
to accept the condescension implied by their superior bearing.
The scene at the 19th Hole, as Sybil Estes argues, emphasizes
the novel's intent to assess the "white bourgeois southern values"
that Simons's father and the golfing set on Hilton Head exem-
plify (480).

Taurus leaves an appropriate gift for Simons when he departs,
"an old wooden stereo-viewer" (160). Simons had initiated their
relationship by engaging Taurus in a false drama viewed through
a rusty telescope; Taurus's gift suggests that he leaves Simons with
a depth of vision he had earlier lacked. Through his relationship
with Taurus, Simons has gained a new way of seeing. If he is Huck
Finn a century later (and Powell's novel was published in 1984,
one hundred years after the publication of *Huck Finn*), Simons is
not one to reject society because it confounds him at the conclusion of his narrative. Rather, he declares that he sees society for
what it is, and he jumps right in.[4]

Powell's novel reevaluates Twain in a contemporary context, ultimately concluding that Twain captured much of the very American confusion over racial relations in his novel. Simons Manigault
is a modern Huck Finn, but when Powell abandons the name
Huckleberry Perry for his protagonist, he takes his character beyond the limitations Twain established. And if Simons finally fails
to develop an ongoing relationship with his Jim, he is unlike earlier protagonists such as Huck in that he retains the moral growth
he takes from the relationship.

Hateful Ways

Ellen Douglas (a pseudonym for Josephine Haxton) has repeatedly centered her fiction on relationships between blacks and whites in the contemporary South, in short stories in *Black Cloud, White Cloud* and in her novel *The Rock Cried Out.* In *Can't Quit You, Baby,* Douglas again examines a cross-racial relationship, though here she pointedly locates her sources in African American culture, taking her title, for instance, from the Willie Dixon blues song. Dixon's songs are ever upon the lips of Tweet, Douglas's primary black character. Set in Mississippi in the 1960s and 1970s, Douglas's novel meditates on the interaction of black and white in the South during the later years of the civil rights movement. Douglas's self-reflexive narrator periodically reviews the extent to which she employs essentialist ideology in developing her narrative, and her self-analysis leads to what growth is possible here. As in *Go Down, Moses* and *Intruder in the Dust,* white and black cultures in Douglas's novel are wholly interdependent, and this union obliges both the narrator and Cornelia to overcome their essentialist impressions of the black housekeeper, Julia Carrier, or "Tweet." Sharing their family stories, Cornelia and Tweet come to recognize the bonds—as well as the enmities—that lie between them and make them unable either to part or to freely embrace. And in this they represent the nation itself.

Douglas establishes familiar racial imperatives from the outset, when Cornelia asks Julia if she knows that Wayne Jones, a local white man, has died. Julia replies only, "Serve him right," before telling Cornelia of the times when she worked for Jones and he attempted to rape her (3). Cornelia's outward indifference to Tweet's plight as a black woman belies her true comprehension: "Cornelia nods, I don't believe it, she says. Julia, I just don't believe it. But of course she does" (10). The novel comes to center upon such indifference: Cornelia must confront her inability to acknowledge Tweet's situation fully before she can transcend the limitations of her own white identity.

Though she recognizes that "there is no getting around in these stories of two lives that the black woman is the white woman's servant" (4), the narrator tells us that her characters "would be uneasy" with the titles "servant" and "mistress" in part because of the implications such titles bring about in a changed day in the South (5). She charges the reader to avoid thinking of the racial stereotypes associated with the Old South in giving titles to her characters: "So, let's settle for housekeeper and employer. Yes, that's better. And try for now to be absentminded about race and class, place and time, even about poverty and wealth, security and deprivation" (5). Still, we are keenly aware that Cornelia's role is akin to that of the good mistress and that the narrator will not address many racial "situations" as such, as when Cornelia assists Tweet in registering to vote, for instance. "Ah well," the narrator whimsically concludes, "I didn't say it was possible [to ignore race altogether]. I said, *Try*" (5).

The narrator recognizes both the impossibility of escaping stereotype and the resultant need to attempt just such an escape, overtly acknowledging what she views as the inevitable failure of liberal intentions in the South. She suggests her characters simply cannot interact without confronting race and racial stereotype: "To them race sounded the endlessly repeated ground bass above and entwined with which they danced the passacaglia (or, as it may sometimes appear, the boogie) of their lives" (5). The language reveals Douglas's larger purpose: rather than allow her comparison to rest on the "passacaglia," a dance of European origin and thus to be defined in strictly Western terminology, she extends her comparison to the "boogie," a description arising out of the black culture at the center of American jazz. The ground for any discussion of race has shifted with the civil rights movement, as the narrator's struggle with the basic terms of her discussion reveals.

Douglas's narrator persistently calls our attention to the condescension inherent in Cornelia's character. Though Cornelia "considered herself a listener" to Tweet's narratives, she mostly takes pride in her ability to suppress the disdain with which she occasionally listens: she "has never by a word or gesture betrayed the boredom, the condescension she sometimes feels, her rejection of the moral code that Tweet's stories sometimes imply, her doubts about the verity of some outlandish set of events" (13–14). In the course of the novel, though, Cornelia comes to accept Tweet's own moral code to a much greater degree than she is able initially: Tweet compels Cornelia to see her own condescension even as Cornelia vainly claims to have overcome it. If, early in the novel, Tweet's stories are, for Cornelia, like "the flowers that she sticks in a jelly glass and sets in the window by the kitchen sink and forgets," by the conclusion they have become essential to her self-definition (14).

While Cornelia values her relationship with Tweet, her near-total deafness symbolizes the way in which she interacts with African Americans: she physically and metaphorically cannot hear Tweet. While she often declines to turn up her hearing aid for members of her family, she does so for Tweet, but only in the context of her role as employer: she listens to "people like her who are—yes, say it—purveyors of services of one kind or another, that is, who in Cornelia's view must be heard, who depend, at the least, upon her direction, but often, too, on her advice, her justice, or her generosity" (15). While Cornelia assumes the hierarchical position to which she felt herself entitled in the South of her youth, Douglas disputes such hierarchies throughout the novel. Indeed, Douglas focuses primarily on her protagonist's moral shift: by the conclusion, Cornelia has rejected her patriarchal posturing as a direct result of Tweet's moral instruction.

As the narrative develops, the narrator reverses her charge to the reader to ignore race, recognizing that ultimately both reader

and writer must challenge expectations of black and white that
confine social reality no less than narrative possibility:

> I want you to believe her [the narrator], but there are pitfalls in
> the path of her narrative that I must make you aware of. You may
> have assumed that she is a white woman. But perhaps you've not
> yet thought how difficult it is for her to be true to her tale.
>
> She begins, as every story teller does, with the illusion of free-
> dom. Whose story will she choose to tell? It's her prerogative to
> decide. . . . [S]he has the power to distort, if she chooses to exercise
> it. She must resist the temptation to satisfy her sense of how Tweet
> and Cornelia *ought* to behave; must resist the need to keep herself
> comfortable. . . . I encourage myself that, although it is difficult,
> it's perhaps not impossible for the tale-teller to rise above her lim-
> itations, escape the straitjacket of her own life. (38–39)

Like Powell's protagonist in the early manuscript of *Edisto*,
Douglas's narrator assesses the dilemmas involved in attempting to portray the interactions of white and black characters in
a southern setting. In acknowledging the "limitations" of race
and class, she challenges the narrow understanding of race that
so often entangles the narratives of southern novelists I've considered. In the process, she acknowledges the difficulties inherent
in her attempt to portray white and black characters interacting
apart from essentializing ideologies. She later professes to be less
certain of her position than Cornelia, who "won't lose her footing,
she's sure of it. She won't [like Tweet] find herself sinking into the
dark water among slimy cypress knees and alligators and alligator
gars" (39). By the end of the novel, Cornelia discovers within herself an ambivalence toward white identity that Douglas's narrator
shares. Both Cornelia and the narrator come to see themselves as
products of both white and black worlds.

Later in the novel, when Cornelia finds herself alone for the
first time in her life, she begins to comprehend the extent to

which she depends upon Tweet. On a plane home, Cornelia's husband, John, dies of a stroke, shortly after she has berated him and their children for protectively keeping the family problems from her throughout their marriage: " 'You bastard. I know. I know. All these years. You . . . You . . . [t]o have secrets with them . . . [t]o conspire with them against me. . . . I hate you. I hate all of you. Every one of you' " (153). Yet Cornelia is overwhelmed with guilt once she learns that John has died, and she cannot tell the stewardess whom to call to drive her home. Finally, after much prodding, she answers: "Call Julia Carrier, she said. Her telephone number is 638–3873. Then, No, she said. That's my number. Her number is 670–1283" (155). For the first time in their relationship, Cornelia overtly recognizes Tweet as a source of moral support, remembering Tweet before her own children and even mistaking her own identity for Tweet's in confusing their phone numbers. Just at the moment she is symbolically parted from her own family, Cornelia turns to Tweet.

Yet immediately after Cornelia comes to accept her dependence on Tweet, she denies her friend, specifically associating Tweet with a black identity she mistrusts in the midst of white society. At John's funeral, Tweet is appalled at the lack of respect she sees for her former employer: " 'You supposed to give somebody a decent burial,' " she says, bemoaning the lack of pomp and circumstance surrounding the funeral, a lacking that she associates with whiteness itself: " '[T]hey're as crazy as any other white people,' " she laments (158). Cornelia quietly ignores Tweet's protests, however, and when Tweet attends the funeral, Cornelia disregards her:

Tweet lit among them all like a painted bunting, a peacock among sparrows, crows, cowbirds, starlings; iridescent in a dress of teal blue, shot, like a peacock's tail, like a grackle's neck feathers, with shining green and purple threads, the skirt full and rustling. Rustling and resplendent, she settled among all those drab birds and mourned John for Cornelia with peacock cries, while all around her the sparrows turned away, hopped to another twig, shielding themselves from her brilliance, and twittered their sad farewells. And Cornelia turned off her hearing aid and gazed at John's face staring out at her from among the laurel leaves. (161)

The passage is notable not only for its revelation of Cornelia's anxious withdrawal from the black world that Tweet represents for her but also for the extent to which it reveals the narrator's own perspective. The terms with which the narrator describes Tweet ("rustling and resplendent," "brilliance") depict the customs of mourning she brings from black culture as superior to those of white culture. Black identity, on the one hand, is vibrant and abundant, while white identity, represented by gloomy "drab birds," is dull and lifeless, accepting death when it comes. This, of course, is but another stereotype of both black and white being, albeit one informed by jazz and Norman Mailer, signifying that the white narrator's engagement with blackness now runs deeper: whites overcome their guilt in seeking moral guidance from their black counterparts. The narrator discovers her own biases and distances herself from her white protagonist, but by the end of the novel, she learns how to join in this black world.

Cornelia's guilt and despondency after John's death remain linked to her engagement with blackness, even when she attempts to escape her loss in New York City. Cornelia finds the city threatening, but her very anonymity there promises refuge from her son's attempts to make her interested in life again. Taking a taxi from the airport to a friend's empty apartment, she is at once terrified and aroused by the "swarthy, bearded" taxi driver: "A sexual thrill of dread tingles in her breasts, her thighs, when she thinks about these possibilities. To be raped, murdered" (184). Once again, she retreats into a fear of the marginal and the unknown, yet, as with her initial trepidation of Tweet, her fears of the taxi driver prove to be unfounded: "In front of her apartment, the driver turns, gazes at her, smiles. See, Lady, he says. Wasn't nothing to worry about. I got you here OK, didn't I?" (185). Like Tweet, the taxi driver must overcome Cornelia's fears of darkness in order to change her thinking.

In New York, Cornelia looks to her relationship with Tweet to overcome her fear of the unknown and of the loneliness she has felt since John died. Tweet's voice comes to her just as she enters her friend's apartment from a darkened stairwell:

> What am I doing here?
>
> Inside her head a swelling and vibration, but no one answered.
>
> She fumbled with a numb hand for her keys, scurried up the dark stairs, down the dingy hall. Something behind her?
>
> The dark!
>
> She feels a crawling weight of darkness moving nearer at her back, for a moment sees Tweet's face close to hers, hears her voice:
>
> Evil out there. I be a fool not to know that. (189)

As we've seen so often in these novels, the white protagonist finds her black guide just at the moment when she is most lost.[5] Tweet is not as comforting as earlier companions have been; she warns Cornelia of danger but does not shield her from it. The "evil" that Cornelia recalls comes from Tweet's narrative, in which she relates her fear of her father. In remembering, Cornelia joins her own narrative with Tweet's, and the two remain linked in the final sections of the novel, though their union is characterized by substantial ambivalence.

When she returns to the South and to Tweet, who has herself been near death and is bedridden, Cornelia attempts to explain what Tweet has done for her: " 'You don't know it yet, but you've . . . you've been *with* me—I mean in New York. I've been in New York and you were—there. Oh, it's hard to tell about, but you were. I *heard* you' " (237). When Tweet rebuffs her attempt to join their two causes, Cornelia implores her, " 'Oh, *listen* to me, please. . . . It's about coming back into the world' " (242).

In an address to the reader late in the novel, Douglas's narrator confesses that she cannot understand Tweet's life: "I thought I was at home in Tweet's life, that when she spoke, I heard her speak with her own authentic voice" (239). She has come to recognize, however, the distance between herself and the black community represented by her character: "But of course I never heard her speak, *except to Cornelia.* Does that trouble you as it does me?" (239). The narrator admits that she, like Cornelia, has not yet taken Tweet out of stereotype, that she has indeed not been able to escape the boundaries of literary essentialism of which she spoke early in the novel. She recalls the point at which she had beseeched her reader to be "absentminded" about race: "Cornelia and Tweet, I wrote, might have other, more complex business with each other. Other business, yes. Sometimes. But surely not more complex business" (240). If the characters themselves occasionally forget the issue of race, the narrator now for the first time recognizes her own inability to portray them in such a way that the reader might forget such stereotypes: "But the truth is that there is no way Tweet could present herself so that *you* would be absentminded. No way. She is black. Cornelia is white. She is servant. Cornelia is mistress. She is poor" (240). The narrator thus comes to recognize the ways in which a reductive perception of racial identity intrudes upon the narrative from the perspective of both reader and writer.

Cornelia's resolve to transform her relationship with Tweet is constantly checked by a return to her earlier biases. Shortly after Tweet regains her voice, which she lost during her illness, Cornelia is shocked to discover that Tweet has stolen a gold barrette. Cornelia confronts Tweet in disbelief. With Tweet's angry response, Cornelia discovers for the first time the extent to which her indifference toward her housekeeper has been matched by Tweet's spite:

Hated you, Tweet says. She rocks back, leans forward in her chair. You ain't got *sense* enough to know I hated you. I hate you all my

life, before I ever know you. . . . Every day, every hour of my entire
life from the day I'm born. Hate you when you acting like you the
only woman in the world ever got sorrow when her husband die.
I hate you, hate you, hate you. And I steal that gold barrette to
remind me of it, in case I forget. She laughs. Sometimes I forget,
she says.

Damn you, then, Cornelia says. I hate you, too. (254)

In none of the narratives of white writers we've examined do
we encounter a black character reacting to a white character with
such vehemence. Tweet reproves Cornelia for her inability to escape white stereotypes of blacks: "Talking all that shit about me
being with you in New York. You ain't never *seen* me, *heard* me
in your entire life and you talking that shit. I wasn't in no New
York. I was down here" (254–55). In refusing to be either mentor
or deliverer, Tweet gains autonomy from the literary stereotypes
of the southern novel and the broader culture.

When she tosses off Cornelia's attempts to gloss over the difficulty of their relationship, Tweet compels us to recognize her
independence from Cornelia and from the model that Twain provides. No longer tied to the white protagonist of the novel, with
the narrator we now view Tweet outside of the parameters of race
we have so far seen.

But as Cornelia walks away from Tweet on the final page of the
novel, the two recognize that the enmity they share is part of their
interdependence. When Cornelia turns to look back at Tweet for
a last time, "Tweet sings out suddenly: Oh, I love you, baby, but
I sure do hate your ways" (256). Tweet's assessment of their relationship, made through Willie Dixon's blues, ironically reverses
the account of Wayne Jones's sexual exploitation of Tweet with
which the novel begins. Tweet directly assesses Cornelia's moral
worth with her implication that Cornelia is "treacherous" and
"low" (recalling Jim's admonishment of Huck after the fog passage: " 'Dat truck dah is trash' " [114]). Still, the words of the song

remind the two of the extent to which they are unable to escape the bonds between them despite their mutual hatred. As Linda Tate writes, "Tweet and Cornelia have formed a new kind of relationship between southern black and white women, based both on now-acknowledged bonds as well as on an essential consciousness of the patriarchally imposed barriers that divide them" (59).

While Huck Finn speaks for Jim throughout his novel, Tweet gains her own voice in *Can't Quit You, Baby*. Having lost her ability to speak during her illness, Tweet regains it when Cornelia begins to make broad assumptions about the nature of their relationship. Tweet demands the right to define her own role in the relationship. At the end of her novel, as at the beginning, Douglas depends upon texts from black culture to comment on the relationship between black and white: Willie Dixon ultimately clarifies the relationship in a way that the narrator admits she cannot. Even at the end of her novel, Douglas's narrator recognizes her own inability to represent fully the experience of her black characters, thus avoiding the farcical nature of Twain's ending and likewise avoiding Twain's return to essentialist ideology.

Ain't Your Brother

Tuscaloosa, W. Glasgow Phillips's first novel, speaks to each of the primary concerns of the southern novels I have considered thus far—race, family, and region, especially—even as it undermines the patinaed structures still supporting those southern institutions. Working in the tradition of twentieth-century southern novelists like Flannery O'Connor and Walker Percy, Phillips's novel plainly looks back to the central work of southern—and American—fiction, Twain's *Huck Finn*.

The protagonist of the novel is Billy Mitchell, the twenty-four-year-old son of a successful psychiatrist who works at a state mental hospital; the Doctor, as Billy calls his father, is dismayed that Billy hasn't yet pursued a career. Billy, for his part, remains sufficiently happy with the titular position of head groundskeeper for the hospital.

At the center of Billy's narration are his visions of his mother's relationship with a black woman, Carmen Rathberry, the Mitchells' long-time servant. When Billy was a child, his mother and Carmen left their families in order to be together, violating multiple southern taboos in the process. The scenes in which Billy imagines the two women driving away from Tuscaloosa are playfully evocative, suggesting that the relationship is a modern Eden in which none of the fruit is forbidden. Their eventual deaths inspire Billy's self-searching throughout the novel.

Among the most hilarious scenes in this comic novel is that in which Billy imagines his father—spurned by his wife for a black woman, he is Phillip's ironic specter of the southern manhood of an earlier day—driving in determined pursuit of the two women. Strapped to the front of the car, his hound bays out the trail: "The hound was not uncomfortable," Phillips writes. "It takes more than that to make a hound uncomfortable; it was probably delighted, squatting up there like a lifesize drooling hood ornament" (85). The Doctor wears nothing but boxer shorts and hunting boots in pursuit, having used the rest of his clothing to protect the dog from the burning metal on the hood of the car. " 'It's hot, ain't it,' " a farmer says to him upon seeing his outfit (152).

Billy believes that the relationship between his mother and Carmen established a permanent tie between himself and his childhood friend Nigel (Carmen's son), but Nigel adamantly refuses to accept this proposition. Nigel reacts to Billy's idealized conception of their relationship much as Ellison's narrator reacted to Mr. Emerson's propositioning, finding in it the seeds of the same racism he encounters every day. Ostensibly involved in acts of sedition such as blowing up the police chief's car, Nigel rejects Billy's innocent overtures and at one point challenges Billy to not return to Paradise—the barbecue joint at the edge of the black part of town where Nigel works and where Billy buys marijuana—until he makes an active commitment to their relationship: " 'You got to figure out where you stand before you come around here again' " (136). It is no accident that the barbecue joint is called Paradise: once again the southern, like the American, Eden is built upon a vision of interracial harmony.

Amidst all of this, improbably but wonderfully, Billy is falling in love with Virginia, a patient at the mental hospital with a mean streak of jealousy that leads her at one point to take a buzzing bee into her mouth and lie in wait for Billy's kiss. Virginia claims to be completely healthy, in contrast to Billy's growing pain over his mother's death. Like other white protagonists we have seen, Billy seeks out Nigel in order to come to terms with the pains of his own experience.

This by now familiar story of the New South reflects the ambivalence of racial identities in America. Despite his outright efforts to understand race and the South in new ways, Billy's relationship with Nigel ultimately founders upon his limited understanding of black culture. Billy comes to the end of his narrative still believing that his life is one with that of his black friend, Nigel. Billy tells Nigel:

"We're intertwined, see, reflections of one another." . . .

"Never mind that shit," says Nigel. "I am fixing to tell you something."

"Anything," I say.

"You're going to hate it," he says.

"Okay," I say.

"I ain't no motif," he says, and pulls my face down and breaks it against the same edge of the fender that his got knocked against. "Ain't your brother. Ain't no mirror neither. Leave me out of that weird shit," he says, and does it again. (186)[6]

Like Powell and Douglas, Phillips demonstrates through pointed irony the failure of liberal intentions on the part of white southerners. It is, of course, a failure that is at the center of *Huck Finn* and so many southern novels that follow it. Phillips suggests that race is the central issue upon which Americans continue to founder. This white protagonist returns his would-be companion to type, but Phillips is more aware than he allows his character to be. And Nigel, for his part, will have none of Billy's essentialist ideology.

A Changed Embrace

Following the African American writers I have examined here, Powell, Douglas, and Phillips move beyond the pattern Mark Twain established even as they often work within it. Their narratives become increasingly self-reflexive as they respond to Twain; no longer lashed to the paradigm that Twain largely established, these three writers undermine Twain's pattern even as they reflect it. Carolyn Porter defines a central crisis of the American writer as one in which the writer "discovers his participation within the world he has thought to stand outside" (xviii). Powell, Douglas, and Phillips employ just such a discovery to overcome the barriers established in the southern novel following Twain, effectively subverting the ideology we have so persistently found in the work of white writers before them. In their novels, the embrace that we find between black and white—no longer nostalgic and removed from the reality of American culture—is tentative and uncertain at best.

CODA

In a Southern Accent

No Huck and Jim, no American novel as we know it.
RALPH ELLISON

We grow uncomfortable with images of racism, as we do
with images of human betrayal, when they are drawn into direct
association with the familiar circumstances of slavery in America.
When Huckleberry Finn threatens to turn Jim over to the
authorities, the fantasy of interracial concord and liberation
seems poised for a fall into American history.
FORREST G. ROBINSON

I have Dutch, nigger, and English in me, and either
I'm nobody, or I'm a nation.
DEREK WALCOTT, in "The Schooner *Flight*"

Chain him, either chain him or expel his black shape from
our midst, before we realize that he is ourselves.
WINTHROP D. JORDAN

Tell me some mo' history, Huck.
FROM TWAIN'S WORKING NOTES TO THE NOVEL

A Blues

Since the 1970s, the taboo against crossing racial boundaries has
waned in American popular culture, and white cultural figures
regularly present public selves complicated and deepened by the
intermingling of racial identities. Crossover has become a marketing tool. In the absence of a widespread taboo, crossover has

become a national and even international obsession (think of the influence of black American culture on British rock of the 1960s and 1970s), and the questions arise: what accounts for its continued popularity in music, television, film, and novels? How can we explain the omnipresence of the crossover theme in our culture?

Some answers may come from a brief look at the burgeoning popularity of blues music, a popularity that serves to demonstrate the commodification and appropriation of African American culture I have discussed throughout this book. In the 1990s, the so-called country blues proved enormously popular among white American audiences, and, in particular, the story of guitarist Robert Johnson has held a mythical fascination. Johnson's death—purportedly at the hands of the jealous husband of one of his many paramours—has been described repeatedly in accounts of his life. Details of his hard-edged life have become inseparable from his music for white blues fans and clearly inform white appreciation of Johnson's music and persona. Writer after writer has described, for instance, how Johnson purportedly barked "like a dog" as he died, and this alone suggests that Johnson's story fascinates his fans precisely because it appalls, giving evidence of the depths of the primitive in a blues life.

White writers on Robert Johnson's blues invariably begin by telling his story and end by telling their own, a pattern we have seen in the southern novel. In claiming to discover Johnson during their journey down Highway 61, it seems, white writers—and perhaps white blues fans by extension—instead discover themselves.[1] As Gene Santoro writes, "Nearly everyone who's ever played that album [Robert Johnson's *King of the Delta Blues*] remembers the first time he or she heard it, usually with a mind-boggling circumstantial vividness—as if Johnson's raggedly keening voice, astonishingly agile guitar, in-your-face creative abundance, and haunted sense of the supernatural's day-to-day power impress itself on listeners so deeply that they become poets-by-proxy" (10). Robert Palmer sees Johnson as a sort of personal muse: "Every listener will finally have to come to terms with that myth in an individual, intuitively personal way" (98).

Johnson's *Complete Recordings* (1990) sold 400,000 copies in its first year and won a Grammy Award. For an impoverished jook joint singer whose greatest previous fame came in 1937, the year before his death, such sales are beyond imagining. *Complete Recordings* was a cash bonanza for Columbia Records, which had to pay no one for the rerelease of music for which the company paid a pittance in the 1930s. As a writer for *Newsweek* wryly put it, "Someone must have their mojo workin' over at Columbia Records" (Leerhsen et al. 72).

Certainly, Johnson's commercial appeal has much to do with widespread interest in blues music, but the level of recent interest has commodified and so transformed both the blues and Johnson. The Robert Johnson we celebrate in America today is both primitive and postmodern: if our image of him is the essence of racial essentialism, then we have at the same time transformed Johnson—and the blues—into a culturally palatable amalgam. The United States Postal Service, for instance, rewrote history when, in a postage stamp memorializing Johnson, it airbrushed out the cigarette hanging from Johnson's lips. (Among blues fans the photograph—one of only two known images of Johnson—was legendary.) In Los Angeles, upscale aficionados listen to the blues in the nine-million-dollar House of Blues on Sunset Strip, complete with its intentionally roughed-up interior designed "to give it that going-down-to-Memphis feel." After the guitarist Beck recently saw African bluesman Ali Farka Tour there, he noticed the dissonance between the music and the context: "The audience was just eating and talking and answering their cell phones," he said. "Tour was just shaking his head" (Dunn 52). Divorced from its context or even sympathy for its context, the bitterest blues becomes our Musak.

Can it get any worse? Anything, of course, is possible in America, and we are perhaps at our most banal when we offer tribute.

A vintage guitar dealer recently made a half-serious proposal to raise money for the Delta Blues Museum in Clarksdale by selling a Robert Johnson board game in which "players would try to get out of the South via Highway 61 without landing on Hard Times and having to go back and start over, one mo' time" (Leerhsen et al. 72). What next? Perhaps the Walt Disney Crossroads theme park? You and the kids get assaulted by the local police and refused admittance to the white hospital? Somewhere Michael Eisner is dreaming the blues.

Bill Cosby certainly is not. In an interview, the actor and jazz fan called for a "moratorium on the blues," suggesting that the music encourages all of the old stereotypes of black identity (Johnson 26). But beyond the essentialism inherent in our contemporary fascination with the blues, what do we miss? In the rush of our own spiritual journeys into blackness, we tend to overlook the spirituality that's already there. Wanting to see the story of the blues as one of heightened sexual pleasure and Robert Johnson as a sort of embittered Dionysus of the Delta, we fail or refuse to see the insistent spirituality of the blues. We want to hear the devil's music and so we miss its soulfulness, its certainty that in human relationships, however fleeting they may be, there is transcendence. The bluesmen may have been running from the devil, but they did so with a deep awareness of the divine potential of the human. Blackness once again becomes fluid in the white mind, a vessel to be filled by white desire.

The "Lincoln of Our Literature"

The appropriation and domestication of black culture as we see it in the recent popularity of Robert Johnson's music is a manifestation of the ambivalence toward African American culture I have identified throughout this book. That several of the literary works I have examined here are among the most memorable of American literature—others are among the most popular—signifies our willingness to engage ourselves again and again in the myth of cross-racial pairings. Just as Americans return repeatedly to *Huckleberry Finn* as the timeless classic of our nation, our writers rewrite and revise it, ostensibly trying to get it right, to look more plainly at the central contradictions of our culture. Their frequent inability to do so reflects upon us all: unable to confront our incongruities, we seek instead familiar ground. Thus we find our writers in some measure repeating the return to type that we find in Twain. When we see in recent years a tendency toward a more critical examination of the pattern on the part of writers like Ellen Douglas, it is because the work of African American writers like Richard Wright and Ralph Ellison has so thoroughly deconstructed the failed vision of racial liberalism to be found in Twain.

When William Dean Howells called Twain the "Lincoln of our literature" (qtd. in Wieck 2), he was thinking not of race but of homespun origins; still, Mark Twain was an emancipator of sorts for American writers. After *Huckleberry Finn*, American fiction has no longer been limited to essentialist portrayals of black characters and black identity, though certainly the years since Twain published his best-known work have provided us with many such examples. Yet when, in the final third of *Huckleberry Finn*, Twain returns Jim to the essentialized view of race from which he had earlier removed him, he draws upon a larger pattern in American culture and establishes a paradigm that would shape southern, and American, literature to come, even as it reflected a similar paradigm in southern, and American, culture. Huck and the protagonists following him seek freedom in their American society, but they do so by restricting that of their marginalized companions; maintaining again and again their racial innocence, they are utterly unable to recognize their own participation in the racial hierarchies they claim to undermine. And, in the end, their identities in the white southern worlds to which they return are defined by their own participation in the marginalization of their companions.

The professed innocence of these protagonists thus grants them their freedom, and this is as it has always been in the United States. Lionel Trilling's assessment that *Huck Finn* "reads us" (qtd. in Carrington 191) is apt: American society measures its moral self by its own engagement with minority culture, and Twain's novel is, of course, engaged with that culture even when Huck abandons Jim to literary minstrelsy at the end. If, as John Seelye suggests, Twain's Jim is the namesake of Jim Crow, we might have expected the betrayal we find in Twain's conclusion. More surprising in so many of the novels that follow *Huckleberry Finn* is that our writers continue to assert the racial innocence of their protagonists. Hence, we see that Americans continue to idealize and then disavow their truest identity, preferring the pain of disavowal to the recognition of a multicultural self.

The texts I have considered here demonstrate the inability of white Americans to acknowledge the significance of otherness in the creation of the American identity. It is as if the notion that "most American whites are culturally part Negro American without even realizing it" is finally too much to bear, and our heroes recoil from the proposition (Ellison, *Shadow and Act* 108). We recoil with them, of course, and, forgetting that bitter denial and betrayal are at the center of these novels, we maintain an intense nostalgia for the supposed innocence that we find in them. Forrest G. Robinson brilliantly demonstrates the force of this cultural repression in our readings of Twain's novel: "This rending tale of drift, betrayal, violence, and injustice is viewed as a national oracle, approached in the anticipation of laughter and affirmation, experienced as something incoherent, disturbing, to varying degrees depressing, yet returned to again and again with the original expectations virtually intact" (*In Bad Faith* 135). It is a repression endemic to American culture. Thus we experience *Huckleberry*

Finn and these later novels in much the same way that we have experienced democracy itself, convincing ourselves time and again
in the face of tremendous contrary evidence that we have indeed
achieved racial innocence.

A Claim of Innocence

As I have suggested throughout, Mark Twain's best novel lies at
the center of an American literary mythology surrounding race
that has been evolving since the earliest European writing on the
New World. Certainly, we find in American history an abundance
of similar betrayals of African American and Native American
identities. Having often declared our minority communities to be
central to our identity as a nation, indeed, to Americanness itself,
we have never been fully content with the idea. Hence, we bear
unbelieving witness to the endless betrayals of those communities, most prominent among them the myriad broken treaties with
Native American populations and the equally numerous broken
promises made to African Americans, especially those promises
associated with Reconstruction, the Great Migration, and *Brown
v. Board of Education.*

Profound hypocrisies over racial identity characterized the for-
mative years of American identity. Early on, "Americans" wished
to differentiate themselves from a European past; obviously, this
was so in the Northeast with the vision of a city on a hill, but it
was true as well in Virginia and throughout the southern colonies.
After the Revolution, Americans were anxious to attest to their
freedom in spite of the burgeoning system of slavery. This contradictory, and primary, mode of racial discourse was most clearly in-
scribed upon the American scene by the Declaration of Independence, in which we find all the well-documented contradictions of
its author with regard to race, contradictions that demonstrate the
pervasive nature of our cultural cognitive dissonance over racial
identity.

Indeed, the process of Jefferson's scripting of the central testament to American freedom offers an instructive model. As John Chester Miller notes, when Jefferson was writing the Declaration, he keenly sensed the discrepancy in a slave-owning people's rebellion against what they viewed as their own enslavement. In his original draft of the Declaration, he accuses King George III of attempting to enslave the colonists and of "inciting *his* slaves to murder freedom-loving white Americans who, had they been free of royal control, would have abolished slavery of their own accord" (Miller 10). While this attempt to blame American slavery on the British—a classic claim for racial innocence that anticipates what we find in *Huck Finn*—would be rejected by the Continental Congress, we see in Jefferson's effort to transfer blame for slavery an insistence upon evasion and a hope for expiation as well.

The democratic impulse that led to Jefferson's Declaration and that so possessed the young nation could, of course, hardly rid the American society of European notions of social division. If the rigidity of Old World social strata was lacking in the New World, the assumptions that created them were not, and those assumptions helped to build the American social hierarchy around the ever-present issue of race. One result of the dissonance between the ideal and the real was lingering guilt over the treatment of racial minorities (and the resultant need for a profession of innocence), for whom the white American cry of freedom has so often meant tyranny.

This paradox explains the prevalence of visions of a noble savage such as we find in Cooper, during the Jacksonian Age, when Native American culture was being obliterated in the name of an expansionism ever tied to freedom. And it explains, too, why hundreds of thousands of impoverished white southerners fought and died for "rights" that were hardly their own. In the presence of the most outrageous racial injustices, our cultural mantra has ever been "freedom," as it is for so many of the protagonists we

encounter here, who must restrict the freedom of their marginalized companions in order to establish their own.

The betrayals and contradictions that we find in these early
examples only became more prevalent following the Civil War.
While Mark Twain wrote *Huckleberry Finn*, the promises of Reconstruction—symbolized by the elusive forty acres and a mule—
were undermined by the Republican party's failure of will and
the concomitant determination of the Southern Redeemers (for
whom, as we have seen, Tom Sawyer is consummate symbol) to
rejoin the fragments of the slave South. Thus the seeds planted
at the beginning of Reconstruction bore bitter fruit at its end
with the sacrifice of southern blacks implicit in the Compromise
of 1877, Rutherford B. Hayes's subsequent withdrawal of federal
troops supporting Reconstruction governments, and the return to
power of the white ruling class. The *Nation* commented plain-
tively at the time that the "extravagant expectations" of Reconstruction had "died out" (qtd. in Foner 587). And, as the novels
we've considered here so pointedly suggest, biting ironies often
accompany these reversals: Eric Foner notes that some of the
same troops leaving Louisiana after the Compromise went west
to hound the Indians after abandoning the project of supporting
the blacks (583). It is all of a piece, and ultimately the demise of
Reconstruction led to the Supreme Court's decision in *Plessy v.
Ferguson*, the decision that legalized segregation and amounted
to a federal endorsement of the revocation of black rights in the
South.[2]

We see in *Plessy* the pattern I am identifying as an American
configuration of race as much as it is a southern one, and we find
such failures of moral resolve throughout the history of race in
America, as we find them in this body of southern novels that
reflects that history. Thus Mark Twain's novel reflects the failure
of Radical Reconstruction, and Elizabeth Spencer's *A Voice at the
Back Door* represents a failed movement toward civil rights for
African Americans at midcentury. More recent works reflect the

ambivalence that remains over racial identity in the American body politic at the beginning of a new millennium. And the literary fascination with transracial transgressions is hardly limited to southern novelists: recent works like Robert Hellenga's *Blues Lessons,* Jeffrey Lent's *In the Fall,* and Kim McLarin's *Meeting of the Waters* trace similar relationships.

American history since 1884 is rife with parallels to the betrayals that we find in our literature, so much so that an extensive review of such failures is hardly necessary here. The promises of a better life in the North that sparked the Great Migration ultimately resulted in the Harlem riots and the failed March on Washington. Likewise, the hopes that were inspired by the 1954 *Brown* decision and that led to such massive social change have ultimately been checked by the rejection of school integration and affirmative action programs in both North and South.[3] As with Reconstruction, what begins as a gesture toward Americans who suffer the burden of racism comes to be perceived as an undeserved encumbrance upon white Americans. And this is what happens in Twain's novel and so many novels that follow it, as white protagonists reject the clear vision of a multicultural self they have so lately taken on.

This pattern of betrayal and denial exists in popular culture as well. Elvis Presley, the "white man who had the Negro sound and the Negro feel," represented the passage of black blues into mainstream American pop.[4] Presley's early, spontaneous denial of his ties to African American musical styles parallels the betrayal that we find at the end of Twain's novel. When Marion Keisker, Sam Phillips's co-manager at Sun Studios, asked the young Presley, "Who do you sing like?" Presley, who had spent years listening to the black blues artists on Beale Street, replied simply, "I don't sing like nobody" (qtd. in Marcus, *Dead Elvis* 159).[5] We find such denials over and over again in our history and in our literature; as we have seen, their repetition forms a litany of denial in the literature of white American authors addressing race.

Norman Mailer, who in "The White Negro" acknowledged the significance of the relationship between black and white to the flourishing of American culture, more recently said that the United States "is so complicated that when I start to think about it I begin talking in a southern accent" (qtd. in Grimes 22). Mailer's derisive intent notwithstanding, his comment is telling: when Americans begin to talk about race, they do so with a distinctly southern accent, if not one of Twain's "Pike County dialects," then something bearing a close resemblance. The nation's idea of the South refuses to die in part because it remains our central metaphor for the hypocrisies and contradictions of American society. And so we continue to recast the relationship between an antebellum southern orphan and a fugitive slave in order to better comprehend ourselves. Thinking we know more of ourselves for the experience, in fact we know less.

Steal Away

What Mark Twain is ultimately up to in *Huckleberry Finn*—like Harriet Beecher Stowe in *Uncle Tom's Cabin*—is neither freeing African American culture nor enslaving it but stealing from it: *Huckleberry Finn* borrows liberally from the motifs of the slave narrative while viewing the slave's experience through the lens of blackface minstrelsy, rendering the narrative acceptable to a white readership. The popular identification of white America with Huck Finn and with the protagonists who follow him has as much to do with guilt as with freedom: as we have seen, Huck's story offers a means of assuaging lingering guilt over the treatment of African Americans and so a means of asserting racial innocence. As Houston Baker suggests, black culture's art forms have "been adjusted to suit the needs of white America—to reinforce stereotypes and sometimes even to justify the victimization of the black American" (135). When the African American writers I consider here repudiate *Huckleberry Finn*, they reclaim the slave narrative and likewise the interplay of black and white America.

In the contemporary southern novel addressing race and interracial union, we find writers who occasionally confront the condescension of the *Huck Finn* model and the apparent failure of many southern white writers to portray autonomous black characters. No longer attempting to pass as black, the white protagonists of these novels recognize the independence of their black companions. These white protagonists retain what moral growth there is beyond the relationship that enables it.

Blue Note

Images of racial union pervade American culture today: one can hardly live in twenty-first-century America and not be aware of a powerful striving toward racial unity. It is the classic American theme, and we read it in our literature as we hear it in rock, jazz, rap, and blues music. We see it at the movies and on television. The list does not end.

Yet made utterly aware of our central cultural ideals through these myriad appeals, we know, too, our failures, the vast divide between these images of our better selves and our reality. Our literature bears witness to this cultural dissonance, reflecting our inability to attain what we envision. We know who we should be and we celebrate that self, yet time and again the revelry ends in a tragic failure of moral vision that is at the heart of the American experience.

NOTES

Introduction

1. Of course, "race" in America cannot be taken to mean only black and white, since as of this writing Hispanics have passed African Americans as the nation's largest minority group.

2. While the works I have chosen to explore in detail are especially effective examples, they represent merely a portion of the southern novels on the subject of racial crossing.

3. Critics have often made the point that Twain resorts to irony in the final section of the novel. In the end, I identify with the school of critics who see Twain more as distracted auteur than sustained ironist in this section.

4. In describing these writers as "liberal," I employ Morton Sosna's definition of southern "racial liberals": white southerners who dissent from conservative southern ideology on race. The southern novelists I consider here demonstrate their dissent in portraying a white character to some degree overcoming, however temporarily, conventional stereotypes of African Americans.

5. John Seelye's provocative assessments of *Huckleberry Finn* and of the American novel challenged me to read the works I discuss here in a broader context. Likewise, his *True Adventures of Huckleberry Finn* and *The Kid*, works in metacriticism both, anticipate many of the arguments I develop regarding Twain's novel.

I am also working in the light cast by three important works of scholarship of the 1980s and 1990s, each of which has contributed in significant ways to the present study. The first is *In Bad Faith: The Dynamics of Deception in Mark Twain's America*, in which Forrest G. Robinson develops the most important textual analysis of *Tom Sawyer* and *Huckleberry Finn* in decades. His assessment of the acts of "bad faith"—deceptions "in the denial of departures from public ideals of the true and just" (2)—of Twain and his readers shaped my thinking of *Huckleberry Finn* and helped me to identify similar acts of denial in the later texts that I consider here.

In *Was Huck Black? Mark Twain and African-American Voices*, Shelly

Fisher Fishkin persuasively argues that at the heart of *Huckleberry Finn* is a union of racial voices reflecting the multicultural American society in which Mark Twain wrote and in which we live. For Fishkin, "Twain's imaginative blending of black voices with white ones (whether conscious or unconscious) effectively deconstructs 'race' as a meaningful category" (144). Fishkin's reader comes to see that Twain's novel has perhaps never been more relevant than it is today as American culture continues to cope with racial enmity, as witnessed in the riots of the 1990s in Crown Heights and Los Angeles and the murder of James Byrd Jr. in 2000. I examine a crossing of racial identities akin to that which Fishkin assesses, though my concern is with a pattern of racial crossing beyond Twain. While I disagree with her assessment of the conclusion of the novel (and certainly the critical debate has demonstrated that there is room for ample disagreement on that topic), her insights into the novel will serve critics of Twain for years to come.

In *Playing in the Dark: Whiteness and the Literary Imagination,* Toni Morrison challenges our understanding of the representation of blackness in the work of white American writers. I take up Morrison's challenge to critics to examine the ways in which African American and Euro-American traditions inform one another.

Finally, I should add that each of these recent works is indebted, as is the present one, to Leslie Fiedler's *Love and Death in the American Novel,* surely the most provocative critique of the American novel in the second half of the twentieth century. Decades after its publication, Fiedler's critique remains essential.

6. As Woodward writes in *The Burden of Southern History,* "The institution that had so recently been blamed for a multitude of the region's ills was now pictured as the secret of its superiority and the reason for its fancied perfection" (179).

7. Writers like Leslie Fiedler, Norman Mailer, and Winthrop D. Jordan long ago identified the persistent pattern of cross-racial companionships in American culture.

8. We see elements of the pattern of denial in some of the earliest exemplars of American literature: Cabeza de Vaca's narrative, for example, and John Smith's writing on Pocahontas. Thomas Morton's *New English Canaan* likewise engages the theme.

9. Roediger writes, "Minstrel entertainers both claimed to be pupils, or even kin, of the Blacks they mocked and as passionately made clear that they were white" (*The Wages of Whiteness* 116).

10. Reed specifically mocks the exotic notions of blackness to be found in works by the Beat writers and Norman Mailer. Kerouac, for example, describes his wish that "I were a Negro, feeling that the best the white world had offered was not enough ecstasy for me, not enough life, joy, kicks, darkness, music, not enough night. I wished I were a Denver Mexican, or even a poor overworked Jap, anything but what I so drearily was, a 'whiteman' disillusioned" (qtd. in Baldwin 297).

11. This list will inevitably be partial, and to it might be added every film in which Whoopi Goldberg has ever appeared. *Adventures of Huckleberry Finn* has itself been made and remade often.

12. We find the pattern in programs as distinct as *The Defiant Ones* and *Six Feet Under,* for example.

13. The meaning of "identity" has spawned a roiling critical debate in the last decade. I use the term in reference to the site at which the social and the psychological meet, drawing upon K. Anthony Appiah's tentative definition of identity as "a coalescence of mutually responsive (if sometimes conflicting) modes of conduct, habits of thought, and patterns of evaluation; in short, a coherent kind of human social psychology" (174).

14. David Roediger's *The Wages of Whiteness* and Toni Morrison's *Playing in the Dark* introduced a series of works in a field of study that has come to be known as whiteness studies. While important work has been done by writers like Richard Dyer, Grace Ellen Hale, and Noel Ignatiev, among many others, the area of study is not so much new as an extension of work such as Fiedler's *Love and Death* and Winthrop Jordan's *White over Black.* As significantly, as Roediger demonstrates in *Black on White*, African American writers have been assessing "whiteness" throughout American history.

1. A Raft of Hope

1. The word "quintessential" hangs on the tongue in such discussions, but it would be a bold critic indeed who would use the term in

the wake of Arac's evisceration of those who have so persistently used it in the past.

2. Most recently, Jane Smiley in a cover article in *Harper's* and Jonathan Arac have addressed the failings of *Adventures of Huckleberry Finn* or, rather, our failings for continuing to read it without regard for the structures of racism to be found there. Stacey Margolis provides a compelling response to Smiley and Arac, claiming the novel articulates "a form of moral action on which individual intention—whether good or bad—finally has no bearing" (331).

3. Clemens's friend William Dean Howells saw him in utter contrast to most southerners of the day:

> The part of him that was Western in his Southwestern origin Clemens kept to the end, but he was the most desouthernized Southerner I ever knew. No man more perfectly sensed and more entirely abhorred slavery, and no one has ever poured such scorn upon the second-hand, Walter-Scotticized, pseudo-chivalry of the Southern ideal. He held himself responsible for the wrong which the white race had done the black race in slavery, and he explained, in paying the way of a negro student through Yale, that he was doing it as his part of the reparation due from every white to every black man. (30)

4. Twain and Cable joined together in 1884–85 for an extended reading tour. Fishkin persuasively demonstrates Twain's racial liberalism in *Was Huck Black?*

5. Robinson's analysis of the passage that follows suggested to me its importance to this study.

6. Tom is depicted in this role from the first page of the novel, in fact, where Huck recollects that it was Tom who first came after him and said he was going to start a band of robbers and that "I might join if I would go back to the widow and be respectable" (2).

7. If the scene strikes us as familiar, it is perhaps because we have encountered something like it before: Jim's deception resembles Tom's masterful escape from whitewashing duties in the earlier novel.

8. The caption (approved by Twain for the W. E. Kemble portrayal of Huck slipping out a window of the Widow's house) suggests that Huck's escape would ultimately be tied to his entry into African American culture. Kemble inaccurately shows Huck climbing out a window

onto a porch (the text calls for him to climb onto the shed roof), and the caption reads: "Huck stealing away" (5). Thus at the outset Huck's travels are linked to those of the slaves for whom "stealing away" was both religious metaphor and physical hope, taken from the famous sorrow song: "Steal away, steal away home / I ain't got long to stay here" (Baker 42).

9. In the scene that follows, Twain stresses Huck's ambivalence over a white identity in his vivid description of Pap: "There warn't no color in his face where his face showed; it was white; not like another man's white, but a white to make a body sick, a white to make a body's flesh crawl—a tree-toad white, a fish-belly white" (23). Pap's whiteness repulses Huck, and such associations with whiteness lead to Huck's climactic decision to steal Jim out of slavery and "go to hell" for doing so. As Toni Morrison writes of whiteness in American literature, Pap's whiteness here is for Huck "mute, meaningless, unfathomable," and from his captivity at Pap's white hands, Huck will go straight into Jim's black arms on Jackson's Island (Morrison 59).

10. Those who do use the term *friend* in the novel are, as here, most often attempting to manipulate. Tom's note from an "UNKNOWN FRIEND" is an example: *"Don't betray me, I wish to be your friend"* (334). And the king's declaration of his own identity is another: "Yes, my friend, it is too true—your eyes is lookin' at this very moment on the pore disappeared Dauphin, Looy the Seventeenth, son of Looy the Sixteenth and Marry Antonette" (163).

11. Robinson argues that Tom's adventures pointedly avoided race as a social question: "It is the omission of slavery that enables *Tom Sawyer* to be a comic novel despite all of the violence and mayhem in it" (*In Bad Faith* 115). For Robinson, Jim's presence in *Huckleberry Finn* "triggers an impulse to 'evasion' that arises out of Tom's cultural incapacity to deal directly with the terrible truth of race-slavery, and that propels him to the limits of his gamesman's capacity for manipulation and make-believe" (*In Bad Faith* 178).

12. Tom removes the threat of otherness, of course, by rendering Jim's plight absurd. In Laurence B. Holland's words, "Tom's antics confer the burden of heroism on Jim but make a cruel and diseased mockery of it" (71).

13. The forty dollars Tom gives Jim matches the amount that the king took for selling Jim.

14. We remember, of course, that Jim had earlier assessed himself at a significantly higher price: " 'I owns mysef, en I's wuth eight hund'd dollars' " (57).

15. Twain's notes were divided and labeled "Group A" and so on by Walter Blair. I am working from photocopies of the notes provided in the Iowa-California edition, 1988. "Uncle" Dan and "Aunt" Hannah were slaves on the farm upon which Twain modeled the Phelps farm. The last quote is a variance on the familiar slave dictum "Bottom rail on top."

16. We know from Alan Gribben's reconstruction of Mark Twain's library, for instance, that Twain had a copy of Charles Ball's *Slavery in the United States: A Narrative of the Life and Adventures of Charles Ball, a Black Man, Who Lived Forty Years in Maryland, South Carolina and Georgia, as a Slave,* which was to become a source for *A Connecticut Yankee in King Arthur's Court.* Further, of course, Twain was familiar with the narratives of many former slaves, Frederick Douglass among them, through the speeches that he had heard.

17. Eric Lott notes that "Twain was himself intrigued by what he called the 'happy and accurate' representations of the minstrel show" (20).

2. Dirty Books for Yankees

1. Surely no critique in the history of American literature has become so widely known as Hemingway's assessment in *Green Hills of Africa* that "all modern American literature comes from one book by Mark Twain called *Huckleberry Finn*" (22). Yet Hemingway, like so many readers after him, was ill at ease with Twain's ending. The last third of the novel troubled him so much that he recommended the reader simply overlook it: "You must stop where the Nigger Jim is stolen from the boys [here Hemingway's memory of the book failed him]. That is the real end. The rest is just cheating." Despite such criticism, however, Hemingway continues his praise in judging that "it's the best book we've had. All American writing comes from that. There was nothing before. There has been nothing as good since" (22).

2. As in Pendleton's *King Tom and the Runaways*, the author's nostalgic impulses differ from the more skeptical response of many of the writers I consider here.

3. *Absalom, Absalom!*, *The Reivers*, and *The Unvanquished* have obvious parallels to *Adventures of Huckleberry Finn* as well.

4. While Faulkner's portrayal of blacks in such stories as "The Fire and the Hearth" and "Pantaloon in Black" provides a significant background to Ike's perspective of Sam Fathers, I focus here only upon that part of the text directly concerning Ike.

5. The imagery of the passage provides strong support for Leslie Fiedler's argument in *Love and Death in the American Novel* that such relationships are homoerotic "marriages" formed so that the white character can atone for his guilt over the persecution of American minorities.

6. The moment recalls the crazy quilt that warms Ishmael and Queequeg.

7. *Go Down, Moses* was published at the beginning of the critical controversy over the conclusion of *Huckleberry Finn*. Faulkner's novel can be read as a supplanted ending for Twain's; this time, the risks are real.

8. Faulkner's contradictory thinking on race, of course, has made for much critical analysis over the years. In his well-known statement to reporter Russell Warren Howe, we find the same sort of tortured ideology we find in Stevens. On the question of civil rights in the South, Faulkner said, "As long as there's a middle road, all right, I'll be on it. But if it came to fighting I'd fight for Mississippi against the United States even if it meant going out in the street and shooting negroes" (qtd. in Blotner 618).

9. Stevens develops into a figure typical of southern fiction in his lengthy and duplicitous pronouncements on race, a type dating back to Augustine St. Clare in Stowe's *Uncle Tom's Cabin*. Like St. Clare before him, Stevens's character claims to represent a reasoned view of race relations even as he works to reassert the old order.

10. It is an ending for Lucas that directly contrasts with the conclusion of *Huckleberry Finn*, in which Tom Sawyer pays Jim forty dollars for his inconvenience and Jim joyfully celebrates wealth regained.

11. In challenging readers' expectations, Spencer anticipates the in-

tertextuality of more recent novels by writers like Padgett Powell and Ellen Douglas, both of whom I consider in my final chapter.

12. Perhaps we are prepared for this act of manipulation: Louis Rubin and others have noted that Jim holds back the news about Pap's death so that Huck will stay with him.

13. The passage reads as follows:

Black people are night people, and you do not drive a Southern road at any unearthly hour without seeing them along the roadsides, going some- where, or marking at a distance across the field the oil lamp burning full wick within the cabin. Sometimes, passing near a cabin that is totally dark as though for sleep, one hears break out again the low mingling of many voices; no crisis has brought them there, but the instinctive motion of their strange society has behaved like a current deep down in the river, and here they are. Savage, they came to a savage land, and it took them in. White people, already appalled by floods and rattlesnakes, malaria, swamps, tor- nadoes, mud, ice, sunstroke, and typhoid fever, felt compelled to levee out the black with the same ruthless patience with which they leveed the Mis- sissippi River. They were driven to do what they did, not by any conviction of right or wrong, but by the simple will to survive. Meanwhile, Negroes married the land. Its image is never complete without them; if they are out of the picture, they are only just around the corner, coming or going, or both. They are not really as afraid in the night as most white people are. Whiteness is a kind of nakedness to the dark world, and Lucy, who had all the fear she could do with, went to no trouble to imagine more. She moved on in her blackness, and her heart, sick and numb, burned tender as the eye of a night creature, alive in the dark. (234–35)

3. Divided Hearts

1. Berenice's association of John Henry with Henry Ford subtly criti- cizes white identity as well: throughout the novel, John Henry acts as an agent provocateur for white identity, since he does not share Frankie's identification with blackness and is much closer in character to Frankie's father than to Berenice.

2. Tom Robinson is implausibly passive in his courtroom description of his fateful meeting with Mayella Ewell:

The witness swallowed hard. "She reached up an' kissed me 'side of th' face. She says she never kissed a grown man before an' she might as well kiss a nigger. She says what her papa do to her don't count. She says, 'Kiss me back, nigger.' I say Miss Mayella lemme outa here an' tried to run but she got her back to the door an' I'da had to push her. I didn't wanta harm her, Mr. Finch, an' I say lemme pass, but just when I say it Mr. Ewell yonder hollered through th' window."

"What did he say?"

Tom Robinson swallowed again, and his eyes widened. "Somethin' not fittin' to say—not fittin' for these folks'n chillun to hear—"

"What did he say, Tom? You *must* tell the jury what he said."

Tom Robinson shut his eyes tight. "He says you goddamn whore, I'll kill ya."

"Then what happened?"

"Mr. Finch, I was runnin' so fast I didn't know what happened." (222)

4. Passing through Darkness

1. Sharon Monteith has explored Carol Dawson's *Body of Knowledge* and Lane von Herzen's *Copper Crown* as well as Kaye Gibbons's *Ellen Foster* and Ellen Douglas's *Can't Quit You, Baby* in her rich study of cross-racial relationships in recent novels by southern white women.

2. Dorothy Scura argues that the cross-racial relationship represents "one of the most significant subjects of fiction of this time" (423).

3. I have listed multiple examples in my introduction. Other examples include *The Jerk* (Steve Martin's character says as the opening credits roll, "I was born a poor black child") and *Forrest Gump*.

4. Ellen's declaration of self calls to mind Huck's plea when a drunken Pap mistakes him for the Angel of Death: "I begged, and told him I was only Huck, but he laughed *such* a screechy laugh, and roared and cussed, and kept on chasing me up" (36).

5. We do not see such recognition on the part of Twain's protagonist.

5. Beautiful Absurdity

1. Lee's earlier works addressing relationships across the color line were somewhat more subtle. In *Bamboozled*, Lee thinks little enough

of his audience that he begins with a voice-over definition of the terms *satire* and *irony*.

2. In studying African American literature and its criticism, we find an enormous repression involved in segregating this body of work—so essential in terms of theme, voice, and character—into a corner of American literature. It is a repression that calls to mind the inversion central to the novels we have read. For this reason, I am cautious in placing these texts in a single chapter: in so doing I mean not to repeat the sequestering tendencies of our scholarship but to demonstrate instead the specific ways in which three African American writers reply to the betrayals we see in the work of white American writers and in American history itself. I show in my next chapter the ways in which this reply comes to shape the dialectic of interracial union in the work of white writers in recent years.

3. Jim also initially meets Huck's apparent benevolence with perfectly justified disbelief and mistrust. The initial suspicion of Twain's character is eventually subsumed by the larger narrative; in Wright's novel, it develops as central focus.

4. In *Pym*, the descent is also into a blinding whiteness.

5. Here we see the influence an African American writer like Richard Wright has on white writers following him. Five years after Wright's novel was published, Carson McCullers would paraphrase Bigger Thomas when Berenice says to Frankie, " '[T]hey done drawn completely extra bounds around all colored people' " (113–14).

6. Ellison rejects the trope that Twain established in *Huckleberry Finn*, even as he mocks Fiedler's famous thesis that the relationships we've seen here are fantasized homosexual marriages.

7. Lynne blends her vision of the South with her vision of the African Americans she finds there:

> To her eyes, used to Northern suburbs where every house looked sterile and identical even before it was completely built[,] . . . the people usually stamped with the seals of their professions[,] to her . . . the South— and the black people living there—was Art. The songs, the dances, the food, the speech. Oh! She was such a romantic, so in love with the air she breathed, the honeysuckle that grew just beyond the door. (130)

8. In the way that Huck is drawn back to a white world, Truman returns to a black one.

6. *"Ain't No Motif"*

1. Simons expresses his desire to have his father come back by removing the fictional titles he has given his parents: "I did not want to call them the Progenitor and the Doctor but my mother and father, the way Jake would call his mother Momma when he went back to see her every afternoon" (145). Even as Simons prepares to return to his white culture, however, he expresses the move in the terms of the black characters he has come to know in the course of the novel: Jake, the bartender at the Baby Grand, provides the criterion by which Simons now assesses his attachment to his own parents.

2. Powell's protagonist mimics the valuation of the primitive to be found in Mailer's "The White Negro" throughout the book.

3. "The Negro," for Mailer, "kept for his survival the art of the primitive, he lived in the enormous present, he subsisted for his Saturday night kicks" (*Advertisements for Myself* 341).

4. In a sequel, *Edisto Revisited*, Simons, lately graduated from college and a failed architect, pursues Taurus, whose real name we never learn, to Louisiana, ostensibly to regain what balance he had earlier possessed. Race remains the central enigma for the adult Simons, and Taurus is unable in the end to give him any sense of certainty: "Who was he for me to find, who was I to find him, who was my mother to be his lover? In all the not knowing it seemed a little speculation was called for, not simply excusable" (100). Simons returns to the Baby Grand as a young man to find that Jinx has died but that Jake remains at the bar. More keenly aware of the boundaries whiteness brings to him, Simons realizes, "I had been a pure accommodation of race and racial difference when I sat under a pinball machine and watched Jinx's unsocked feet" (139). And he reasserts that difference while acknowledging the value in the interracial connection. Jake praises Simons on the beauty of his companion, the lovely Patricia Hod (Simons's cousin):

"You in some cotton."

"I am in cotton like . . . like a pistol in a Crown Royal bag." This was how Jake kept—and operated—his bar pistol.

"You got cheetah on your side," he said.

"What?"

"Say you got cheetah, man."

"Okay." I had no idea what this meant, either, and Jake knew that, but that was partly his point. It was a compliment that was better for my not entirely getting it. In my current intellectualizing mode, I was ironically less of a chump if I let it go and did not dig for it, white topical anthropologist. I tried one out myself: "All the snow in the world won't change the color of the pine needles."

"Heard that." (140)

Powell asserts again the certainty of racial difference, emphasizing it now with none of the irony we may have attached to his assertion in the earlier novel. For Powell, race remains an enigma at the end, a category that cannot of itself be a conduit to selfhood.

5. As Huck casts about on Jackson's Island, dead to all the world, he happens upon Jim. Just as all appears lost for Duncan Harper, he establishes the relationship with Beckwith Dozer.

6. Phillips appears to borrow from Henry Louis Gates's story of walking out of the Schomburg Library in Harlem with Anthony Appiah and Houston Baker and trying to hail a taxi. There they were, three preeminent African American scholars, and no cab would stop for them. Appiah and Gates scream out together to the passing taxis: "But sir, it's only a trope!"

Coda

1. Highway 61 was the road out of the Delta to the northern Promised Land for thousands of African Americans.

2. Irony doesn't fail us in *Plessy* either: the one vote in dissent of the decision was, of course, cast by a southerner and former advocate of slavery, John Marshall Harlan. Justice Harlan's declaration that "[o]ur Constitution is color-blind, and neither knows nor tolerates classes among citizens" was echoed half a century later in the Court's decision in *Brown v. Board of Education* and helped to guide the civil rights movement (qtd. in Woodward, "The Case" 156).

3. More recently, we have seen the affirmative action programs begun by one liberal southern president, Lyndon Johnson, during his War on Poverty bitterly dismissed as "quotas" by the president who brought

us Willie Horton and then dismantled by his erstwhile liberal and southern successor.

4. According to Marion Keisker, Sam Phillips said, "If I could find a
white man who had the Negro sound and the Negro feel, I could make
a billion dollars" (qtd. in Marcus, *Dead Elvis* 52).

5. In the course of his career, Presley *would* come to acknowledge
explicitly the influence blues artists had upon him.

WORKS CITED

Allison, Dorothy. *Bastard out of Carolina.* New York: Dutton, 1992.

Appiah, K. Anthony. *In My Father's House.* New York: Oxford University Press, 1992.

Arac, Jonathan. *Huckleberry Finn as Idol and Target: The Function of Criticism in Our Time.* Madison: University of Wisconsin Press, 1997.

Baker, Houston. *Long Black Song.* Charlottesville: University Press of Virginia, 1972.

Baldwin, James. "The Black Boy Looks at the White Boy." *The Price of the Ticket: Collected Nonfiction, 1948–1985.* New York: St. Martin's Press, 1985. 289–303.

Bamboozled. Dir. Spike Lee. New Line, 2000.

Beaver, Harold. *Huckleberry Finn.* London: Allen and Unwin, 1987.

———. "Run, Nigger, Run: *Adventures of Huckleberry Finn* as a Fugitive Slave Narrative." *Journal of American Studies* 8 (1974): 339–61.

The Birth of a Nation. Dir. D. W. Griffith. Madacy Entertainment, 1915.

Blair, Walter. Introduction. *Adventures of Huckleberry Finn.* By Mark Twain. Ed. Walter Blair et al. Berkeley: University of California Press, 1988. xxiv–l.

Blair, Walter, and Victor Fischer, eds. *Adventures of Huckleberry Finn.* By Mark Twain. 1884. Berkeley: University of California Press, 1988.

Blotner, Joseph. *Faulkner: A Biography.* New York: Random House, 1984.

Booth, Wayne. *The Company We Keep: An Ethics of Fiction.* Berkeley: University of California Press, 1988.

Bulworth. Dir. Warren Beatty. Twentieth Century–Fox, 1998.

Cabeza de Vaca, Alvar Núñez. *Castaways: The Narrative of Alvar Núñez Cabeza de Vaca.* 1542. Ed. Enrique Pupo-Walker. Trans. Frances M. López-Morillas. Berkeley: University of California Press, 1993.

Caldwell, Erskine. *In Search of Bisco.* 1965. New York: Pocket Books, 1966.

Callahan, John F. "The Hoop of Language: Politics and the Restoration of Voice in *Meridian.*" *Alice Walker.* Ed. Harold Bloom. New York: Chelsea House Publishers, 1989. 153–84.

Carr, Virginia Spencer. *The Lonely Hunter: A Biography of Carson Mc-Cullers.* Garden City, NY: Doubleday, 1975.

Carrington, George C. *The Dramatic Unity of "Huckleberry Finn."* Columbus: Ohio State University Press, 1976.

Cash, W. J. *The Mind of the South.* 1941. New York: Vintage, 1960.

Chakovsky, Sergei. "Lucas Beauchamp and Jim: Mark Twain's Influence on William Faulkner." *Faulkner and Race.* Ed. Doreen Fowler and Ann J. Abadie. Jackson: University Press of Mississippi, 1987. 236–54.

Changing Lanes. Dir. Roger Michell. Paramount Home Video, 2002.

Clara's Heart. Dir. Robert Mulligan. Warner, 1988.

Cobb, James C. *The Most Southern Place on Earth: The Mississippi Delta and the Roots of Regional Identity.* New York: Oxford University Press, 1992.

Cook, Martha. "Old Ways and New Ways." *The History of Southern Literature.* Ed. Louis D. Rubin, Blyden Jackson, S. Moore Rayburn, and Lewis P. Simpson. Baton Rouge: Louisiana State University Press, 1985. 527–34.

Cooper, James Fenimore. *The Last of the Mohicans.* 1826. New York: Dodd, Mead, 1951.

———. *The Leatherstocking Tales.* Vol. 2. Library of America. New York: Literary Classics of the U.S., 1985.

Cox, Elizabeth. *Night Talk.* St. Paul: Graywolf Press, 1997.

Cox, James. *Mark Twain: The Fate of Humour.* Princeton, NJ: Princeton University Press, 1966.

Crews, Harry. *All We Need of Hell.* New York: Harper and Row, 1987.

Davis, Reuben. *Shim.* Jackson: University Press of Mississippi, 1995.

Dawson, Carol. *Body of Knowledge.* Chapel Hill, NC: Algonquin Books, 1994.

Douglas, Ellen. *Black Cloud, White Cloud: Two Novellas and Two Stories.* Boston: Houghton Mifflin, 1963.

———. *Can't Quit You, Baby.* 1988. New York: Penguin, 1989.

———. *The Rock Cried Out.* New York: Harcourt Brace Jovanovich, 1979.

Doyno, Victor A. *Writing Huck Finn: Mark Twain's Creative Process.* Philadelphia: University of Pennsylvania Press, 1991.

Driving Miss Daisy. Dir. Bruce Beresford. Warner Bros., 1989.

Du Bois, W. E. B. *The Souls of Black Folk.* 1903. New York: Penguin, 1982.

Dunn, Jancee. "Beck: Resident Alien." *Rolling Stone* 11–25 July 1996: 51–53.

Edgerton, Clyde. *Raney: A Novel.* Chapel Hill, NC: Algonquin Books, 1985.

Ehle, John. *The Journey of August King.* New York: Harper and Row, 1971.

Ellison, Ralph. Introduction. 1981. *Invisible Man.* New York: Modern Library, 1992. xi–xxviii.

———. *Invisible Man.* 1952. New York: Modern Library, 1992.

———. *Shadow and Act.* New York: Random House, 1964.

———. "What America Would Be Like without Blacks." 1970. *Going to the Territory.* New York: Vintage, 1987. 104–12.

Eminem. "Without Me." *The Eminem Show.* Aftermath Records, 2002.

Estess, Sybil. "The Eden of *Edisto:* The Fall into the Then-Next." *Southwest Review* 69 (1984): 477–81.

The Family Man. Dir. Brett Ratner. Universal, 2000.

Faulkner, William. *Absalom, Absalom!* 1936. New York: Vintage, 1972.

———. *Go Down, Moses.* 1942. New York: Vintage, 1990.

———. *Intruder in the Dust.* 1948. New York: Random House, 1991.

———. "A Letter to the North." *Reader's Digest* May 1956: 75–78.

———. *Light in August.* 1932. New York: Random House, 1972.

———. *The Reivers, a Reminiscence.* New York: Random House, 1962.

———. *The Sound and the Fury.* 1929. New York: Random House, 1954.

———. *The Unvanquished.* 1934. New York: Random House, 1966.

Fiedler, Leslie. "Come Back to the Raft Ag'in, Huck Honey!" *Partisan Review* 15 (1948): 664–71.

———. "*Huckleberry Finn:* The Book We Love to Hate." *Proteus* 1 (1984): 1–8.

———. *Love and Death in the American Novel.* 1966. New York: Anchor Books, 1992.

Fishkin, Shelley Fisher. *Was Huck Black? Mark Twain and African-American Voices.* New York: Oxford University Press, 1993.

Flanigan, Sara. *Sudie.* 1986. New York: St. Martin's Press, 1990.

Foner, Eric. *Reconstruction: America's Unfinished Revolution, 1863–1877.* New York: Harper and Row, 1988.

Ford, Jesse Hill. *The Liberation of Lord Byron Jones.* 1965. Athens: University of Georgia Press, 1993.

Forrest Gump. Dir. Robert Zemeckis. Paramount, 1994.

48 Hrs. Dir. Walter Hill. Paramount, 1982.

Gates, Henry Louis, Jr. *Loose Canons: Notes on the Culture Wars.* New York: Oxford University Press, 1992.

―――. *The Signifying Monkey.* New York: Oxford University Press, 1988.

―――. "The White Negro." *New Yorker* 11 May 1998: 62–65.

Gibbons, Kaye. *Ellen Foster.* 1988. New York: Vintage Contemporaries, 1990.

Gone with the Wind. Dir. George Cukor and Victor Fleming. Warner, 1939.

Grau, Shirley Ann. *The Keepers of the House.* 1964. New York: Avon Books, 1985.

Gribben, Alan. *Mark Twain's Library: A Reconstruction.* 2 vols. Boston: G. K. Hall, 1980.

Griffin, John Howard. *Black Like Me.* 1960. New York: Signet, 1961.

Grimes, William. "What Debt Does Hollywood Owe to Truth?" *New York Times* 5 March 1992, late ed.: C20+.

Gubar, Susan. *Racechanges: White Skin, Black Face in American Culture.* Oxford: Oxford University Press, 1997.

Guess Who's Coming to Dinner. Dir. Stanley Kramer. Columbia/Tristar, 1967.

Hale, Grace Elizabeth. *Making Whiteness: The Culture of Segregation in the South, 1890–1940.* New York: Pantheon Books, 1998.

Happy Gilmore. Dir. Dennis Dugan. Universal, 1996.

Harris, Joel Chandler. *Uncle Remus: His Songs and His Sayings.* 1880. New York: D. Appleton, 1881.

Hellenga, Robert. *Blues Lessons.* New York: Scribner's, 2002.

Hemingway, Ernest. *Green Hills of Africa.* New York: Scribner's, 1938.

Holland, Laurence B. "A 'Raft of Trouble': Word and Deed in *Huckleberry Finn.*" *American Realism: New Essays.* Ed. Eric Sundquist. Baltimore, MD: Johns Hopkins University Press. 1982. 66–81.

Howells, William Dean. *My Mark Twain: Reminiscences and Criticisms.* 1910. Ed. Marilyn Austin Baldwin. Baton Rouge: Louisiana State University Press, 1967.

Hyman, John H. *The Relationship.* Manassas, VA: EM Press, 1995.

Ignatiev, Noel. *How the Irish Became White.* New York: Routledge, 1995.

The Jerk. Dir. Carl Reiner. Universal, 1979.

Johnson, Robert E. "Bill and Camille Cosby: First Family of Philanthropy." *Ebony* May 1989: 25+.

Jones, Rhett S. "Nigger and Knowledge: White Double-Consciousness in *Adventures of Huckleberry Finn.*" *Mark Twain Journal* 22 (1984): 28–37.

Jordan, Winthrop D. *White over Black: American Attitudes toward the Negro, 1550–1812.* Williamsburg: University of North Carolina Press, 1968.

Jungle Fever. Dir. Spike Lee. Universal, 1991.

Kaplan, Justin. Introduction. *Adventures of Huckleberry Finn.* By Mark Twain. New York: Fawcett Columbine, 1996. vii–xi.

———. *Mr. Clemens and Mark Twain.* New York: Simon and Schuster, 1966.

Kenan, Randall. *Walking on Water: Black American Lives at the Turn of the Twenty-First Century.* New York: Vintage, 2000.

Kerman, Cynthia Earl, and Richard Eldridge. *The Lives of Jean Toomer.* Baton Rouge: Louisiana State University Press, 1987.

Kincaid, Nanci. *Crossing Blood.* New York: Putnam, 1992.

Kreyling, Michael. *Inventing Southern Literature.* Jackson: University Press of Mississippi, 1998.

Lauber, John. *The Inventions of Mark Twain.* New York: Hill and Wang, 1990.

Lee, Harper. *To Kill a Mockingbird.* 1960. New York: Harper Collins, 1995.

Leerhsen, Charles, et al. "There's Blues in the News." *Newsweek* 12 November 1990: 72–74.

The Legend of Bagger Vance. Dir. Robert Redford. Dreamworks, 2000.

Lent, Jeffrey. *In the Fall.* New York: Vintage, 2001.

Lethal Weapon. Dir. Richard Donner. Warner, 1987.

Lewis, R. W. B. "The Hero in the New World: William Faulkner's *The Bear.*" *Kenyon Review* 13 (1951): 641–60.

Limerick, Patricia Nelson. *The Legacy of Conquest: The Unbroken Past of the American West.* New York: Norton, 1987.

Lott, Eric. *Love and Theft: Blackface Minstrelsy and the American Work-ing Class.* New York: Oxford University Press, 1993.

MacKethan, Lucinda. "*Huck Finn* and the Slave Narratives: Lighting Out as Design." *Southern Review* 20 (1984): 247–64.

Mailer, Norman. *Advertisements for Myself.* New York: G. P. Putnam's Sons, 1959.

———. *The White Negro.* San Francisco: City Lights Books, 1957.

Marcus, Greil. *Dead Elvis: A Chronicle of a Cultural Obsession.* New York: Doubleday, 1991.

———. *Mystery Train: Images of America in Rock 'n' Roll Music.* New York: Plume, 1990.

Margolis, Stacey. "Huckleberry Finn; or, Consequences." *PMLA* 116 (2001): 329–43.

Mason, Ernest D. "Attraction and Repulsion: Huck Finn, 'Nigger' Jim, and Black Americans Revisited." *College Language Association Jour-nal* 33 (1989): 36–48.

McCullers, Carson. *The Member of the Wedding.* 1946. New York: Ban-tam Books, 1979.

McDowell, Margaret B. *Carson McCullers.* Boston: Twayne Publishers, 1980.

McLarin, Kim. *Meeting of the Waters.* New York: William Morrow, 2001.

Melville, Herman. *Moby-Dick, or, The Whale.* 1851. New York: Penguin, 2001.

Michaels, Walter Benn. *Our America: Nativism, Modernism and Plural-ism.* Durham, NC: Duke University Press, 1995.

Miller, John Chester. *The Wolf by the Ears: Thomas Jefferson and Slav-ery.* 1977. New York: Meridian, 1980.

Monster's Ball. Dir. Marc Forster. Lions Gate Home Entertainment, 2002.

Monteith, Sharon. *Advancing Sisterhood? Interracial Friendships in Con-temporary Southern Fiction.* Athens: University of Georgia Press, 2000.

Moody, Anne. *Coming of Age in Mississippi.* 1968. New York: Dell, 1984.

Morgan, Ted. *Wilderness at Dawn: The Settling of the North American Continent.* New York: Simon and Schuster, 1993.

Morrison, Toni. *Playing in the Dark: Whiteness and the Literary Imagi-nation.* Cambridge, MA: Harvard University Press, 1992.

Morton, Thomas. *New English Canaan: or, New Canaan.* 1637. New York: Arno Press, 1972.

Nadel, Alan. *Invisible Criticism: Ralph Ellison and the American Canon.* Iowa City: University of Iowa Press, 1988.

Nagel, James. "*Huck Finn* and *The Bear:* The Wilderness and Moral Freedom." *English Studies in Africa* 12 (1969): 59–63.

Palmer, Robert. "King of the Delta Blues Singers." *Rolling Stone* 18 October 1990: 97–98.

Pendleton, Louis Beauregard. *King Tom and the Runaways.* New York: D. Appleton, 1890.

Phillips, W. Glasgow. *Tuscaloosa.* New York: William Morrow, 1994.

Poe, Edgar Allan. *The Narrative of Arthur Gordon Pym.* 1838. New York: Heritage Press, 1930.

Porter, Carolyn. *Seeing and Being.* Middletown, CT: Wesleyan University Press, 1981.

Powell, Padgett. "Edisto." *Ms.* 1983.

———. *Edisto.* 1984. New York: Henry Holt, 1985.

———. *Edisto Revisited.* New York: Henry Holt, 1996.

———. Personal interview. 30 March 1996.

Prenshaw, Peggy Whitman. *Elizabeth Spencer.* Boston: Twayne Publishers, 1985.

Railton, Stephen. "Jim and Mark Twain: What Do Dey Stan' For?" *Virginia Quarterly Review* 63 (1987): 393–408.

Rampersad, Arnold. "*Adventures of Huckleberry Finn* and Afro-American Literature." *Mark Twain Journal* 22 (1984): 47–56.

Reed, Lou. "I Wanna Be Black." *Street Hassle.* Arista, 1978.

———. "Walk on the Wild Side." *Transformer.* RCA, 1972.

Robinson, Forrest G. *In Bad Faith: The Dynamics of Deception in Mark Twain's America.* Cambridge, MA: Harvard University Press, 1986.

———. "Uncertain Borders: Race, Sex, and Civilization in *The Last of the Mohicans.*" *Arizona Quarterly* 47.1 (1991): 1–28.

Roediger, David, ed. *Black on White: Black Writers on What It Means to Be White.* New York: Schocken Books, 1998.

———. *Colored White: Transcending the Racial Past.* Berkeley: University of California Press, 2002.

———. *The Wages of Whiteness: Race and the Making of the American Working Class.* Rev. ed. New York: Verso, 1999.

Rousseau, Jean-Jacques. *Emile: or, On Education*. 1762. Trans. Allan Bloom. New York: Basic Books, 1979.

Rowley, Hazel. *Richard Wright: The Life and Times*. New York: Henry Holt, 2001.

Rubin, Louis D., Jr. *The Edge of the Swamp: A Study of Literature and Society in the Old South*. Baton Rouge: Louisiana State University Press, 1989.

Rubin, Louis D., Jr., Blyden Jackson, S. Moore Rayburn, and Lewis P. Simpson, eds. *The History of Southern Literature*. Baton Rouge: Louisiana State University Press, 1985.

Santoro, Gene. *Dancing in Your Head: Jazz, Blues, Rock, and Beyond*. New York: Oxford University Press, 1994.

Schmitz, Neil. "Twain, *Huckleberry Finn*, and the Reconstruction." *American Studies* 12 (1971): 59–67.

Scura, Dorothy. Review of *Advancing Sisterhood? Interracial Friendships in Contemporary Southern Fiction*. By Sharon Monteith. *Mississippi Quarterly* 54.3 (2001): 420–24.

Seelye, John. *Beautiful Machine: Rivers and the Republican Plan, 1755–1825*. New York: Oxford University Press, 1991.

———. Introduction. *The Adventures of Huckleberry Finn*. By Mark Twain. Ed. John Seelye. New York: Penguin, 1985. ix–xxix.

———. *The Kid*. Lincoln: University of Nebraska Press, 1972.

———. *The True Adventures of Huckleberry Finn*. Urbana: University of Illinois Press, 1987.

Smiley, Jane. "Say It Ain't So, Huck: Second Thoughts on Mark Twain's 'Masterpiece.' " *Harper's* January 1996: 61–67.

Smith, David L. "Huck, Jim, and American Racial Discourse." *Mark Twain Journal* 22 (1984): 4–12.

Smith, Henry Nash, and William B. Gibson. *Mark Twain–Howells Letters: The Correspondence of Samuel L. Clemens and William D. Howells, 1872–1910*. Cambridge: Oxford University Press, 1960.

Smith, John. *The Complete Works of Captain John Smith (1580–1631)*. Ed. Philip L. Barbour. 3 vols. Chapel Hill: University of North Carolina Press, 1986.

Sosna, Morton. *In Search of the Silent South: Southern Liberals and the Race Issue*. New York: Columbia University Press, 1977.

Southern, Terry. *Red-Dirt Marijuana and Other Tastes.* New York: New American Library, 1967.

Spencer, Elizabeth. *The Voice at the Back Door.* 1956. New York: Time, 1965.

Stowe, Harriet Beecher. *Uncle Tom's Cabin.* 1852. New York: Penguin, 1987.

Sundquist, Eric J. *To Wake the Nations: Race in the Making of American Literature.* Cambridge, MA: Harvard University Press, 1993.

Tate, Allen. *Essays of Four Decades.* Chicago: Swallow Press, 1968.

Tate, Linda. *A Southern Weave of Women: Fiction of the Contemporary South.* Athens: University of Georgia Press, 1994.

Taylor, Robert Lewis. *A Journey to Mattecumbe.* London: Hutchinson, 1961.

Training Day. Dir. Antoine Fuqua. Warner Home Video, 2001.

Trilling, Lionel. "Huckleberry Finn." *The Liberal Imagination: Essays on Literature and Society.* 1950. New York: Viking Press, 1951. 104–17.

Twain, Mark. *Adventures of Huckleberry Finn.* 1884. Ed. Victor Fischer, Lin Salamo, Harriet Elinor Smith, and Walter Blair. Berkeley: University of California Press, 2001.

———. *The Adventures of Tom Sawyer.* 1876. New York: Penguin Books, 1986.

———. *Pudd'nhead Wilson and Those Extraordinary Twins.* 1894. Ed. Sidney E. Berger. New York: Norton, 1980.

Uhry, Alfred. *Driving Miss Daisy.* 1987. New York: Theatre Communications Group, 1988.

Von Herzen, Lane. *Copper Crown.* New York: William Morrow, 1991.

Walker, Alice. *Meridian.* New York: Pocket Books, 1976.

Wieck, Carl F. *Refiguring Huckleberry Finn.* Athens: University of Georgia Press, 2000.

Wilson, Harriet E. *Our Nig, or, Sketches from the Life of a Free Black, in a Two-story White House, North, Showing that Slavery's Shadows Fall Even There / by "Our Nig."* 1859. New York: Vintage, 1983.

Woodward, C. Vann. *The Burden of Southern History.* Baton Rouge: Louisiana State University Press, 1960.

———. "The Case of the Louisiana Traveler." *Quarrels That Have*

Shaped the Constitution. Ed. John A. Garraty. New York: Harper and Row, 1962. 145–58.

Wright, Richard. *Native Son.* 1940. New York: Harper and Row, 1989.

Zappa, Frank. "Uncle Remus." *Apostrophe.* Rykodisc, 1974.

Zinn, Howard. *The Southern Mystique.* New York: Knopf, 1964.

INDEX